云南省国家级非物质文化遗产文献资料汇编

（汉英对照）

The Documentary Compilation of the State-level Intangible Cultural Heritage of Yunnan Province (Chinese-English Versions)

李新新 主编

李新新 译审

李新新 向晓红 于云飞 向兰 译

本书由教育部人文社会科学研究规划基金项目『云贵川地区国家级非物质文化遗产的对外译介研究』（项目编号：19YJA850009）资助

四川大学出版社

SICHUAN UNIVERSITY PRESS

图书在版编目（CIP）数据

云南省国家级非物质文化遗产文献资料汇编 ：汉英对照 / 李新新主编 ； 李新新等译． -- 成都 ： 四川大学出版社， 2024. 9. -- (国家级非物质文化遗产文献资料汇编). -- ISBN 978-7-5690-7266-2

Ⅰ. G127.74

中国国家版本馆 CIP 数据核字第 2024P3F392 号

书　　名：云南省国家级非物质文化遗产文献资料汇编（汉英对照）
Yunnan Sheng Guojiaji Feiwuzhi Wenhua Yichan Wenxian Ziliao Huibian（Han-Ying Duizhao）
主　　编：李新新
译　　者：李新新　向晓红　于云飞　向　兰
丛 书 名：国家级非物质文化遗产文献资料汇编

丛书策划：刘　畅
选题策划：喻　震　刘　畅
责任编辑：刘　畅
责任校对：敬雁飞
装帧设计：墨创文化
责任印制：李金兰

出版发行：四川大学出版社有限责任公司
地址：成都市一环路南一段 24 号（610065）
电话：（028）85408311（发行部）、85400276（总编室）
电子邮箱：scupress@vip.163.com
网址：https://press.scu.edu.cn
印前制作：成都墨之创文化传播有限公司
印刷装订：四川煤田地质制图印务有限责任公司

成品尺寸：170mm×240mm
印　　张：19.5
插　　页：2
字　　数：469 千字

版　　次：2024 年 10 月 第 1 版
印　　次：2024 年 10 月 第 1 次印刷
定　　价：98.00 元

扫码获取数字资源

四川大学出版社
微信公众号

编者序

作为四大文明古国之一，中国拥有五千年的文明历史。作为统一的多民族国家，中国拥有56个民族共同造就的多姿多彩的文明。悠久的历史和灿烂的文明给中华民族留下了极其丰富的文化遗产，这既包括有形文化遗产（即物质文化遗产），又包括无形文化遗产（即非物质文化遗产，简称“非遗”）。我国政府历来重视文化遗产的保护工作，作为文化遗产的一种，非物质文化遗产的保护也受到高度重视。

当前，随着经济全球化和社会现代化，我国非物质文化遗产的生存环境渐趋恶化，尤其是濒临消亡的或人口数量少的民族的非物质文化遗产的抢救、挖掘、保护、保存及传承与发展面临极大挑战，现状堪忧。正是在这一新的时代背景下，我国政府加大对各省、市、县的非遗项目的抢救、挖掘与保护力度，其标志性事件是2004年我国政府正式批准联合国教科文组织通过的《保护非物质文化遗产公约》。第二年，国务院发布了《关于加强文化遗产保护的通知》，制定了“国家+省+市+县”四级保护体系，为我国非遗确立了系统的保护体系。2011年《中华人民共和国非物质文化遗产法》的通过，标志着我国非遗的抢救、挖掘、保护、保存、传承与发展有了成体系的法律保障。近年来，我国的非遗保护工作开展得如火如荼。2006、2008、2011和2014年，国家文化部牵头分别组织了第一、二、三、四批次的国家级非遗名录的申报工作，提交国务院审批通过。我国各省、市、县也相继推出各级非遗名录，加大力度推进各级非遗的抢救、挖掘、保护、保存及传承工作。

迄今为止，我国非遗的挖掘、整理、保护、传承、传播等的相关研究已取得累累硕果，但大部分成果仅限于汉语文献，其传播也仅限于中华民族内部的非遗宣传。这种将已挖掘、整理和保护完善了的非遗珍宝囿于国内的举措绝非智举，跟不上当下的中国文化“走出去”战略。为了扩大我国非遗研究前期阶段性成果的国际影响力，将中华文化精华对外传播至世界各地，弘扬光大，我国非遗的对外译介便成为当务之急。新的时代语境下，我国的非遗研究将迈入一个新阶段——深度对外译介阶段，即以前期阶段性成果为依托，将已挖掘、整理和保护完善了的非遗项目逐渐分批次、分阶段地译介给国际社会，这是新时代下非物质文化遗产保护的必由之路。正是在这一时代背景下，西华大学李新新副教授牵头，组建研究团队，以“云贵川地区国家级非物质文化遗产的对外译介研究”为题申报了2019年度教育部人文社会科学研究规划基金项目，并于2019年3月15日获得立项，项目编号：19YJA850009。该课题顺应了非遗研究的发展新趋势，是我国非遗对外译介迈出的尝试性的一步。《四川省国家级非物质文化遗产文献资料汇编（汉英对照）》［The Documentary Compilation of the State-level Intangible Cultural Heritage of Sichuan Province (Chinese-English Versions)］、《云南省国家级非物质文化遗产文献资料汇编（汉英对照）》［The Documentary Compilation of the State-level Intangible Cultural Heritage of Yunnan Province (Chinese-English Versions)］、《贵州省国家级非物质文化遗产文献资料汇编（汉英对照）》［The Documentary Compilation of the State-level Intangible Cultural Heritage of Guizhou Province (Chinese-English Versions)］正是该立项课题的研究成果。

这些研究成果主要是云、贵、川三省在前四批次中审批通过的国家级非遗名录项目已取得的阶段性成果的对外译介，是对这三省国家级非遗文献资料缺乏英译文现状的弥补。非物质文化遗产具有鲜明的民族性，云贵川地区分布着中华民族的55个少数民族，堪称是整个中华民族的缩影，蕴藏着我国的非遗“富矿”，这些丰富的非物质文化遗产便是中华民族文化精华的浓缩。在新的时代语境下，要深入推动中国文化“走出去”，使其发扬光大，离不开对云贵川地区这些民族文化浓缩精华的优质对外译介。作为我国非遗对外译介宏伟工程的先期研究，云贵川地区国家级非物质文化遗产的优质对外译介肩负着重要的历史使命，是对外弘扬、传播中华民族优秀传统文化必不可少的一部分。

本课题的成果主要涉及云、贵、川三省1—4批次348项国家级非物质文化遗产（含新增项目和扩展项目）的中英文版文献资料汇编，其中四川125项，云南113项，贵州110项。对应非遗项目的十个类别，《四川省国家级非物质文化遗产文献资料汇编（汉英对照）》［The Documentary Compilation of the State-level Intangible Cultural Heritage of Sichuan Province (Chinese-English Versions)］、《云南省国家级非物质文化遗产文献资料汇编（汉英对照）》［The Documentary Compilation of the State-level Intangible Cultural Heritage of Yunnan Province (Chinese-English Versions)］、《贵州省国家级非物质文化遗产文献资料汇编（汉英对照）》［The Documentary Compilation of the State-level Intangible Cultural Heritage of Guizhou Province (Chinese-English Versions)］除“引言”外，正文部分均分为十章，即“第一章民间文学”“第二章传统音乐”“第三章传统舞蹈”“第四章传统戏剧”“第五章曲艺”“第六章传统体育、游艺与

杂技”“第七章传统美术”“第八章传统技艺”“第九章传统医药”“第十章民俗”。中文部分主要搜集整理了相关非遗项目目前已取得的阶段性成果，框架式地概述其基本内容，并附直观图片，为广大非遗爱好者和研究者们提供一个便于快速检索的文献资料集锦。英文部分为国际非遗爱好者提供了了解中国非遗文化，尤其是云贵川三省非遗文化的平台，使更多热爱中华文化的国际友人有机会了解中国的非遗文化，从而助力中国文化“走出去”。

课题负责人李新新副教授对云、贵、川三省所涉及的国家级非遗项目的中文介绍资料进行搜集、汇编、整理，并撰写“引言”。之后，和课题组成员一起进行翻译工作，具体的分工为：李新新副教授负责《四川省国家级非物质文化遗产文献资料汇编》的翻译；向晓红教授负责《贵州省国家级非物质文化遗产文献资料汇编》的翻译，由向兰协助；于云飞博士负责《云南省国家级非物质文化遗产文献资料汇编》的翻译。最后，李新新副教授负责所有译文的审校工作，并撰写“编者序”和“后记”，整理了书末的词汇表。

本课题的研究成果具有重要的学术价值和现实意义。首先，该系列成果系统整理了云、贵、川三省前四批次批准的国家级非物质文化遗产项目的中、英文文献资料，是对这三省国家级非遗文献资料缺乏英译文现状的弥补，具有重要的学术价值。这些成果将相关非遗在抢救、挖掘、整理、保护、传承、开发利用及传播等方面取得的前期阶段性成果转化为对外弘扬、传播这三个多民族聚居区所富含的中华民族优秀传统文化的外宣成果，能够在一定程度上促进我国非遗的保护、传承与传播向“深度对外译介”新阶段的转变，为最终实现对外弘扬、传播中华民族优秀传统文化和提升中国文化软实力作出基础性贡献。其次，作为我国非遗深度对外译介阶段的前期阶段性成果，这些成果可以为我国其他省、市、县少数民族非遗的对外译介提供一定的借鉴，助力各省、市、县的非遗对外译介向纵深推进，加快我国非遗的保护、传承与传播向“深度对外译介”新阶段实现转变，从而推动我国非遗的对外译介迈向高潮，为中国文化精华的深度对外译介打下一定的基础。最后，这些成果能够为英语国家的中国文化爱好者，尤其是中国非遗文化的爱好者提供深入了解中国非物质文化遗产及中国少数民族文化精髓的渠道。从这一层面来说，本课题的研究成果也具有重要的现实意义。

课题组在整理和翻译本系列文献资料汇编的过程中，主要遇到了三方面的困难。一是部分文献资料收集困难。在这些国家级非遗项目中，部分非遗项目的文字资料在权威的非物质文化保护中心官网、政府官网、新闻网上的介绍过于简单，尤其是第四批次通过的非遗项目，资料很少，因此需要到非遗所在地进行现场搜集。但是，课题立项九个多月后便遇上三年的疫情，出行极为不便，这使得文献资料的现场采集陷入困境。鉴于此，课题负责人查阅了大量高质量的期刊论文，购买了一批与所涉非遗项目有关的书籍、省志、县志等，详细研读后，进行汇编整理，补充了缺失的文献资料。二是字数多，翻译任务重。由于该课题的成果涉及三个省 348 项国家级非物质文化遗产，文献资料字数很多，因此翻译任务繁重。三是汉语文化负载词多，翻译难度大，审校任务重。在这些文献资料中，独具中国特色，尤其是云贵川三省少数民族特色的文化负载词很多，翻译难度很大，因为要将这些国家级非遗蕴含的西南少数民族文化尽可能“不失真”“不走样”地译介给英语读者，以达到优质地对外传播我国民族文化精髓和云、贵、川三省国家级非物质文化遗产的目的，译者必须查阅大量资料，求其准确含义，才能准确翻译，因此翻译工作十分耗时，难度很大，审校任务也很重。

本着译介、传播中国文化的目的，在翻译独具中国文化特色，尤其是云、贵、川三省少数民族特色的文化负载词时，课题负责人和团队成员灵活采用了多种翻译方法，以确保英译文既能最大程度展示中国的语言文字特点、文化内涵，又能让英语读者快速、准确地理解相关表达的含义。例如，在翻译“第九章传统医药”中的非遗文献资料时，会涉及很多中国少数民族特有的药材，这些药材名在英语中缺少对应的表达，但在拉丁语中却有相应的表达。鉴于此，课题负责人和团队成员主要采用了音译（汉语拼音）+ 直译 + 拉丁译文、音译（汉语拼音）+ 增译 + 拉丁译文、直译 + 音译（汉语拼音）+ 拉丁译文等翻译方法，这样翻译出的英译文既保证了相关药材名称翻译的科学性，又向英语读者传达了其汉语拼音的语言文字特点，而且还补充了必要的中药材文化信息。再如，在该章里有很多中药名，这些中药名也是中国文化所特有的，独具中国特色，因而在英语和拉丁语中都没有相对应的表达。鉴于此，课题负责人和团队成员主要采用了直译、音译（汉语拼音）+ 直译、直译 + 音译（汉语拼音）+ 直译、直译 + 音译（汉语拼音）+ 增译等翻译方法，这样翻译出的英译文或直译出原药名的字面意思，或既保留了原药名汉语拼音的语言文字特点又直译出其字面意思，又或在此基础上增补了必要的中医药文化信息。

在翻译这些非遗项目的文献资料时，课题组所采用的基本原则如下：

（1）有约定俗成译文的，则采用约定俗成的译文。如“同济堂”是中华老字号的医药品牌，闻名中外，其药品外包装 Logo 上的英文为“TONGJI TANG”。由于该中药品牌的英文已经被中外消费者广泛接受，故课题组便采用这一约定俗成的译文。

（2）有些独具少数民族特色的非遗名称，在翻译时则采用保留其少数民族音的译文。如“侗族大歌”译为“Al Laox of the Dong Nationality”，“苗族贾理”译为“*Jaxlil of the Miao Nationality*”，“刻道”译为“*Kheik Det (carved song stick) Epic*”等。

（3）如果采用直译法能准确传达原文化负载词之意的，则采用直译法。如“秦皮”译为“ash bark”，“小儿救急丹”译为“Infant Emergency Pellets”，“接骨消炎丸”译为“Pills for Bonesetting and Diminishing Inflammation”，“八味秦皮丸”译为“Eight-flavor Ash Bark Pills”等。

（4）如果采用直译法达不到预期效果，则采用其他灵活多变的组合式翻译方法，如音译（汉语拼音）+ 释译 + 直译法、音译（汉语拼音）+ 释译 + 增译法、音译（汉语拼音）+ 增译法、音译（汉语拼音）+ 直译法、音译（汉语拼音）+ 直译 + 增译法、音译（汉语拼音）+ 释译法。采用这些翻译方法可以使英译文既保留原文化负载词的汉语拼音，又能适当增补其所蕴含的独特的中国少数民族文化内涵，为英语读者呈现原汁原味的具有异域风味的中国文化负载词的英译文，从而达到在英语世界优质地传播我国云贵川地区少数民族文化，尤其是非物质文化遗产的目的。例如，课题组采用音译（汉语拼音）+ 释译 + 直译法，将“口弦音乐”译为“Kouxian (a kind of buccal reed) Music”；采用音译（汉语拼音）+ 释译 + 增译法，将“司岗里”译为“*Sigangli (Out of the Cliff-cave) Epic*”；采用音译（汉语拼音）+ 增译法，将“仰阿莎”译为“*Yang'asha Poem*”；采用音译（汉语拼音）+ 直译法，将“黄龙溪火龙灯舞”译为“Huanglongxi Fire Dragon Lantern Dance”；采用音译（汉语拼音）+ 直译 + 增译法，将“滚山珠”译为“Gunshan Bead (also called Gunshan Worm)”；采用音译（汉语拼音）+ 释译法，将“寨老”译为“Zhailao (a head of a stockaded village)”，将“坯胎”译为“Pitai (a product that already has the required shape but still needs processing)”，将“甑子”译为“Zengzi (a wooden container used for steaming)”等。

（5）对于查阅很多资料仍无法获得准确含义的文化负载词，课题组只能通过汉语拼音进行音译。虽然此举使得译文无法传达原文化负载词的字面含义及文化内涵，但至少保留了其原汁原味的汉语拼音特征，虽有遗憾，却是不得已而为之。

（6）原文逻辑欠妥之处，译文中采用增译或适度改译的方法，以确保英译文逻辑正确。由于篇幅有限，不一一举例赘述。

漫长而艰巨的资料搜集、整理、翻译、审校工作接近尾声，课题组成员的心情既激动又忐忑。激动的是，四年多来的辛苦耕耘即将收获，付梓问世；忐忑的是，担心拙译在广大读者的慧眼下显出不妥之处。课题组成员深知我们在非物质文化遗产方面的学识和翻译能力有限，因此拙译中疏漏、舛误在所难免，祈请国内外非遗专家、翻译家及同行不吝批评赐教。

李新新

2023 年 12 月 31 日于西华大学

引言

本书主要涉及云南省1—4批国家级非物质文化遗产的文献资料汇编，搜集整理了云南省相关非遗项目目前已取得的阶段性成果，框架式地概述了各项目的基本内容，并附上图片，以期为广大非遗爱好者和研究者们提供一个便于快速检索的云南省1—4批国家级非遗文献资料集锦。

根据中华人民共和国中央人民政府分别于2006年5月20日、2008年6月16日、2011年6月9日和2014年12月3日公布的《国务院关于公布第一批国家级非物质文化遗产名录的通知》《国务院关于公布第二批国家级非物质文化遗产名录和第一批国家级非物质文化遗产扩展项目名录的通知》《国务院关于公布第三批国家级非物质文化遗产名录的通知》和《国务院关于公布第四批国家级非物质文化遗产代表性项目名录的通知》，云南省第一、二、三、四批次分别入围34项，41项（新增38项、扩展3项），21项（新增12项、扩展9项）和17项（新增9项、扩展8项）非物质文化遗产，共计113项。

根据批次，云南省国家级非物质文化遗产名录（1—4批）的详细统计数据如表1。

表1　云南省国家级非物质文化遗产名录（1—4批）分批次汇总表

省份	批次				
	第一批（项）	第二批（项）	第三批（项）	第四批（项）	总计（项）
云南省	34	41（其中新增项38项，扩展项3项）	21（其中新增项12项，扩展项9项）	17（其中新增项9项，扩展项8项）	113

根据项目类别，云南省国家级非物质文化遗产名录（1—4批）的详细统计数据如表2。

表2　云南省国家级非物质文化遗产名录（1—4批）分类别汇总表

序号	项目类别	数量（单位：项）
1	民间文学	17
2	传统音乐	10
3	传统舞蹈	26

序号	项目类别	数量（单位：项）
4	传统戏剧	10
5	曲艺	1
6	传统体育、游艺与杂技	1
7	传统美术	5
8	传统技艺	19
9	传统医药	5
10	民俗	19
	总计	113

针对本汇编的正文部分，特做如下说明：

第一，根据项目类别，本汇编分为十章，相同类别的非遗项目归为一章，对其文献资料进行汇总。

第二，非遗项目的类型有两种：新增项目和扩展项目。前者指首次进入国家级非遗名录的非遗项目；后者指此前已进入上一批国家级非遗名录，而在后续批次申报时，由于申报地区和单位不同，只能将其列入扩展项目名录的非遗项目。

第三，对于两个名称相同，但分别属于新增项目和扩展项目两个不同类型的非遗项目，由于申报批次、申报地区和申报单位不同，仍按两个项目统计，因此在正文中也分项列出。但是，二者的文献资料是合二为一，还是分别单独介绍，将视情况而定。如果二者涉及的文献资料大致相同，则合二为一，汇总起来一并介绍；如果二者涉及的文献资料独具当地特色，则单独介绍。

第四，本汇编中名称相同的两项非遗项目合二为一介绍的有：第一章“民间文学”中的“第 11 项：司岗里”和“第 12 项：司岗里”。

第五，本汇编中名称相同的两项非遗项目分别单独介绍的有：第十章“民俗”中的“第 1 项：傣族泼水节”和“第 2 项：傣族泼水节”。

本汇编涉及的非遗项目是在云南省定居的各少数民族及汉族所创造的文化珍宝，具有多学科的研究价值。

第一章“民间文学”中，有 17 项非遗，主要涉及彝、哈尼、佤、阿昌、拉祜、藏、德昂、傣、壮、景颇和纳西等 11 个少数民族的创世史诗或英雄史诗。其中，大部分都是用本民族语记录或诵唱有关本民族、自然万物及人类的起源与发展史，或者总结本民族的生产生活技能和经验，有的还涉及相关民族的婚恋生死、原始崇拜和风俗习惯等。这些都是历史学、文化学和民俗学研究的“活化石”。

第二章“传统音乐”中，有10项非遗，主要涉及傈僳、哈尼、彝、布朗、白和纳西等6个少数民族以及汉族的民歌、酒歌、洞经音乐和古典音乐等，具有鲜明的民族特征和地域性，对音乐学相关研究具有重要价值。

第三章“传统舞蹈”中，有26项非遗，主要涉及彝族、哈尼、傣族、藏、佤、壮、拉祜、基诺、纳西、布朗、普米、德昂、怒、白和傈僳等15个少数民族的传统舞蹈，其中彝族的多达10项。这些非遗主要是有关各少数民族崇拜之物的舞蹈，如木鼓舞、水鼓舞、铜鼓舞、大鼓舞、象脚鼓舞、铓鼓舞、蜂桶鼓舞、芦笙舞和老虎笙等，体现了各民族的历史观、道德观、价值观和思维方式，是维系其民族精神的纽带，对增强民族团结，促进文化交流具有重要意义。

第四章“传统戏剧”中，有10项非遗，主要涉及汉、傣、佤、彝、白和壮等6个民族的传统戏剧。其中，有些戏剧是云南多民族文化融合的产物，如玉溪花灯戏、花灯戏、滇剧、白剧和腾冲皮影戏等，体现了多民族文化相互交融的特点。而有些戏剧是某少数民族独有剧种，极具民族特色，如傣剧、佤族清戏、彝剧和壮剧等。这些传统戏剧是研究相关民族戏剧文化的宝贵材料。

第五章“曲艺”中，仅有1项非遗，即傣族章哈，是傣族独特的曲艺形式，是傣族文化不可或缺的组成部分，具有鲜明的傣族特色，对研究傣族曲艺文化具有极其重要的价值。

第六章“传统体育、游艺与杂技”中，也仅有1项非遗，即彝族摔跤，是石林彝族人最热爱的传统体育活动，体现了当地彝民热爱运动、勇敢坚强的民族性格。

第七章“传统美术”中，有5项非遗，主要涉及纳西、傣、彝和白等4个少数民族的传统美术，体现了这四个民族高超的艺术创造力和独特的审美情趣，具有很强的实用价值，在当地少数民族的社会生活中占据着重要的地位。

第八章“传统技艺”中，有19项非遗，主要涉及傣族、白、哈尼、彝、苗、阿昌、藏和汉等8个民族的传统技艺。其中，傣族最多，有5项，主要涉及制陶、造纸、织锦、贝叶经制作和象脚鼓制作技艺等，体现了傣族人民高超的传统技艺水平。其他民族的传统技艺主要有茶制作、银（铜）器锻制、扎染、芦笙制作以及食物制作，如过桥米线和火腿的制作等。这些传统技艺是傣族、白、哈尼、彝、苗、阿昌、藏和汉等民族集体智慧的结晶，与其日常生活息息相关，是其传统文化的重要组成部分。

第九章“传统医药”中，有5项非遗，主要涉及彝、傣、藏和汉等4个民族的传统医药。其中，一些非遗是相关少数民族独特的医药精华，如彝医水膏药疗法、拨云锭制作技艺、睡药疗法和藏医骨伤疗法等。汉民族的昆中药传统中药制剂则是传统中医与当地少数民族医学的融合，是多民族医药文化交融的见证。

第十章“民俗”中，有 19 项非遗，主要涉及白、傣、彝、苗、景颇、独龙、怒族、傈僳、德昂、哈尼、藏、壮和汉等 13 个民族的民俗活动。其中，很多民俗活动源于少数民族的祭祀活动，如傣族泼水节、彝族火把节、怒族仙女节、德昂族浇花节、祭寨神林、梅里神山祭祀和女子太阳山祭祀等，具有浓厚的宗教祭祀、祖先祭祀或神灵祭祀的文化内涵；有些民俗活动体现了少数民族对英雄人物的崇拜情怀，如傈僳族刀杆节；而有些民俗活动则体现了少数民族的礼仪文化习俗，如白族三道茶等。这些民俗活动不仅是少数民族凝聚人心、加强团结的纽带，更是其民族传统文化展示与传承的舞台，对民俗学的相关研究具有宝贵的价值。

值得一提的是，本汇编中涉及的一些非遗项目，由于受到社会现代化进程加快的影响，年轻人不愿意学习和传承，因此面临濒危的境地；有些则是濒临消亡的民族或人口基数小的民族所独有的珍奇非遗项目，其本身就面临着传承乏人的困境；而有些非遗项目由于其技术难度大，对传承者的条件要求极其苛刻，因此其传承亦面临濒危的困境。因此，对这些濒危非遗项目的尽早抢救、挖掘和保护便显得尤为重要。

Introduction

This book mainly involves the documentary compilation of the state-level intangible cultural heritage of Yunnan Province (Batches 1-4), which has collected and sorted out the interim results that have been achieved currently concerning the related intangible cultural heritage items in Yunnan Province, outlining the basic content of each item with appropriate pictures. It aims to provide a collection of literature of the state-level intangible cultural heritage of Yunnan Province (Batches 1-4) that is easy for intangible cultural heritage lovers and researchers to access quickly.

The Notice of the State Council on Publishing the 1st-batch State-level Intangible Cultural Heritage List, The Notice of the State Council on Publishing the 2nd-batch State-level Intangible Cultural Heritage List and the 1st-batch Extended Item List of the State-level Intangible Cultural Heritage, The Notice of the State Council on Publishing the 3rd-batch State-level Intangible Cultural Heritage List and The Notice of the State Council on Publishing the 4th-batch Representative Item List of the State-level Intangible Cultural Heritage were published on the official website of the Central People's Government of the People's Republic of China respectively on May 20th, 2006, June 16th, 2008, June 9th, 2011 and December 3rd, 2014. According to these four notices, 34 items, 41 items (38 new items plus 3 extended items), 21 items (12 new items plus 9 extended items) and 17 items (9 new items plus 8 extended items) of the intangible cultural heritage of Yunnan Province have been shortlisted respectively in the 1st, 2nd, 3rd and 4th batches. There are 113 items in total.

According to the batches, the detailed statistics of the state-level Intangible Cultural Heritage List of Yunnan Province (Batches 1-4) are shown in Table 1:

Table 1 Summary Table of the State-level Intangible Cultural Heritage List of Yunnan Province in Batches (Batches 1-4)

Province	Batch				
	Batch 1 (Items)	Batch 2 (Items)	Batch 3 (Items)	Batch 4 (Items)	Total (Items)
Yunnan	34	41（38 New Items, 3 Extended Items）	21（12 New Items, 9 Extended Items）	17（9 New Items, 8 Extended Items）	113

According to the categories of items, the detailed statistics of the State-level Intangible Cultural Heritage List of Yunnan Province (Batches 1-4) are shown in Table 2.

Table 2 Summary Table of the State-level Intangible Cultural Heritage List of Yunnan Province in Categories (Batches 1-4)

No.	Categories of the Items	Amount (Unit: items)
1	Folk Literature	17
2	Traditional Music	10
3	Traditional Dance	26
4	Traditional Opera	10
5	Quyi (a general term for all Chinese talking-and-singing art forms)	1
6	Traditional Sports, Recreations and Acrobatics	1
7	Traditional Fine Arts	5
8	Traditional Craft	19
9	Traditional Medicine	5
10	Folk Custom	19
	Total	113

For the main body of this compilation, some specifics are explained as follows.

Firstly, according to categories of the items, this compilation is divided into ten chapters, with the same category of intangible cultural heritage items falling under one chapter and their literature summarized together.

Secondly, intangible cultural heritage items are divided into two types: New Item and Extended Item. The former refers to the intangible cultural heritage items that have been shortlisted in the State-level Intangible Cultural Heritage List for the first time; and the latter refers to the ones that have been shortlisted in the State-level Intangible Cultural Heritage List of the previous batch but have to be listed again due to different application regions and units in the subsequent batches.

Thirdly, as to two intangible cultural heritage items which have the same name but fall under different types of New Item and Extended Item, they are counted as two items due to different application batches, application regions and application units. Consequently, they are listed separately in the body part. However, whether to introduce their literature together or separately depends on specific situations: if the literature concerning them is roughly the same, the literature will be introduced together; and if the literature involved has unique local characteristics, the literature will be introduced separately.

Fourthly, in this compilation, two items of intangible cultural heritage with the same name introduced together are: "Item 11: *Sigangli (out of the cliff-cave) Epic*" and "Item 12: *Sigangli (out of the cliff-cave) Epic*" in Chapter One "Folk Literature".

Fifthly, in this compilation, two items of intangible cultural heritage with the same name introduced separately are: "Item 1: the Water-splashing Festival of the Dai Nationality" and "Item 2: the Water-splashing Festival of the Dai Nationality" in Chapter Ten "Folk Custom".

The intangible cultural heritage items involved in this compilation are cultural treasures created by the ethnic minorities and the Han nationality living in Yunnan Province, having multi-disciplinary research value.

In Chapter One "Folk Literature", there are 17 items of intangible cultural heritage, which mainly involve the epics of creation or the heroic epics of the eleven ethnic minorities of Yi, Hani, Wa, Achang, Lahu, Zang, De'ang, Dai, Zhuang, Jingpo and Naxi. Among them, most are in their native languages, recording or chanting the origins and development history of their nationalities, all things in nature and human beings, or summarizing the production and life skills and experiences of their nationalities; and some are concerned with the marriage, love, life, death, primitive worship, as well as social customs and habits of relevant nationalities. All of them are the "living fossils" for studying the history, culturology and folklore of related nationalities.

In Chapter Two "Traditional Music", there are ten items of intangible cultural heritage of the six ethnic minorities of Lisu, Hani, Yi, Bulang, Bai and Naxi, as well as the Han nationality, which mainly involve the folk songs, Toasting Songs, Dongjing Music, classical music, etc. They have distinctive national features and regionalism, with great value in studying the musicology of relevant nationalities.

In Chapter Three “Traditional Dance”, there are 26 items of intangible cultural heritage, which mainly involve the traditional dances of the 15 ethnic minorities of Yi, Hani, Dai, Zang, Wa, Zhuang, Lahu, Jinuo, Naxi, Bulang, Pumi, De’ang, Nu, Bai and Lisu, with as many as ten items belonging to the Yi nationality. These dances are mainly related to things worshiped by relevant ethnic minorities, such as the Wooden-drum Dance, the Water Drum Dance, the Bronze-drum Dance, the Big Drum Dance, the Elephant-foot Drum Dance, Manggu Drum Dance, the Bee-barrel Drum Dance, Lusheng Dance and the Tiger Sheng Dance, which reflect the historical outlook, moral concepts, values and thinking patterns of relevant nationalities, function as the bond for maintaining their national spirit and are of great significance in enhancing national unity and promoting cultural exchanges.

In Chapter Four “Traditional Opera”, there are ten items of intangible cultural heritage, which mainly involve the traditional operas of the six nationalities of Han, Dai, Wa, Yi, Bai and Zhuang. Among them, some operas, such as Yuxi Lantern Opera, the Lantern Opera, Yunnan Opera, Bai Opera and Tengchong Shadow Play, are the products of the integration of multiple ethnic cultures in Yunnan Province, showing the characteristics of multiple ethnic cultures blending with each other. And some operas, such as Dai Opera, Qing Opera of the Wa Nationality, Yi Opera and Zhuang Opera, are unique to certain ethnic minority and have special ethnic characteristics. These traditional operas are “living materials” for the study of the operatic culture of related nationalities.

In Chapter Five “Quyi (a general term for all Chinese talking-and-singing art forms)”, there is only one item of intangible cultural heritage, namely Zhangha of the Dai Nationality. With distinctive characteristics of the Dai nationality, it is a form of Quyi (a general term for all Chinese talking-and-singing art forms) unique to this ethnic group and an indispensable part of the Dai culture, which is of great value to the study of the Quyi culture of the Dai nationality.

In Chapter Six “Traditional Sports, Recreations and Acrobatics”, there is also only one item of intangible cultural heritage, namely Wrestling of the Yi Nationality. It is a traditional sport activity deeply loved by the Yi people in Shilin County, reflecting their love for fitness exercises and their national characters of bravery and toughness.

In Chapter Seven “Traditional Fine Arts”, there are five items of intangible cultural heritage, which mainly involve the traditional fine arts of the four ethnic minorities of Naxi, Dai, Yi and Bai. They reflect the superb artistic creativity and unique aesthetic taste of these four nationalities, having great utility value and occupying an important position in the social life of local ethnic minorities.

In Chapter Eight "Traditional Craft", there are 19 items of intangible cultural heritage, which mainly involve the traditional crafts of the eight nationalities of Dai, Bai, Hani, Yi, Miao, Achang, Zang and Han. Among them, the Dai nationality has the largest number with as many as five items, which mainly include the crafts of making pottery, paper, brocade, Pattra-leaf Scriptures and the Elephant-foot Drum, reflecting the superb traditional crafts of the Dai people. The traditional crafts of other nationalities mainly include tea making, silverware (bronze ware) forging, Tie Dyeing, Lusheng Musical Instruments making and food making, such as Guoqiao Rice Noodles making and ham making. These traditional crafts are the crystallization of the collective wisdom of the Dai, Bai, Hani, Yi, Miao, Achang, Zang and Han nationalities, which is closely related to their daily life and is an important part of their traditional cultures.

In Chapter Nine "Traditional Medicine", there are five items of intangible cultural heritage, which mainly involve the traditional medicine of the four nationalities of Yi, Dai, Zang and Han. Among them, some are the medical essence unique to ethnic minorities, such as the Therapy of Ointments Mixed with Water of the Yi Nationality, the Craft of Making Boyun Pastille, the Therapy of Sleeping in Herbs and the Therapies for Bone Injuries of the Zang Medicine; while the Preparations of Kun Traditional Chinese Medicine of the Han nationality are the integration of the traditional Chinese medicine and the medicines of local ethnic minorities, and are an evidence of the integration of the medical cultures of multiple nationalities.

In Chapter Ten "Folk Custom", there are 19 items of intangible cultural heritage, which mainly involve the folk activities of the 13 nationalities of Bai, Dai, Yi, Miao, Jingpo, Dulong, Nu, Lisu, De'ang, Hani, Zang, Zhuang and Han. Among them, many folk activities have originated from the sacrificial activities of ethnic minorities, such as the Water-splashing Festival of the Dai Nationality, the Torch Festival of the Yi Nationality, the Fairy Maiden Festival of the Nu Nationality, the Flower-watering Festival of the De'ang Nationality, Offering Sacrifices to Gods of Stockaded Villages, Offering Sacrifices to the Meili Sacred Mountain and Women's Offering Sacrifices to the Sun Mountain, which have rich cultural connotations of religious sacrifices, ancestor sacrifices or god sacrifices; some folk activities reflect their adoration of heroes, such as the Daogan (knife ladder) Festival of the Lisu Nationality; while some folk activities reflect the etiquette culture and custom of ethnic minorities, such as the Three-course Tea of the Bai Nationality. These folk activities are not only a tie for ethnic minorities to unite people and strengthen unity, but also a stage for exhibiting and inheriting their traditional cultures, which is valuable for the study of folklore of related nationalities.

It is worth mentioning that, due to the impact of the accelerated process of social modernization, young people are not willing to learn and pass them on, so some items of intangible cultural heritage involved in this compilation face an endangered situation; some of them are unique to the ethnic minorities that are on the verge of extinction or have very small populations, so they themselves are in a dilemma of lacking inheritors; and some of them are technically difficult and require extremely stringent requirements for inheritors, so their inheritance also faces the dilemma of being endangered. Therefore, it is particularly important to rescue, document and protect the endangered intangible cultural heritage as early as possible.

目录 Contents

第四章 传统戏剧

第五章 曲 艺

第六章 传统体育、游艺与杂技

第七章 传统美术

第十章　民　俗

附录

后记

第一章 民间文学

Chapter One

Folk Literature

第 1 项：遮帕麻和遮咪麻

“活祀”（祭司）念诵《遮帕麻和遮咪麻》
a Priest Reciting *Zhepama and Zhemima Myth*

项目序号：3	项目编号：Ⅰ-3	公布时间：2006（第一批）	类别：民间文学
所属地区：云南省	类型：新增项目	申报地区或单位：云南省梁河县	

《遮帕麻和遮咪麻》是阿昌族的长篇诗体创世神话，主要流传在云南省德宏傣族景颇族自治州梁河县阿昌族人民中，以唱诗和口头白话两种形式传承至今。故事中的盐婆神话是研究古代西南民族游牧文化的第一手资料。

天公遮帕麻和地母遮咪麻是阿昌族心目中的神话人物，不仅是人类的始祖、开天辟地的大神、补天治水的巨匠、杀妖降魔和保护众生的英雄，更是最受崇拜的至尊善神和护佑所有寻常人家的神灵，同时也是阿昌族祭祀活动的主掌之神。史诗中的魔王腊訇则是最大的恶神。[①]《遮帕麻和遮咪麻》讲述了阿昌族始祖遮帕麻和遮咪麻造天织地、制服洪荒、创造人类、智斗邪魔腊訇，使宇宙恢复和平景象的过程。阿昌族在宗教活动、民俗活动以及建房、迎候亲戚、娶亲迎候媒人和丧葬仪式时都要念诵《遮帕麻和遮咪麻》，以求屋舍平安、家人清吉，或请求为死者的魂灵引路。开头的唱词为追溯家谱，首先唱颂阿昌族的始祖遮帕麻和遮咪麻创造了人类，使族人得以联姻并繁衍传承。遮帕麻和遮咪麻的传说，不论是唱诗还是白话故事，内容基本一致。《遮帕麻和遮咪麻》生动地反映了人类从母权制向父权制过渡的状况，是阿昌族文化发展的一座丰碑，阿昌族将其称为“我们民族的歌”。[②]

Item 1: *Zhepama and Zhemima Myth*

Item Serial Number: 3	Item ID Number: Ⅰ-3	Released Date: 2006 (Batch 1)	Category: Folk Literature
Affiliated Province: Yunnan Province	Type: New Item	Application Province or Unit: Lianghe County, Yunnan Province	

Zhepama and Zhemima Myth is a long poetic creation myth of the Achang nationality. It is mainly circulated among the people of the Achang nationality in Lianghe County, Dehong Dai and Jingpo Autonomous Prefecture, Yunnan Province. It has been handed down to the present in two forms: poem for singing and oral vernacular. The Yanpo Myth in the story is the first-hand material to study the nomadic culture of the ancient southwestern ethnic groups.

The Heaven Father Zhepama and the Earth Mother Zhemima are the mythological figures in the eyes of the Achang people. They are not only the ancestors of mankind, the great gods who have created the heaven and the earth, the masters who repaired the sky and brought water under control, and the heroes who kill demons and devils and protect all living creatures, but also the supreme benevolent

① 《阿昌族史诗〈遮帕麻和遮咪麻〉》，云南非物质文化遗产保护网，http://www.ynich.cn/view.php?id=1231&cat_id=11110，检索日期：2019 年 9 月 2 日。

② 《遮帕麻和遮咪麻》，中国非物质文化遗产网，http://www.ihchina.cn/Article/Index/detail?id=12181，检索日期：2019 年 9 月 2 日。

gods who have been worshipped most and everyone's gods who protect all ordinary families. They are also the major gods in charge of the sacrificial activities of the Achang nationality. Demon Lahong in the epic is the biggest evil god. This myth tells the process of the creation of the heaven and the earth, the ending of chaos, the creation of mankind, the fighting against Demon Lahong, and the restoration of the peace of the universe, done by the Achang people's ancestors Zhepama and Zhemima. In religious activities, folk activities, building houses, welcoming relatives, welcoming matchmakers in marriage ceremony and funeral ceremonies, the Achang people must recite ***Zhepama and Zhemima Myth*** to pray for the safety of houses and the auspiciousness of the family, or to pray for leading the way for the souls of the deceased. The beginning lines introduce the genealogy of the Achang people, which first pay tribute to their ancestors, Zhepama and Zhemima, who have created human beings, enabling the Achang people to get married and reproduce. The content of the poem for singing and the story in oral vernacular of this myth are roughly same. ***Zhepama and Zhemima Myth*** vividly reflects the transition of human beings from matriarchy to patriarchy. It is a monument to the cultural development of the Achang nationality, regarded as "the song of our ethnic group".

第 2 项：牡帕密帕

拉祜族民间史诗《牡帕密帕》
Mupa Mipa Myth, the folk epic of the Lahu nationality

项目序号：4	项目编号：Ⅰ-4	公布时间：2006（第一批）	类别：民间文学
所属地区：云南省	类型：新增项目	申报地区或单位：云南省思茅市	

《牡帕密帕》是拉祜族“波阔嘎阔”（一种民间演唱叙事古歌的形式）演唱的一部长篇诗体创世神话，形成于拉祜族漫长的古代社会，流传于云南省思茅市澜沧拉祜族自治县。

拉祜族在长期游猎采集和迁徙过程中，产生了万物有灵的信仰，创造了包括厄萨产生、造天地、造日月、物种的起源和人种由来等神话传说。[①]《牡帕密帕》全诗共 17 个篇章，2300 行，内容包括造天地日月、造万物和人类以及人类初始阶段的生存状况等，是拉祜族人民传承历史悠久的口述文学精品。《牡帕密帕》由“嘎木科”（会唱诗的人）和“魔巴”（宗教活动主持者）主唱，也可有多人伴唱或多人轮唱；歌词通俗简练，格律固定，对偶句居多。曲调优美动听，调式因地域不同而有差异，演唱以字行腔，有说唱的特点。《牡帕密帕》在拉祜族的传统节日、宗教活动或农闲期间说唱，说唱往往通宵达旦，参加者无不兴致盎然。[②]

---

① 《拉祜族史诗〈牡帕密帕〉》，云南非物质文化遗产保护网，http://www.ynich.cn/view.php?id=1230&cat_id=11110，检索日期：2019 年 9 月 3 日。

② 《牡帕密帕》，中国非物质文化遗产网，http://www.ihchina.cn/Article/Index/detail?id=12182，检索日期：2019 年 9 月 3 日。

Item 2: *Mupa Mipa Myth*

Item Serial Number: 4	Item ID Number: Ⅰ-4	Released Date: 2006 (Batch 1)	Category: Folk Literature
Affiliated Province: Yunnan Province	Type: New Item	Application Province or Unit: Simao City, Yunnan Province	

Mupa Mipa Myth is a long poetic creation myth sung by the Lahu nationality in the form of "Bokuo Gakuo" (a form of folk narrative ancient song). It has been created in the long ancient society of the Lahu nationality and circulated in Lancang Lahu Autonomous County, Simao City, Yunnan province.

In the process of long-term hunting, food gathering and migration, the Lahu people have developed the belief in animism. Myths and legends, including the birth of God Esa, the creation of the heaven and the earth, the creation of the sun and the moon, and the origins of species and human race, have emerged. The whole epic consists of 17 chapters with 2,300 lines. It describes the creation of the heaven, the earth, the sun, the moon, all things on earth and human beings, as well as their living conditions at the initial stage. It is a masterpiece of oral literature passed down by the Lahu people for a long history. ***Mupa Mipa Myth*** is sung mainly by "Gamuke" (a verse singer) and "Moba" (a presider of religious activities), sometimes with many supporting singers. It can also be sung by many people in turns. Its lyrics are popular and concise, with fixed rhythm and many couplets. Its melody is beautiful and melodious, and its musical mode varies from region to region. Its singing is performed with clear articulation and a mellow and full tune according to the words in it, having the feature of talking and singing. ***Mupa Mipa Myth*** is performed at traditional festivals and in religious activities or during the slack period of farming. Its performance usually lasts all night till dawn, and all participants are full of interests.

第 3 项：四季生产调

节庆场合演唱四季生产调
Singing the Four-season Production Tune on a Festival Occasion

项目序号：24	项目编号：Ⅰ-24	公布时间：2006（第一批）	类别：民间文学
所属地区：云南省	类型：新增项目	申报地区或单位：云南省红河哈尼族彝族自治州	

四季生产调流传于云南省红河哈尼族彝族自治州红河、元阳、绿春、金平、建水等县的哈尼族聚居区，传承历史悠久。

哈尼族无文字，其先民将积累的关于自然、动植物、生产生活的丰富技能和经验形成一套完整的农业生产生活和民间文化知识体系，经过总结提炼，以通俗易懂的歌谣“四季生产调”代代传承，使哈尼族农耕生产、生活的传统文化一直延续至今。四季生产调分为引子、冬季三月、春季三月、夏季三月和秋季三月五个部分。[①] 引子部分有 41 行，强调祖先传承下来的四季生产调对哈尼族的生存所具有的意义，其余部分按季节顺序讲述梯田耕作的程序、技术要领及相关的天文历法知识、自然物候变化规律、节庆祭典知识和人生礼节规范等。其传承方式主要是“莫批”（哈尼族民间文化传承人）收徒弟、家庭传承及在节庆或公众场合演唱等。其体系严整，通俗易懂，可诵可唱，语言生动活泼，贴近生产、生活。四季生产调不仅是梯田生产技术的全面总结，也是哈尼族社会伦理道德规范的集大成之作，见证了哈尼族梯田稻作文明的变迁历程。[②]

① 《哈尼族四季生产调》，云南非物质文化遗产保护网，http://www.ynich.cn/view.php?id=1229&cat_id=11110，检索日期：2019 年 9 月 3 日。

② 《四季生产调》，中国非物质文化遗产网，http://www.ihchina.cn/Article/Index/detail?id=12224，检索日期：2019 年 9 月 3 日。

Item 3: The Four-season Production Tune

<table>
<tr><td>Item Serial Number: 24</td><td>Item ID Number:
Ⅰ-24</td><td>Released Date:
2006 (Batch 1)</td><td>Category:
Folk Literature</td></tr>
<tr><td>Affiliated Province: Yunnan Province</td><td>Type:
New Item</td><td colspan="2">Application Province or Unit:
Honghe Hani and Yi Autonomous Prefecture, Yunnan Province</td></tr>
</table>

The Four-season Production Tune, with a long history of inheritance, is mainly spread in areas inhabited by the Hani nationality in Honghe, Yuanyang, Lüchun, Jinping, Jianshui and other counties in Honghe Hani and Yi Autonomous Prefecture of Yunnan Province.

The Hani nationality has no written language. The abundant skills and experience accumulated by its ancestors about nature, animals, plants, production and life have developed into a rounded knowledge system of agricultural production, life, and folk culture. After summarization and refinement, the knowledge has been passed down from generation to generation in the form of a popular and easy-to-understand ballad, known as "**the Four-season Production Tune**", making the traditional culture of farming, production and life of the Hani people inherited till today. **The Four-season Production Tune** consists of five parts: the introduction, three winter months, three spring months, three summer months and three autumn months. The introduction part has 41 lines, emphasizing the significance of **the Four-season Production Tune** that is inherited from ancestors for the survival of the Hani people. The remaining parts describe, in the order of seasons, the procedures and technical essentials of terrace farming, related knowledge of astronomical calendar, laws of natural and phenological changes, knowledge of festival celebrations and sacrificial rituals, norms of life etiquette, etc. It is mainly imparted and inherited in three ways: "Mopi" (the inheritor of the folk culture of the Hani nationality) teaching his disciples, family impartment and inheritance, and singing at festivals or in public places. Its structure is well-organized, and its content is easy to understand. It can be either recited or sung, and its lyrics are lively and closely related to production and life. **The Four-season Production Tune** is not only a comprehensive summarization of the terrace farming technology, but also a collection of the social ethics and moral norms of the Hani nationality, which has witnessed the evolution of the cultivation civilization of rice in terrace fields of the Hani people.

第 4 项：格萨（斯）尔

格萨（斯）尔王雕像
the Statue of King Gesar

项目序号：27	项目编号：Ⅰ-27	公布时间：2006（第一批）	类别：民间文学
所属地区：云南省	类型：新增项目	申报地区或单位：云南省	

史诗《格萨（斯）尔》是广泛流传于藏族地区的一部家喻户晓、人人喜爱的长篇英雄史诗，其诗行约 30 万～150 万行，被誉为世界最长的史诗。在云南主要流传于迪庆藏族自治州及丽江等地广大藏族、普米族和部分纳西族、傈僳族。

格萨尔是藏族民间文学中的一个典型人物，人们采用浪漫主义手法，通过各种神奇的故事来歌颂这位藏族人民理想中的古代英雄。史诗《格萨（斯）尔》体现了爱国、爱民、反对头人和反对宗教压迫的精神。[①] 其主旨是“降妖伏魔，为民除害”，基本章节有：1. 格萨尔的诞生；2. 智斩魔虎；3. 固穆可汗；4. 降伏十二头魔王；5. 大战锡来河三汗；6. 力战蟒古斯喇嘛；7. 大闹地狱；8. 英雄再生；9. 奋战昂都拉玛魔汗；10. 铲除二十一颗头颅魔王；11. 消灭固么布魔汗；12. 那钦汗的覆灭等。[②] 云南省已搜集到《格萨（斯）尔》各种资料 20 多种，有些与其他省区相同，有些较为独特。如在德钦县发掘出版的《加岭传奇之部》，以歌颂藏汉友谊为主要内容，书中的山名、地名和风俗都是云南独有的，具有地方特色。[③]

① 《格萨尔史诗》，云南非物质文化遗产保护网，http://www.ynich.cn/view-11110-1228.html，检索日期：2019 年 8 月 30 日。

② 《格萨（斯）尔》，迪庆非物质文化遗产保护网，http://www.dqich.cn/baohuminglu/detail/22/66，检索日期：2019 年 8 月 31 日。

③ 《格萨尔史诗》，云南非物质文化遗产保护网，http://www.ynich.cn/view-11110-1228.html，检索日期：2019 年 8 月 30 日。

Item 4: *Gesar Epic*

Item Serial Number: 27	Item ID Number: Ⅰ-27	Released Date: 2006 (Batch 1)	Category: Folk Literature
Affiliated Province: Yunnan Province	Type: New Item	Application Province or Unit: Yunnan Province	

Gesar Epic is a well-known long heroic epic beloved by many people, which is widely circulated in areas inhabited by the Zang nationality, with about 300,000 to 1,500,000 lines, acclaimed as the longest epic in the world. In Yunnan Province, it is predominantly spread among the ethnic groups of Zang, Pumi, Naxi and Lisu in Diqing Zang Autonomous Prefecture, Lijiang City, etc.

Gesar is a typical character in the folk literature of the Zang nationality. People use romantic techniques to sing the praises of this ancient hero in the ideal of the Zang people through various magical stories. This epic reflects the spirit of patriotism, love for people, and opposition to headmen and religious oppression. Its main theme is "subduing demons and monsters, and getting rid of evils for the people". Its basic chapters are: 1. The Birth of Gesar; 2. Wisely Killing Devil Tiger; 3. Gumu Khan; 4. Subduing the Twelve-head Demon; 5. Fighting against Three Khans of the Xilai River; 6. Fighting Hard against Manggusi Lama; 7. Causing Havoc in the Hell; 8. The Rebirth of the Hero; 9. Bravely Combating the Demon Khan of Angdu Lama; 10. Eliminating the 21-head Demon King; 11. Annihilating the Demon Khan of Gumobu; 12. The Fall of Naqin Khan, etc. In Yunnan Province, more than 20 versions of *Gesar* have been collected. Some of them are the same as those in other provinces, and some are rather unique. For example, *The Legend of Jialing,* discovered and published in Deqin County, mainly focuses on singing the praises of the friendship between the Zang and Han nationalities. The mountain names, place names and customs mentioned in this book are unique to Yunnan Province, having local characteristics.

第 5 项：阿诗玛

《阿诗玛》
Ashima Poem

项目序号：28	项目编号：Ⅰ-28	公布时间：2006（第一批）	类别：民间文学
所属地区：云南省	类型：新增项目	申报地区或单位：云南省石林彝族自治县	

《阿诗玛》是流传于云南省石林彝族自治县彝族支系撒尼人的一部叙事长诗。它使用口传形式的诗体语言，讲述或演唱阿诗玛不屈不挠地同强权势力作斗争的故事，揭示了光明终将代替黑暗、善美终将代替丑恶、自由终将代替压迫与禁锢的人类理想，反映了彝族撒尼人“断得弯不得”（宁折不弯）的民族性格和民族精神。[①]

《阿诗玛》以撒尼彝语创作，分为南北两个流派。南部流派分布在圭山镇、亩竹箐乡和尾则乡，北部流派分布在北大村乡、西街口乡和石林镇。两个流派大同小异。《阿诗玛》可讲述也可传唱，演唱所占比例较大，有独唱、对唱、一人领唱众人合唱几种形式。《阿诗玛》曲调有“喜调”“老人调”“悲调”“哭调”“骂调”等，演唱者根据其年龄、性别选用相应的曲调。《阿诗玛》以五言句传唱，在技巧上使用了伏笔、夸张和讽刺等手法，在艺术形式上使用了谐音、顶真、拈连和比喻等形式，主要在节日、婚嫁、祭祀、葬仪、劳动、生活等不同场合传唱和讲述，尤以婚礼时演唱最为盛行。[②]自 20 世纪 50 年代初其汉文整理本发表后，《阿诗玛》已被翻译成英、法、德、西班牙、俄、日、韩等多种语言在海外流传。[③]

---

① 《阿诗玛》，中国非物质文化遗产网，http://www.ihchina.cn/Article/Index/detail?id=12241，检索日期：2019 年 9 月 3 日。

② 《彝族叙事长诗〈阿诗玛〉》，云南非物质文化遗产保护网，http://www.ynich.cn/view-11110-1227.html，检索日期：2019 年 8 月 30 日。

③ 《阿诗玛》，中国非物质文化遗产网，http://www.ihchina.cn/Article/Index/detail?id=12241，检索日期：2019 年 9 月 3 日。

Item 5: *Ashima Poem*

<table>
<tr><td>Item Serial Number: 28</td><td>Item ID Number:
Ⅰ-28</td><td>Released Date:
2006 (Batch 1)</td><td>Category:
Folk Literature</td></tr>
<tr><td>Affiliated Province: Yunnan Province</td><td>Type:
New Item</td><td colspan="2">Application Province or Unit:
Shilin Yi Autonomous County, Yunnan Province</td></tr>
</table>

Ashima Poem is a long narrative poem circulated among the Sani branch of the Yi nationality in Shilin Yi Autonomous County, Yunnan Province. Using oral poetic language, it narrates or sings the story of Ashima's indomitable struggle against powerful forces. The poem reveals the ideals of mankind that brightness will eventually replace darkness, that goodness and beauty will finally replace ugliness, and that freedom will replace oppression and imprisonment in the end. It reflects the national character and spirit of the Sani people of the Yi nationality, that is, they will never be bended and conquered.

Ashima Poem, which was written in Sani dialect, is divided into two genres, the northern genre and the southern genre. The southern genre is distributed in Guishan, Muzhujing and Weize townships, while the northern genre is distributed in Beidacun, Xijiekou and Shilin townships. The two genres are largely identical with only minor differences. ***Ashima Poem*** can be performed by means of narrating or singing. Singing takes up a larger proportion. There are several forms of singing: solo singing, antiphonal singing, and one person leading the singing with others singing in chorus. The tunes of ***Ashima Poem*** include "happy tune", "senior's tune", "sorrowful tune", "crying tune" and "curse tune". A performer selects a corresponding tune according to his/her age and gender. ***Ashima Poem*** is sung in five-character lines, using the techniques of foreshadowing, exaggeration, satire, etc, as well as the rhetorical devices of homophonic rhetoric, anadiplosis, zeugma, metaphor, etc. It is mainly sung and narrated on different occasions, such as festivals, weddings, sacrifices, funerals, laboring and living. Especially at weddings, singing ***Ashima Poem*** is the most popular. Since the publication of the Chinese version in the early 1950s, ***Ashima Poem*** has been translated into many foreign languages, such as English, French, German, Spanish, Russian, Japanese and Korean, and has been in circulation overseas.

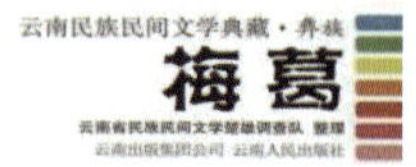

第 6 项：梅葛

《梅葛》专著
Meige Epic (a monograph)

项目序号：550	项目编号：Ⅰ-63	公布时间：2008（第二批）	类别：民间文学
所属地区：云南省	类型：新增项目	申报地区或单位：云南省楚雄彝族自治州	

《梅葛》是一部古老的彝族长篇说唱史诗，无文字记载，主要靠口耳相传、沿袭演唱保存下来。其内容是彝族人对开天辟地、万物起源的理解以及生产劳动、婚丧嫁娶、风情习俗的记述，被视为彝族人民的“根谱”。① 姚安口传彝族《梅葛》起源于云南省楚雄彝族自治州姚安县官屯乡。

《梅葛》长达 5770 余行，分为“创世”“造物”“婚事和恋歌”“丧葬”四个部分。梅葛有老年梅葛、中年梅葛、青年梅葛、娃娃梅葛四种类型。老年梅葛主要唱述开天辟地、创世立业的内容，同时也反映彝族群众的劳动和生活；中年梅葛唱述青年男女成家后生产生活的艰难，内容忧伤，曲调凄婉；青年梅葛反映彝族青年男女的纯真情爱，属于恋爱山歌性质；娃娃梅葛是彝族“儿歌”，由成群结伙的彝族青少年和儿童对唱。《梅葛》演唱有单人、双人和集体三种形式，伴奏乐器有葫芦笙、口弦、笛子和月琴等。《梅葛》用彝汉两种语言演唱，唱词以七字句、五字句为常见，讲求彝语声韵，诙谐风趣。②

① 《彝族梅葛》，云南非物质文化遗产保护网，http://www.ynich.cn/view.php?id=1156&cat_id=11111，检索日期：2019 年 9 月 3 日。

② 《梅葛》，中国非物质文化遗产网，http://www.ihchina.cn/Article/Index/detail?id=12296，检索日期：2019 年 9 月 3 日。

Item 6: *Meige Epic*

Item Serial Number: 550	Item ID Number: Ⅰ-63	Released Date: 2008 (Batch 2)	Category: Folk Literature
Affiliated Province: Yunnan Province	Type: New Item	Application Province or Unit: Chuxiong Yi Autonomous Prefecture, Yunnan Province	

Meige Epic is an ancient long talking-and-singing epic of the Yi nationality, which has no written record. It has been preserved and passed on mainly by word of mouth and traditional singing. Its content is about the Yi people's understanding of the creation of the heaven and the earth, the origin of all things, as well as the narration of their production and labor, weddings and funerals, and customs, which is regarded as "the root genealogy" of the Yi people. The orally-transmitted ***Meige Epic*** of the Yi nationality originates from Guantun Township, Yao'an County, Chuxiong Yi Autonomous Prefecture, Yunnan Province.

Meige Epic consists of more than 5770 lines, and is divided into four parts: "The Creation of the World", "The Creation of All Things", "Marriages and Love Songs", and "Funerals". It has four types, namely ***Meige Epic*** for the old, ***Meige Epic*** for the middle-aged, ***Meige Epic*** for the young and ***Meige Epic*** for kids. ***Meige Epic*** for the old mainly sings the creation of the heaven and the earth and the establishment of careers. Besides, it also reflects the production and life of the Yi people. ***Meige Epic*** for the middle-aged mainly sings the difficulties in production and life of young men and women after getting married, with a melancholic content and melody. ***Meige Epic*** for the young reflects the pure love of young men and women, which belongs to romantic folk songs. ***Meige Epic*** for kids is children's songs, sung in antiphonal style by groups of teenagers and children of the Yi nationality. The singing of ***Meige Epic*** has three forms, one-person singing (solo), two-person singing (duet), and collective singing (chorus). The accompaniment instruments include Hulusheng (a gourd-made musical instrument), Kouxian (a kind of buccal reed), flutes and Yueqin (a four-stringed plucked musical instrument with a full-moon-shaped sound box). It is sung in Yi and Mandarin languages. Its lyrics are commonly composed of seven-character and five-character sentences, emphasizing the rhyme of the Yi language and being humorous and witty.

《查姆》专著
Chamu Epic (a monograph)

第 7 项：查姆

项目序号：551	项目编号：Ⅰ-64	公布时间：2008（第二批）	类别：民间文学
所属地区：云南省	类型：新增项目	申报地区或单位：云南省双柏县	

《查姆》是流传于云南省双柏县大麦地镇、安龙堡乡等彝族地区的彝族民间创世史诗。查姆在彝语中为“大”和“起源”之意，意译为“万物的起源”。

《查姆》以神话传说的方式记述了人类、万物的起源和发展历史，提出了猴子变人的朴素观点，由通晓彝文的毕摩（彝族祭司）用彝文记录在书笺上进行传承，结构庞杂、神话色彩浓厚。据彝族《毕摩经》记载，最早的《查姆》有一百二十多个“查”，分为上部和下部。上部内容包括开天辟地、洪水泛滥、人类起源、万物起源等；下部内容包括天文地理、占卜历算、诗歌文学等，是一部名副其实的彝族百科全书，彝族人称之为“根谱”。[①]《查姆》用老彝文记载，基本上是五言句式，讲究押韵。原来只在丧葬、祭祀场合由毕摩吟唱，现在当地彝族群众逢年过节、婚丧祭祀、盖房起屋、播种收割等都请毕摩吟唱《查姆》，常用曲调优美的“阿噻调”来配唱，现在当地彝族群众逢年过节、婚丧祭祀、盖房起屋、播种收割等都请毕摩吟唱《查姆》。常用曲调优美的“阿噻调”来配唱，有时亦用大四弦伴奏，有唱有述，载歌载舞。[②]

---

① 《查姆》，中国非物质文化遗产网，http://www.ihchina.cn/Article/Index/detail?id=12297，检索日期：2019 年 9 月 3 日。

② 《彝族史诗〈查姆〉》，云南非物质文化遗产保护网，http://www.ynich.cn/view.php?id=1110&cat_id=11111，检索日期：2019 年 9 月 3 日。

Item 7: *Chamu Epic*

Item Serial Number: 551	Item ID Number: Ⅰ-64	Released Date: 2008 (Batch 2)	Category: Folk Literature
Affiliated Province: Yunnan Province	Type: New Item	Application Province or Unit: Shuangbai County, Yunnan Province	

Chamu Epic is a folk creation epic of the Yi nationality circulated in areas inhabited by the Yi people in Damaidi Township, Anlongbu Township, etc. of Shuangbai County, Yunnan Province. *Chamu* means "grand" and "origin" in the Yi language, and can be translated into "the origin of all things".

Chamu Epic gives an account of the origin and development history of human beings and all things in the form of myths and legends, and puts forward the simple yet profound theory of monkeys turning into humans. It is passed down by Bimo (the priest of the Yi nationality), who is proficient in the Yi language and record it on book notes in the Yi language. With a complex structure, it is full of strong mythological color. According to the records of *Bimo Scripture* of the Yi nationality, the earliest version of ***Chamu Epic*** has more than 120 *cha* (one "*cha*" refers to one origin of a creature), which is divided into two parts. The first part includes the creation of the heaven and the earth, flooding, the origin of human beings and the origin of all things. The second part involves astronomy, geography, divination, calendar, calculation, poetry, literature, etc. It is a veritable encyclopedia of the Yi nationality, regarded as "the root genealogy" by the Yi people. ***Chamu Epic*** is recorded in the old Yi language, which basically adopts the five-character sentence pattern and stresses rhyming. Originally, it was sung by Bimo only at funerals and on sacrificial occasions. Now, the local Yi people will invite Bimo to sing it on the occasions of festivals, weddings, funerals, offering sacrifices, building houses, sowing, harvesting, etc. It is often sung to the accompaniment of "the mode of Asai" that has a beautiful melody. Sometimes, it is performed to the accompaniment of Big Sixian (a four-stringed plucked musical instrument), integrating singing, narration and dancing.

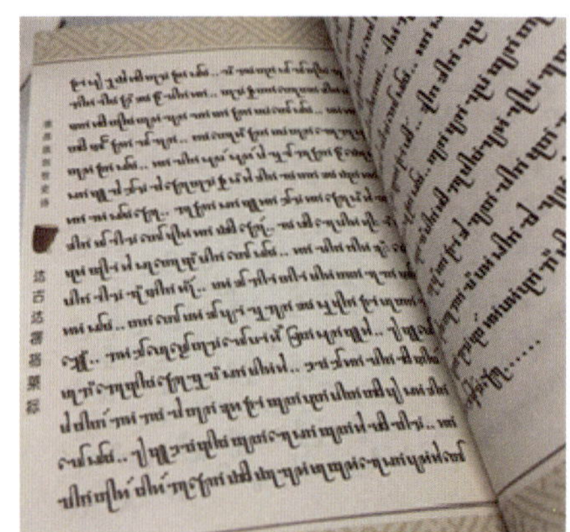

第 8 项：达古达楞格莱标

傣文版《达古达楞格莱标》
Dagu Daleng Gelaibiao Epic in the Dai Script

项目序号：552	项目编号：Ⅰ-65	公布时间：2008（第二批）	类别：民间文学
所属地区：云南省	类型：新增项目	申报地区或单位：云南省德宏傣族景颇族自治州	

《达古达楞格莱标》是德昂族民间创世神话史诗，流传于云南省德宏傣族景颇族自治州、保山市隆阳区潞江坝乡和临沧市镇康县、耿马县、永德县、双江县及缅甸掸邦、佤邦一带。

《达古达楞格莱标》是德昂族先民植物崇拜（茶神）的自然产物，是“集体创作的部落故事”。14 世纪以来，德昂族艺人借用傣族文字对其进行了整理、记录，使这一古老的史诗能够同时以傣文抄本和口传的形式流布和传承。原傣文抄本长约 2000 行，由“序歌”“茶神下凡诞生人类”“光明与黑暗的斗争”“战胜洪水和恶势力”“百花百果的由来与腰箍的来历”及“先祖的诞生和各民族的繁衍”六部分组成。史诗主要讲述德昂民族的诞生与发展，以及德昂人同大自然顽强斗争的艰苦历史，揭示了德昂族的悠久茶文化及其“古老茶农”称谓的历史渊源。①

① 《达古达楞格莱标》，中国非物质文化遗产网，http://www.ihchina.cn/Article/Index/detail?id=12298，检索日期：2019 年 9 月 3 日。

Item 8: *Dagu Daleng Gelaibiao Epic*

Item Serial Number: 552	Item ID Number: Ⅰ-65	Released Date: 2008 (Batch 2)	Category: Folk Literature
Affiliated Province: Yunnan Province	Type: New Item	Application Province or Unit: Dehong Dai and Jingpo Autonomous Prefecture, Yunnan Province	

Dagu Daleng Gelaibiao Epic is a folk creation epic of the De'ang nationality, circulated in Dehong Dai and Jingpo Autonomous Prefecture, Lujiangba Township of Longyang District in Baoshan City, and Zhenkang County, Gengma County, Yongde County and Shuangjiang County of Lincang City in Yunnan Province, as well as Shan State and Wa State in Myanmar.

This epic is a natural product of plant worship (the God of Tea) of the ancestors of the De'ang nationality and a "tribal story created collectively". Since the 14th century, some De'ang artists have sorted and recorded it by using the Dai script, which has enabled this ancient epic to be imparted and inherited in the forms of a Dai-script handwritten copy and oral transmission. The original Dai-script handwritten copy is about 2,000 lines, consisting of six parts: "Preface", "The God of Tea's Descending to the World and Mankind's Birth", "Battles between Light and Darkness", "Overcoming Floods and Evil Forces", "Origins of Flowers, Fruits and Waist Belts" and "The Birth of Ancestors and the Reproduction of Various Ethnic Groups". The epic mainly tells the birth and development of the De'ang nationality and the arduous history of the De'ang people's tenacious struggle against nature, revealing the long-standing tea culture of the De'ang nationality and the historical origin of its appellation as "the ancient tea farmer".

第 9 项：哈尼哈吧

哈尼哈吧演唱

the Singing of *Haba (ancient songs) of the Hani Nationality*

项目序号：553	项目编号：Ⅰ-66	公布时间：2008（第二批）	类别：民间文学
所属地区：云南省	类型：新增项目	申报地区或单位：云南省元阳县	

《哈尼哈吧》，哈尼语意为“哈尼古歌”，是哈尼族社会生活中流传广泛、影响深远的民间歌谣，是一种有别于哈尼族山歌、情歌、儿歌等的庄重、典雅的古老歌唱形式。主要在云南省南部红河和澜沧江之间的元江、墨江、绿春、金平、江城等哈尼族聚居县流传，思茅县、澜沧县、西双版纳傣族自治州等地也有。

其内容涉及哈尼族古代社会的生产劳动、原始宗教祭典、人文规范、伦理道德、婚嫁丧葬、吃穿用住和文学艺术等方面，是世代以梯田农耕生产生活为核心的哈尼族人教化风俗、规范人生的百科全书。从目前收集整理的资料来看，哈尼古歌《窝果策尼果》《哈尼阿培聪坡坡》《十二奴局》《木地米地》是其代表性作品。《哈尼哈吧》主要由民间歌手在祭祀、节日、婚丧和建房等隆重场合的酒席间演唱，表达节日祝贺、吉祥如意的心愿。其内容丰富，结构严谨，歌手可以连续演唱几天几夜。演唱方式有一人主唱、众人伴唱或一问一答、二人对唱加众人和声等。①

① 《哈尼哈吧》，中国非物质文化遗产网，http://www.ihchina.cn/Article/Index/detail?id=12299，检索日期：2019 年 9 月 3 日。

Item 9: *Haba (ancient songs) of the Hani Nationality*

Item Serial Number: 553	Item ID Number: Ⅰ-66	Released Date: 2008 (Batch 2)	Category: Folk Literature
Affiliated Province: Yunnan Province	Type: New Item	Application Province or Unit: Yuanyang County, Yunnan Province	

Haba (ancient songs) of the Hani Nationality, meaning "ancient song" in the Hani language, is a widely-circulated folk song that has a far-reaching influence on the social life of the Hani nationality. It is a solemn and elegant ancient singing form that is different from mountain songs, love songs and children's songs of the Hani nationality. It is mainly spread in the counties inhabited by the Hani nationality, such as Yuanjiang, Mojiang, Lüchun, Jinping and Jiangcheng between the Honghe River and the Lancang River in the southern part of Yunnan Province, as well as in Simao County, Lancang County, Xishuangbanna Dai Autonomous Prefecture and other places.

Its content involves the production and labor, primitive religious sacrificial rites, humanistic norms, ethics and morality, weddings and funerals, food, clothing, housing, literature, art, etc. of the ancient Hani society. It is an encyclopedia for the Hani people who live on terraced field production for generations to indoctrinate customs and normalize life. Seen from the material currently collected and sorted out, its representative works are the ancient songs of the Hani nationality, such as *Woguo Ceniguo* (*Twelve Tunes of Ancient Songs*), *Hani Apei Congpopo* (*The Epic of the Migration of the Hani Nationality*), *Shi'er Nuju* (*Twelve Chapters*), *Mudi Midi* (*The Creation of the Heaven and the Earth*). ***Haba (ancient songs) of the Hani Nationality*** is mainly performed by folk singers at banquets on grand occasions, such as sacrifices, festivals, weddings and funerals, as well as house construction, to express holiday congratulations and auspicious wishes. It is abundant in content, and well-knit in structure. Singers can sing continuously for several days and nights. It can be sung by a lead singer to the accompaniment singing of a group of singers, or by two singers singing in antiphonal style with many other singers singing in harmony.

第10项：召树屯与喃木诺娜

《召树屯与喃木诺娜》绘画作品
a Painting of *Zhaoshutun and Nanmu Nuona Poem*

项目序号：554	项目编号：Ⅰ-67	公布时间：2008（第二批）	类别：民间文学
所属地区：云南省	类型：新增项目	申报地区或单位：云南省西双版纳傣族自治州	

《召树屯与喃木诺娜》是傣族的一部以爱情为主线的口传叙事长诗，也是傣族最著名、流传最广的爱情赞美诗，在西双版纳傣族地区和东南亚地区广为流传。其版本众多，不仅有口头传承的说唱韵文（长诗）和散文体长篇故事，还被民间画师用作佛寺壁画、经画的创作题材。

相传在古老的勐版加国有一位英俊勇敢的王子叫召树屯，成年后，为反对父王订下的婚事，他离开宫殿，四处寻找自己理想的伴侣。当他来到风景秀丽的金湖时，恰逢孔雀国的七位公主到金湖沐浴，七公主喃木诺娜漂亮、高贵，深深地打动了王子。正当王子愁眉不展时，湖中的神龙把留住小公主的秘密告诉王子，于是王子趁七位公主沐浴时藏起了她的孔雀羽衣，让她飞不回去，两人一见钟情，擦出了爱情的火花。《召树屯与喃木诺娜》由傣泐文记载、吟唱，以傣族独特的艺术手法栩栩如生地塑造了召树屯和喃木诺娜这两个代表傣家人典型性格、怀有傣族人民理想追求的完美形象。该长诗不仅着力描绘他们外在的美，更揭示出他们忠于爱情、热爱家乡的高尚品德，歌颂了他们勇敢顽强、坚忍不拔的刚毅精神。①

① 《召树屯与喃木诺娜》，中国非物质文化遗产网，http://www.ihchina.cn/Article/Index/detail?id=12300，检索日期：2019年9月3日。

Item 10: *Zhaoshutun and Nanmu Nuona Poem*

Item Serial Number: 554	Item ID Number: I -67	Released Date: 2008 (Batch 2)	Category: Folk Literature
Affiliated Province: Yunnan Province	Type: New Item	Application Province or Unit: Xishuangbanna Dai Autonomous Prefecture, Yunnan Province	

Zhaoshutun and Nanmu Nuona Poem is an orally-transmitted long narrative poem of the Dai nationality with love as the main theme. It is also the most famous and most widely-circulated love hymn of the Dai people, widely spread in areas inhabited by the Dai nationality in Xishuangbanna Dai Autonomous Prefecture and Southeast Asia. It has many versions, including orally-transmitted talking-and-singing verse (long poem) and prose-style long story. It is also used as material by folk painters for Buddhist temple murals and scripture paintings.

According to legend, in the ancient country of Mengbanjia, there was a handsome and brave prince named Zhaoshutun. When he became an adult, to oppose the marriage arranged by his Father King, he left the palace and looked around for his ideal partner. When he came to the picturesque Golden Lake, the seven princesses of the Peacock Kingdom happened to come to the Golden Lake to bathe. The seventh princess, Nanmu Nuona, was beautiful and noble, so the prince was deeply attracted by her. When he knitted his brows in anxiety and didn't know what to do, the magic dragon in the lake told him the secret of detaining the little princess. Then, the prince hid her peacock-feather robe while the seven princesses were bathing so that the little princess could not fly back. The two fell in love at first sight, lighting the spark of love. ***Zhaoshutun and Nanmu Nuona Poem*** is recorded and sung in the Daile language. By using the unique artistic technique of the Dai nationality, it vividly portrays the perfect images of Zhaoshutun and Namu Nona, who represent the typical personalities of the Dai people and harbor their ideals and pursuit. This long poem not only focuses on portraying their external beauty, but also reveals their noble character of being faithful to love and loving their hometown, and praises their brave, tenacious and persevering spirit.

第 11–12 项：司岗里

《司岗里》（著作）
Sigangli (out of the cliff-cave) Epic (a work)

项目序号：561	项目编号：Ⅰ-74	公布时间：2008（第二批）	类别：民间文学
所属地区：云南省	类型：新增项目	申报地区或单位：云南省沧源佤族自治县	

项目序号：561	项目编号：Ⅰ-74	公布时间：2011（第三批）	类别：民间文学
所属地区：云南省	类型：扩展项目	申报地区或单位：云南省西盟佤族自治县	

《司岗里》是广泛流传于佤族民间的口述文学，是一部佤族创世史诗，是佤族历史、道德、宗教、哲学、风俗等民间传统文化的综合载体，流传于云南省的沧源佤族自治县和西盟佤族自治县。

“司岗”是崖洞的意思，“里”是出来，“司岗里”就是从岩洞里出来。传说远古时，人被囚禁在密闭的大山崖洞里出不来，万能的神灵莫伟委派小米雀啄开岩洞，老鼠引开守在洞口咬人的老虎，蜘蛛堵住不让人走出山洞的大树，人类才得以走出山洞，到各地安居乐业、生息繁衍。该诗 5700 余行，涵盖了神话、传说、故事等诸多佤族民间文学样式，描述了人类从“司岗”出来后发生的各种故事，包括人类起源，以及与之密切相关的动植物的产生、祖先事迹、村寨史、家族史、民族史、民族关系、英雄故事和爱情故事等。内容涉及佤族的自然现象、动植物、生产生活、家族历史、传统习俗、部落战争、祭祀和繁衍生息等方面。《司岗里》通过佤族先民对宇宙万物和人类起源的独特阐释，描述了劳动创造世界的过程和原始宇宙观，表达了各民族友好相处、团结和睦的愿望。由于佤族没有文字，《司岗里》先以讲故事的方式口述传承，逐步发展为吟唱歌咏的形式，至今已有上千年的历史。①

Items 11-12: *Sigangli (out of the cliff-cave) Epic*

Item Serial Number: 561	Item ID Number: Ⅰ-74	Released Date: 2008 (Batch 2)	Category: Folk Literature
Affiliated Province: Yunnan Province	Type: New Item	Application Province or Unit: Cangyuan Wa Autonomous County, Yunnan Province	

Item Serial Number: 561	Item ID Number: Ⅰ-74	Released Date: 2011 (Batch 3)	Category: Folk Literature
Affiliated Province: Yunnan Province	Type: Extended Item	Application Province or Unit: Ximeng Wa Autonomous County, Yunnan Province	

Sigangli (out of the cliff-cave) Epic is an oral literature widely circulated among the people of the Wa nationality. It is a creation epic of the Wa nationality, and a comprehensive carrier of the folk traditional culture of history, morals, religion, philosophy, customs, etc. of the Wa people. It is spread in Cangyuan Wa Autonomous County and Ximeng Wa Autonomous County of Yunnan Province.

"Sigang" means cliff cave, "li" means coming out, so "Sigangli" means coming out from the cave. It is said that in ancient times, human beings were imprisoned in a large cliff cave and could not get out. The almighty god, Mowei, sent a Xiaomique Bird to peck a hole in the cave, a mouse to lure away the tiger that guarded the entrance to the cave and bit people, and a spider to block the tree that prevented people from leaving the cave, so that human beings could walk out of the cave, live and work in peace, thrive and breed in various places. The epic consists of more than 5,700 lines, covering many folk literary styles of the Wa nationality, such as myths, legends and stories. It describes various stories that occurred after humans came out of "Sigang", including the origin of mankind, the emerging of animals and plants closely related to human beings, ancestral deeds, village history, family history, ethnic history, ethnic relations, heroic stories and love stories. Its content involves the

① 《司岗里》，中国非物质文化遗产网，http://www. ihchina. cn/Article/Index/detail?id=12311，检索日期：2019 年 9 月 3 日。

natural phenomena, animals and plants, production and life, family history, traditional customs, tribal wars, sacrifices and the reproduction of the Wa nationality. Through the unique interpretation of the ancestors of the Wa nationality on the origins of the universe, all things and mankind, ***Sigangli (out of the cliff-cave) Epic*** describes the process of labor creating the world and the primitive views on the universe, and expresses the desire of all ethnic groups to live together friendly, in unity and in harmony. Since the Wa people have no written words, ***Sigangli (out of the cliff-cave) Epic*** was first passed on orally in the form of storytelling and gradually developed into a form of singing. It has a history of over a thousand years up to now.

第 13 项：坡芽情歌

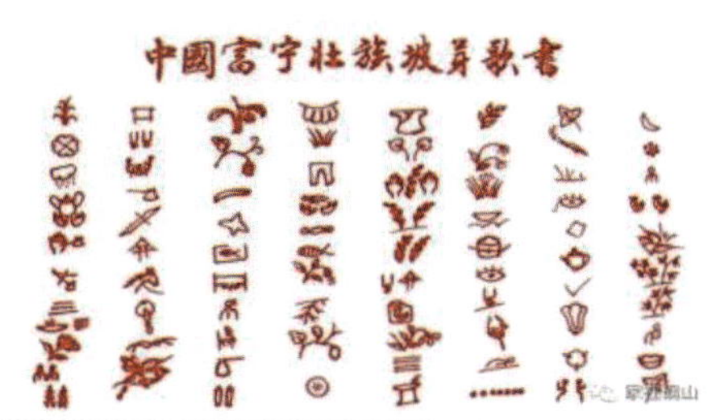

坡芽情歌
Poya Love Songs

项目序号：1057	项目编号：Ⅰ-113	公布时间：2011（第三批）	类别：民间文学
所属地区：云南省	类型：新增项目	申报地区或单位：云南省富宁县	

坡芽情歌是一部由 81 个图画符号记录在土布上的爱情民歌集，壮族语称“布瓦吩”，意为“把花纹图案画在土布上的山歌”（当地人称“坡芽歌书”），情歌所采用的图画符号被文字学专家称为“文字之芽”，流传于云南省富宁县的壮族村寨，以剥隘镇坡芽村为中心。

图画符号有月、星、树、稻谷、犁、斧、禽、马、人、衣、鸟、房屋、枫叶等，每一个图画符号代表一首情歌或同一类情歌。歌集详细地描绘了一对青年男女从相识、相知、相恋到白头偕老的动人故事。歌集采用联曲式的结构方式，层层迭进，有情节的连贯性和完整性，主人公曲折的爱情过程反映了古代壮族的生产生活和民情风俗，融合了文学、音乐、图画等多种民间艺术。情歌以壮族北部方言演唱，男女对唱，一唱一和。曲调以“分打捞”“分标”“分呃哎”“分戈麻”等壮族山歌小调为主。句式多为五言，每首歌四句或数十句不等，以首尾韵、腰尾韵和尾韵为主要押韵方式，韵律严密和谐。①

Item 13: Poya Love Songs

Item Serial Number: 1057	Item ID Number: Ⅰ-113	Released Date: 2011 (Batch 3)	Category: Folk Literature
Affiliated Province: Yunnan Province	Type: New Item	Application Province or Unit: Funing County, Yunnan Province	

① 《坡芽情歌》，中国非物质文化遗产网，http://www.ihchina.cn/Article/Index/detail?id=12358，检索日期：2019 年 9 月 3 日。

Poya Love Songs are a collection of love folk songs recorded on homespun cloth by using 81 pictorial symbols. It is called "Buwafen" in the Zhuang language, which means "mountain songs with decorative patterns drawn on the homespun cloth" (referred to as "A Book of Poya Songs" by local people). The pictorial symbols adopted in the love songs are called "the buds of characters" by philologists, which are circulated in the Zhuang villages of Funing County, Yunnan Province, with Poya Village in Bo'ai Township as the center.

These pictorial symbols include the moon, stars, trees, rice in the husk, plows, axes, fowls, horses, people, clothing, birds, houses and maple leaves. Each pictorial symbol represents a love song or the same kind of love song. The collection of songs describes in detail the touching stories of a pair of young men and women from meeting, getting to know, falling in love and growing old together. This collection of songs adopts the joint-tune music structure, and develops step by step, coherent and complete in plots. The protagonists' winding love stories reflect the production, life and folk customs of the Zhuang nationality in ancient times, integrating a variety of folk arts, such as literature, music and drawing. The love songs are sung in the northern dialect of the Zhuang nationality, with men and women performing antiphonal singing, echoing each other. The main musical modes are the minor modes of mountain songs of the Zhuang nationality, such as "Fendalao", "Fenbiao", "Fen'e'ai" and "Fengema". The sentence pattern is largely five-character, with four or dozens of sentences per song. The main rhyming patterns include head-and-end rhymes, middle-and-end rhymes, and end rhymes, and the rhymes are rigorous and harmonious.

《目瑙斋瓦》（著作）
Munao Zhaiwa Epic (a work)

第14项：目瑙斋瓦

项目序号：1063	项目编号：Ⅰ-119	公布时间：2011（第三批）	类别：民间文学
所属地区：云南省	类型：新增项目	申报地区或单位：云南省德宏傣族景颇族自治州	

《目瑙斋瓦》是景颇族的创世史诗，是研究景颇族诞生、迁徙、原始宗教起源、婚姻制度演变、山官制度产生及民族交往的珍贵资料，内容涵盖了景颇族的政治、历史、哲学、文学、艺术、习俗和伦理道德等领域，堪称景颇族传统文化的经典。流传于德宏州各县（市）景颇族居住地，包括盈江县的五个乡，陇川县的七个乡镇，潞西市的六个乡镇以及瑞丽市的两个乡。

据有关专家研究，《目瑙斋瓦》最早滥觞于原始社会父系氏族时期，是景颇族先民祭祀天神、太阳神的祭词，长8900行，分为六章。第一章讲述了天地万物的形成及人类的诞生。第二章讲述了景颇族的创世英雄宁贯杜率领天下豪杰改造自然，使土壤肥沃、庄稼生长的奋斗过程。第三章讲述大地洪水泛滥。第四章讲述宁贯杜寻找财富，娶龙女扎圣为妻。第五章讲述景颇族跳“目瑙纵歌”舞的来历。第六章讲述大地上的生活，包括钻木取火、寻找水源、制造生产生活用具、学会穿衣裤、种谷、建房、男婚女嫁等等。①

① 《目瑙斋瓦》，中国非物质文化遗产网，http://www.ihchina.cn/Article/Index/detail?id=12367，检索日期：2019年9月3日。

Item 14: *Munao Zhaiwa Epic*

Item Serial Number: 1063	Item ID Number: Ⅰ-119	Released Date: 2011 (Batch 3)	Category: Folk Literature
Affiliated Province: Yunnan Province	Type: New Item	Application Province or Unit: Dehong Dai and Jingpo Autonomous Prefecture, Yunnan Province	

Munao Zhaiwa Epic is the creation epic of the Jingpo nationality. It is a precious material for studying the birth, migration, origin of primitive religion, evolution of marriage system, the formation of Shanguan system ("Shanguan" means the hereditary headman and the presider of sacrificial activities in the villages of the Jingpo nationality) and ethnic intercourse of the Jingpo nationality. Its content covers the politics, history, philosophy, literature, art, customs, ethics, morality, etc. of the Jingpo nationality, which can be called a classic of its traditional culture. It is spread in areas inhabited by the Jingpo nationality in all counties (cities) of Dehong Dai and Jingpo Autonomous Prefecture, including five townships in Yingjiang County, seven townships in Longchuan County, six townships in Luxi City and two townships in Ruili City.

According to research by some experts, the origin of ***Munao Zhaiwa Epic*** can be traced back to the patrilineal clan period of the primitive society. It is the sacrificial oration used by the ancestors of the Jingpo nationality when offering sacrifices to the god of the heaven and the god of the sun. It consists of 8900 lines and is divided into six chapters. Chapter One talks about the formation of the heaven, the earth and everything in the world, as well as the birth of mankind. Chapter Two tells the struggling process of all heroes in the world transforming the heaven and the earth, and making the land fertile and crops grow under the leadership of Ningguandu, the creator hero of the Jingpo nationality. Chapter Three describes the flood disasters on land. Chapter Four talks about Ningguandu's search for wealth and his marriage to Zhasheng, the daughter of dragon. Chapter Five tells the origin of performing Munao Zongge Dance of the Jingpo Nationality. Chapter Six talks about the life on land, including drilling wood to make fire, seeking the source of water, making production tools and living utensils, learning to wear clothes, planting grains, building houses and getting married.

第 15 项：洛奇洛耶与扎斯扎依

《洛奇洛耶与扎斯扎依》（著作）
Luoqi Luoye and Zhasi Zhayi Poem (a published work)

项目序号：1064	项目编号：Ⅰ-120	公布时间：2011（第三批）	类别：民间文学
所属地区：云南省	类型：新增项目	申报地区或单位：云南省墨江哈尼族自治县	

《洛奇洛耶与扎斯扎依》是哈尼族碧约人口传叙事长诗，涉及哈尼族生产生活、婚恋生死、原始崇拜、风俗习惯和精神信念等，流传于云南省滇南的哈尼族聚居地区，主要在普洱市墨江哈尼族自治县、江城哈尼族彝族自治县、宁洱哈尼族彝族自治县及红河州、玉溪市的哈尼族碧约人支系聚居的村寨中。

洛奇洛耶与扎斯扎依是长诗中的两位青年，男为英雄智慧的化身，女为美丽纯真的代表。全诗分为“开头的歌”“扎斯扎依”“洛奇洛耶”“赶街相会”“秧田对歌”“串门求亲”“成家立业”“领头抗租”“不死的魂”和“结尾的歌”，共十章，近 2000 行。故事的结尾部分，特别是抗租失败后，主人公被砍成肉块、剁成肉酱后依然复活，被铜钉钉在山崖下，淌了七天七夜的血仍然不屈服的情节，将哈尼族人民对英雄的爱戴之情表现得淋漓尽致，充分体现了哈尼族坚强的民族性格。作品以吟唱的方式传承。在一代代人的吟唱中，内容不断丰富，成为哈尼族优秀的口传文学作品。[①]

① 《洛奇洛耶与扎斯扎依》，中国非物质文化遗产网，http://www.ihchina.cn/Article/Index/detail?id=12368，检索日期：2019 年 9 月 3 日。

Item 15: *Luoqi Luoye and Zhasi Zhayi Poem*

Item Serial Number: 1064	Item ID Number: Ⅰ-120	Released Date: 2011 (Batch 3)	Category: Folk Literature
Affiliated Province: Yunnan Province	Type: New Item	Application Province or Unit: Mojiang Hani Autonomous County, Yunnan Province	

Luoqi Luoye and Zhasi Zhayi Poem is a long narrative poem of the Biyue branch of the Hani nationality, which involves the Hani people's production and living, marriage and love, life and death, primitive worship, habits and customs, spiritual beliefs, etc. It is circulated in areas inhabited by the Hani nationality in southern Yunnan Province, mainly in Mojiang Hani Autonomous County, Jiangcheng Hani and Yi Autonomous County, and Ning'er Hani and Yi Autonomous County of Pu'er City, as well as the stockaded villages where the Biyue branch of the Hani nationality lives in Honghe Hani and Yi Autonomous Prefecture and Yuxi City.

Luoqi Luoye and Zhasi Zhayi are two young people in the long poem. The male figure is the embodiment of bravery and wisdom, and the female one is the representative of beauty and innocence. The whole poem is divided into ten chapters, with nearly 2000 lines. These chapters include "The Song at the Beginning", "Zhasi Zhayi", "Luoqi Luoye", "Meeting Unexpectedly When Going to Market", "Singing in Antiphonal Style on the Rice Field", "The Proposal of Marriage", "Getting Married and Starting a Career", "Taking the Lead in Refusing to Pay for the Land Rent", "the Immortal Soul" and "the Ending Song". At the end of the story, especially after the failure of the refusal to pay for the land rent, the protagonists were chopped into pieces, but they still came back to life. Even nailed to the cliff by copper nails and bleeding for seven days and nights, they were still unyielding. This poem vividly reflects the Hani people's love and esteem for heroes and their tough national character. It has been passed down in the form of singing. Through generations of singing, it has been constantly enriched in content, becoming an excellent orally-transmitted literary work of the Hani nationality.

第16项：阿细先基

《阿细的先基》（著作）
Axi Xianji Poem (a published work)

项目序号：1065	项目编号：Ⅰ-121	公布时间：2011（第三批）	类别：民间文学
所属地区：云南省	类型：新增项目	申报地区或单位：云南省弥勒县	

《阿细先基》，又名《阿细人的歌》，是彝族支系阿细人的创世史诗，口头流传于云南省弥勒县西山地区的阿细人聚居地。由于长诗是由艺人用阿细语创作并演唱，散落于民间，所以长期不被外界所闻。20世纪40年代，经诗人光未然、语言学家袁家骅先后搜集整理出版，才得以广为外界所知。

诗篇全文约计2000行，由“引子”“最古的时候”“男女说合成一家”和“尾声”四部分组成。内容包括阿细人的神话传说（天地万物的起源、自然现象的成因等）、男女爱情与婚姻以及早期的民族生活（人类早期的艰苦生活和所经受的磨难）和阿细人的风俗习惯。《阿细先基》是阿细人的“根谱”，体现了阿细人探寻自然、认识自然的执著、勇武与睿智，折射出朴素的唯物主义思想。由于其很大篇幅以男女情爱为主线，描述了阿细人对纯真爱情、美好事物的热烈追求与憧憬，对现实社会的各种见解，故而在阿细人村落里，男女青年们常在耕作之暇互相对唱，成为求偶的手段。[①]

Item 16: *Axi Xianji Poem*

Item Serial Number: 1065	Item ID Number: Ⅰ-121	Released Date: 2011 (Batch 3)	Category: Folk Literature
Affiliated Province: Yunnan Province	Type: New Item	Application Province or Unit: Mile County, Yunnan Province	

① 《阿细先基》，中国非物质文化遗产网，http://www.ihchina.cn/Article/Index/detail?id=12369，检索日期：2019年9月3日。

Axi Xianji Poem, also known as “the Song of the Axi People”, is the creation epic of the Axi branch of the Yi nationality. It is circulated orally in areas inhabited by the Axi people in Xishan region of Mile County, Yunnan Province. Because this long poem has been composed and sung by artists in Axi dialect, scattered among the people, it has remained unknown to the outside world for a long time. In the 1940s, after the poet Guang Weiran and linguist Yuan Jiahua collected, sorted out and published this poem successively, it became widely known to the outside world.

The full text of the poem is about 2,000 lines, consisting of four parts: “Introduction”, “In Ancient Times”, “Men and Women Getting Married” and “Ending”. Its content includes the myths and legends of the Axi people (the origins of the heaven, the earth and all creatures, the causes of natural phenomena, etc.), the love and marriage of men and women, early ethnic life (the hard life and suffering experienced by early human beings), and the customs and habits of the Axi people. ***Axi Xianji Poem*** is “the root genealogy” of the Axi people, which reflects their persistence, courage and wisdom for exploring and getting to know nature, as well as their world view of simple materialism. With a large proportion of the poem focusing on love stories between men and women, it describes the Axi people’s passionate pursuit of and longing for pure love and beautiful things, as well as their various insights into the real society. Therefore, in Axi villages, young men and women often sing it to each other during the leisure time after their farming, which has become a means of courtship.

第17项：黑白战争

《黑白战争》（著作）
The Battle between the Black and the White (a published work)

项目序号：1247	项目编号：Ⅰ-153	公布时间：2014（第四批）	类别：民间文学
所属地区：云南省	类型：新增项目	申报地区或单位：云南省丽江市古城区	

《黑白战争》是记载在东巴经卷中的一部长诗，共3000行左右，被称为纳西族英雄史诗，由纳西族东巴祭司以古纳西象形文书写，仅出现于由纳西族东巴祭司主持的特定宗教仪式上。①

《黑白战争》的纳西书名叫“董岩术岩”，直译为“董与术之间的仇和冤”。因为董的一方的日月山川飞禽走兽一切呈白色，而术的一方则恰巧相反，一切皆黑，故把它汉译为《黑白战争》。史诗展现了古代纳西部落为争夺日月星辰而展开的浩大频繁的战争场面，歌颂了格拉茨姆和董若瓦璐一对青年男女的生死恋情，阐述了宇宙的起源、天地的形成、人类的诞生、万物的繁衍、万象观、人生观、善恶观、荣辱观和价值观。② 该史诗被称为纳西版“罗密欧与朱丽叶”。《黑白战争》将战争的发端归咎于盗取日月，用太阳和月亮象征胜利者白的一方，从某种意义上讲，这场战争又可称为“争夺日月之战”，反映了古人类原始的天体崇拜观。③

① 陈烈，《论纳西族英雄史诗〈黑白战争〉》，载《民族文学研究》，1988年第6期，第65-69，59页。

② 吴晓东，《纳西族史诗〈黑白战争〉连环画在北京展出》，载《中国青年报》，2017年6月19日第5版。

③ 戈阿干，《〈黑白战争〉文化内涵探索》，载《民族艺术研究》，1995年第5期，第3-8页。

Item 17: *The Battle between the Black and the White*

Item Serial Number: 1247	Item ID Number: Ⅰ-153	Released Date: 2014 (Batch 4)	Category: Folk Literature
Affiliated Province: Yunnan Province	Type: New Item	Application Province or Unit: Ancient City District, Lijiang City, Yunnan Province	

The Battle between the Black and the White is a long poem recorded in Dongba Scripture, with a total of about 3,000 lines. It is called the heroic epic of the Naxi nationality, written in the ancient Naxi pictograph by Dongba, the priest of the Naxi nationality. This epic will be sung only in specific religious ceremonies presided over by Dongba, the priest of the Naxi nationality.

The Battle between the Black and the White in the Naxi language is known as "Dongyan Shuyan", which is literally translated as "the Hatred between Dong and Shu". Because the sun, the moon, mountains, rivers, birds and animals on Dong's side are all white, while Shu's side is just the opposite, with everything black, it is translated into Chinese as ***The Battle between the Black and the White***. The epic shows the massive and frequent war scenes of the ancient Naxi tribes fighting for the sun, the moon and stars. It praises the eternal love between a young couple, Gela Cimu and Dongruo Walu, and expounds the origin of the universe, the formation of the heaven and the earth, the birth of human beings, the reproduction of all things, views on all phenomena, outlook on life, outlook on good and evil, outlook on honor and disgrace, and outlook on values. This epic is known as the Naxi version of "Romeo and Juliet". ***The Battle between the Black and the White*** attributes the origin of the war to the stealing of the sun and the moon, with them symbolizing the victor—the white side. In a sense, this war can also be called "the battle for the sun and the moon", reflecting the primitive view of celestial worship of the ancient people.

第二章 传统音乐

Chapter Two Traditional Music

第 1 项：傈僳族民歌

傈僳族民歌“摆时”大赛
the Contest of “Baishi”, a Folk Song of the Lisu Nationality

项目序号：48	项目编号：Ⅱ-17	公布时间：2006（第一批）	类别：传统音乐
所属地区：云南省	类型：新增项目	申报地区或单位：云南省怒江傈僳族自治州	

傈僳族民歌包括“木刮”“摆时”和“优叶”等歌种。“木刮”流传于云南省怒江傈僳族自治州的傈僳族聚居区；“摆时”广泛流传于泸水县和兰坪县傈僳族地区；“优叶”主要流传于福贡县的傈僳族村寨。

“木刮”是傈僳族最重要、流传最广的民歌歌种之一，在傈僳语中原指所有的歌和调，后来逐渐成为叙事古歌的专称，主要用于内容严肃、气氛庄重的传统叙事长诗，并多在民族节日、集会等时间和场合歌唱。一般由中老年男性分为两方，盘腿围坐火塘边，各以男、女身份一问一答对唱。对唱时双方都由一人领唱，众人伴唱，领唱者唱一句，伴唱者和一句，吟唱中以酒助兴，边饮边歌。“摆时”多为集体性的男女对唱，也可由一人作自娱性独唱，在平时及节日集会、庆祝丰收、男婚女嫁等喜庆的场合都有歌唱，歌词内容广泛，曲调热情奔放，宜于表露内心激情，深受傈僳族人民喜爱。其歌唱内容分为“朵我”“辖我”两类。“朵我”主要歌唱传统叙事长诗，“辖我”则根据对歌对象即兴编唱，多以爱情、时事为主要内容。“优叶”按歌唱内容及形式分为两类：一类由中老年人围坐火塘边一面饮酒一面对唱，主要内容是追述旧时的悲伤、苦难，曲调低沉、速度徐缓、旋律平稳；另一类曲调轻松、活泼，是青年男女传情表意的主要方式，可男女对唱，也可在同性间对唱。①

Item 1: Folk Songs of the Lisu Nationality

Item Serial Number: 48	Item ID Number: Ⅱ-17	Released Date: 2006 (Batch 1)	Category: Traditional Music
Affiliated Province: Yunnan Province	Type: New Item	Application Province or Unit: Nujiang Lisu Autonomous Prefecture, Yunnan Province	

Folk Songs of the Lisu Nationality include song types of “Mugua”, “Baishi” and “Youye”. “Mugua” is circulated in the Lisu settlements of Nujiang Lisu Autonomous Prefecture in Yunnan Province; “Baishi” is widely spread in areas inhabited by the Lisu nationality in Lushui County and Lanping County; and “Youye” is mainly spread in Lisu villages in Fugong County.

“Mugua” is one of the most important and widely-circulated types of folk songs of the Lisu nationality. In the Lisu language, it originally referred to all songs and tunes. Later, it has gradually become a proper name for narrative ancient songs. It is mainly used for traditional narrative long poems that are serious in content and solemn in atmosphere, and often performed on the occasions of ethnic festivals, gatherings, etc. Generally, middle-aged and elderly men are divided into two groups, sitting cross-legged around the Fire Pit, with one group acting as the male and the other acting as the female, performing antiphonal singing in the form of asking

① 《傈僳族民歌》，中国非物质文化遗产网，http://www.ihchina.cn/Article/Index/detail?id=12431，检索日期：2019 年 9 月 1 日。

and answering questions. When performing antiphonal singing, both sides are led by one leading singer respectively, accompanied by others. The leading singer sings one sentence, and the accompaniment vocalists echo it accordingly. In the process, singers will drink liquor when singing to add to the fun. “Baishi” is mostly a collective antiphonal singing performed by male and female singers, and it can also be sung by one person for self-entertainment. It is sung at ordinary times and on festive occasions, such as festival gatherings, harvest celebrations and weddings. The lyrics are extensive in content and the tunes are passionate and unrestrained, which is suitable for expressing inner passion and deeply loved by the Lisu people. The content of the songs is divided into two categories: “Duowo” and “Xiawo”. “Duowo” is mainly to sing traditional narrative long poems, and “Xiawo” is the songs improvised by singers according to the target who performs antiphonal singing, mostly with love and current affairs as the main content. According to the content and the form of singing, “Youye” is divided into two categories. The first category is the songs performed by middle-aged and elderly people who sit around the Fire Pit performing antiphonal singing while drinking. The main content is to recount the sadness and suffering of the past, with low tunes, slow speed and stead melody. The other category is relaxed and lively in tunes, which is the main way for young men and women to express their feelings. It can be sung in the antiphonal style by men and women or between the same sex.

第 2 项：哈尼族多声部民歌

哈尼族多声部民歌表演
the Performance of Polyphonic Folk Songs of the Hani Nationality

项目序号：61	项目编号：Ⅱ-30	公布时间：2006（第一批）	类别：传统音乐
所属地区：云南省	类型：新增项目	申报地区或单位：云南省红河哈尼族彝族自治州	

哈尼族多声部民歌历史悠久，主要流传于云南省红河哈尼族彝族自治州红河县以普春村为中心的数个哈尼族村落中，其产生与哈尼族的社会生产，尤其是梯田稻作农耕劳动有密切的关系。

哈尼族多声部民歌包括歌颂劳动、赞美爱情和讴歌山野田园美景等方面的内容。曲目以《吾处阿茨》（栽秧山歌）和《情歌》最具代表性。演唱方式分为有乐器伴奏和无乐器伴奏人声帮腔两种。哈尼族多声部民歌的演唱场合多样，梯田、山林和村寨都可以是其表演空间。伴奏乐器均由民间歌手自己制作，三弦、小二胡只在普春村使用。其唱词结构以开腔用词、主题唱词和帮腔用词三部分构成一个小的基本段落，其音乐形态在歌节结构、调式音列、调式色彩、调式组合和多声部组成等方面都显示出鲜明的民族和地域特征，既凝聚着哈尼族的音乐智慧和才能，又展现出哈尼族文化及其民族性格和审美观念。[①]

Item 2: Polyphonic Folk Songs of the Hani Nationality

Item Serial Number: 61	Item ID Number: Ⅱ-30	Released Date: 2006 (Batch 1)	Category: Traditional Music
Affiliated Province: Yunnan Province	Type: New Item	Application Province or Unit: Honghe Hani and Yi Autonomous Prefecture, Yunnan Province	

① 《哈尼族多声部民歌》，中国非物质文化遗产网，http://www.ihchina.cn/Article/Index/detail?id=12471，检索日期：2019 年 8 月 11 日。

Polyphonic Folk Songs of the Hani Nationality have a long history and are mainly circulated in several Hani villages centered on Pucun Village in Honghe County, Honghe Hani and Yi Autonomous Prefecture, Yunnan Province. Their origin is closely related to the social production of the Hani nationality, especially the terraced rice farming.

The content of **Polyphonic Folk Songs of the Hani Nationality** includes praising labor, love and the beauty of mountains and fields. "Wuchu Aci"(a mountain song of transplanting rice seedlings) and "A Love Song" are the most representative songs. The singing methods are divided into two types: the one with the accompaniment of musical instruments, and the one with vocal accompaniment instead of musical instruments. The occasions for singing **Polyphonic Folk Songs of the Hani Nationality** are varied, including terraced fields, mountains, forests and villages. The accompaniment instruments are all made by folk singers themselves, with Sanxian (a three-stringed plucked musical instrument) and Small Erhu (a two-stringed bowed instrument) only used in Pucun Village. Their lyric structure is composed of three parts, with opening lyrics, topic lyrics and accompaniment lyrics forming a small basic passage. In terms of verse structure, mode and sound sequence, mode color, mode combination, multi-voice part composition, etc., their music form reflects distinctive ethnic and regional characteristics. They not only showcase the musical wisdom and talents of the Hani nationality, but also demonstrate the Hani culture and its ethnic character and aesthetic concepts.

第 3 项：彝族海菜腔

彝族海菜腔表演
the Performance of Haicai Tone of the Yi Nationality

项目序号：62	项目编号：Ⅱ-31	公布时间：2006（第一批）	类别：传统音乐
所属地区：云南省	类型：新增项目	申报地区或单位：云南省红河哈尼族彝族自治州	

彝族海菜腔是云南彝族特有的民歌形式，又称“大攀桨”“倒扳桨”，俗称“石屏腔”，主要流传于云南省红河哈尼族彝族自治州石屏县彝族尼苏人村落。[①]

彝族海菜腔通常由 1～2 人领唱，众人（三人以上）帮腔，一般是男女对唱。其演唱形式包含了领唱、对唱、合唱和说唱等。曲调通常由拘腔、空腔、正七腔、擫腔及白话腔等组成，结构复杂，篇幅宏大，唱词工整，内容丰富，可谓曲中有曲，有“民歌中的套曲”之说。民间歌手演唱一套完整的海菜腔，少则四十多分钟，多则需一个多小时。其唱词大体分为“正词”“衬词”两大类。其中，“正词”只有固定的 28 个字，格式相当于一首七绝诗。而“衬词”多为演唱者即兴编创，内容涉及广泛。由于历史上彝汉文化的交融，现在民间演唱海菜腔基本上以汉语为主。[②]海菜腔代表性曲目有《哥唱小曲妹来学》《石屏橄榄菜》等。

① 《彝族海菜腔》，中国非物质文化遗产网，http://www.ihchina.cn/Article/Index/detail?id=12481，检索日期：2019 年 9 月 1 日。

② 《彝族海菜腔》，云南非物质文化遗产保护网，http://www.ynich.cn/view.php?id=1232&cat_id=11110，检索日期：2019 年 9 月 1 日。

Item 3: Haicai Tone of the Yi Nationality

Item Serial Number: 62	Item ID Number: Ⅱ-31	Released Date: 2006 (Batch 1)	Category: Traditional Music
Affiliated Province: Yunnan Province	Type: New Item	Application Province or Unit: Honghe Hani and Yi Autonomous Prefecture, Yunnan Province	

Haicai Tone of the Yi Nationality is a type of folk song unique to the Yi people in Yunnan Province, which is also called "Dapanjiang" and "Daobanjiang", commonly known as "Shiping Tone". It is mainly circulated in villages inhabited by the Nisu branch of the Yi nationality in Shiping County, Honghe Hani and Yi Autonomous Prefecture, Yunnan Province.

Haicai Tone of the Yi Nationality is usually sung by 1-2 leading singers, accompanied by many (more than three) other singers, in the form of antiphonal singing of male and female singers. The singing forms include leading singing, antiphonal singing, chorusing, as well as talking and singing. The tunes are usually composed of Juqiang Tone, Kongqiang Tone, Zhengqi Tone, Yaqiang Tone, Baihua Tone, etc. It is complex in structure, grand in scale, neat and orderly in lyrics, and rich in content. It can be said that there are tunes in tunes, known as "a song cycle in folk songs". It will take a folk singer 40-60 minutes to finish singing a complete set of Haicai Tone. The lyrics are roughly divided into two categories: "main lyrics" and "foil lyrics". Among them, "main lyrics" have only 28 fixed characters, the format of which is equivalent to a Seven-character Quatrain; while "foil lyrics" are mostly improvised by singers, covering a wide range of content. Due to the fusion of the Yi and Han cultures in history, at present, Haicai Tone is sung mainly in Chinese among the people. The representative songs of Haicai Tone include "Brother Sings Ditties and Litttle Sister Learns to Sing" and "Shiping Olive Dish".

第 4 项：
姚安坝子腔

国家级传承人刘彩菊、州级传承人钱成忠演唱姚安坝子腔
the Performance of Bazi Tone of Yao'an by Liu Caiju, the State-level Inheritor of Intangible Cultural Heritage and Qian Chengzhong, the Prefecture-level Inheritor of Intangible Cultural Heritage

项目序号：595	项目编号：Ⅱ-96	公布时间：2008（第二批）	类别：传统音乐
所属地区：云南省	类型：新增项目	申报地区或单位：云南省姚安县	

姚安坝子腔是云南省楚雄彝族自治州西北部特有的民间歌曲样式，主要流传于姚安县境内以汉族聚居的村寨中，多在春耕栽种季节和秧苗拔绿时由汉族青年男女以对唱方式演唱。

姚安坝子腔主要分为上坝子腔和下坝子腔两种。上坝子腔融入了山区彝族的情歌小调音律，演唱时声音圆润柔和，音律低沉优雅；下坝子腔声音高亢，音域在 d1 至 a2 之间，音符跳度大，音域宽广。其唱词分主词和副词两部分，两者的内容区别较大，但在整个唱腔中与旋律密不可分，互相衬托。副词又叫“垛板”，即演唱中的绕口令，沿用了京剧、滇剧中的“垛板”，在“数”加“唱”时一气呵成，中间无半点停顿，要求演唱者音域高、口齿清、吐字好。“垛板”演唱时，常将姚安坝子的村庄和地名数说在里面，充分展现出演唱者的语言能力。姚安坝子腔多在野外和田间演唱，演唱时以笛子、二胡和打击乐器伴奏，代表性曲调有“十二属”“十二月采花”“猜调”“数姚州”和“数地名”等。①

① 《姚安坝子腔》，中国非物质文化遗产网，http://www.ihchina.cn/Article/Index/detail?id=12627，检索日期：2019 年 9 月 1 日。

Item 4: Bazi Tone of Yao'an

Item Serial Number: 595	Item ID Number: Ⅱ-96	Released Date: 2008 (Batch 2)	Category: Traditional Music
Affiliated Province: Yunnan Province	Type: New Item	Application Province or Unit: Yao'an County, Yunnan Province	

Bazi Tone of Yao'an is a unique folk song style in the northwestern part of Chuxiong Yi Autonomous Prefecture, Yunnan Province. It is primarily spread in villages inhabited by the Han nationality in Yao'an County. It is mostly performed by the young men and women of the Han nationality in the form of antiphonal singing during the spring-planting season or when the seedlings are budding.

Bazi Tone of Yao'an is mainly divided into two types: Upper Bazi Tone and Lower Bazi Tone. Upper Bazi Tone incorporates the minor melody of love songs of the Yi nationality in mountainous areas. The voice of singing is mellow and soft, and the melody is low and elegant. Lower Bazi Tone is high-pitched, with a wide vocal range from d1 to a2, and musical notes fluctuating greatly. The lyrics are divided into two parts: major lyrics and secondary lyrics. The content of the two is quite different, but they are inseparable from the melody in the whole singing and complement each other. Secondary lyrics are also called "Duoban", a tongue twister in singing. They adopt the "Duoban" in Peking Opera and Yunnan Opera. When singers perform "listing" while "singing", they will finish them without any pause in the middle, which requires singers to have a high vocal range, clear articulation and good pronunciation in singing. When "Duoban" is performed, names of villages and places in Yao'an Bazi are often listed, fully demonstrating the singer's language ability. **Bazi Tone of Yao'an** is mostly performed in the wild and fields to the accompaniment of flutes, Erhu (a two-stringed bowed instrument) and percussion instruments. The representative tunes are "Twelve Zodiac Signs", "Picking Flowers in December", "Guessing the Tunes", "Counting Yaozhou", "Counting Place Names", etc.

第 5 项：彝族民歌（彝族酒歌）

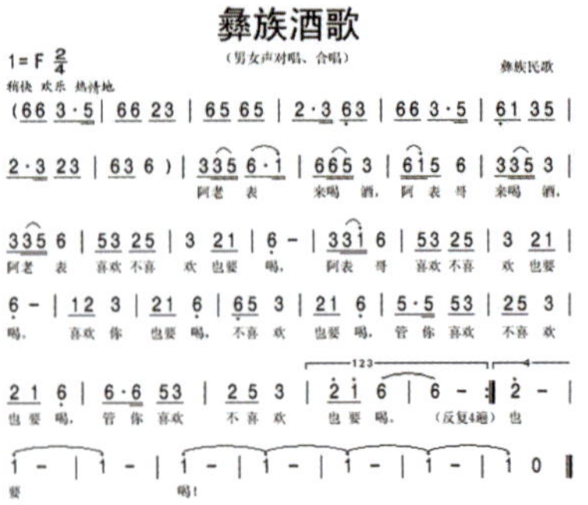

彝族酒歌曲谱
the Music Score of Toasting Songs of the Yi Nationality

项目序号：612	项目编号：Ⅱ-113	公布时间：2008（第二批）	类别：传统音乐
所属地区：云南省	类型：新增项目	申报地区或单位：云南省武定县	

彝族酒歌是武定彝族一种古老的民歌艺术形式，主要流行于云南省楚雄彝族自治州武定县。

武定彝族酒歌有“挪衣”“道嘎”“起除挪衣八”“命熬”“起除”“早除”“南嘎”“所稳切答除”之分。其中“挪衣”意为听古代流传的歌，内容古老，通常源自历史和传说；“道嘎”意指用清楚易懂的语言唱小调，内容多为格言、警句；“起除挪衣八”意为将“嫁调”与“挪衣”合在一起，即将宫调式和商调式二者有机统一；“命熬”中的“命”为诗，“熬”为见，“命熬”意即唱起歌词如同眼见一样，其内容多为叙事诗；“起除”即“嫁调”，其曲调有 140 余首，歌词不固定；“早除”是歌颂的调子，多表现祝贺、赞美和恭维等内容；“南嘎”属对唱形式，有时也有齐唱；“所稳切答除”系贵宾敬酒调，以《祝酒歌》《迎客调》等为代表。彝族酒歌演唱时一般不用器具伴奏，祭祀酒歌使用树叶、羊皮鼓和法铃伴奏，在庄重的迎宾场合则以月琴、大三弦、大号和地筒等乐器伴奏。[①]

① 《彝族民歌（彝族酒歌）》，中国非物质文化遗产网，http://www.ihchina.cn/Article/Index/detail?id=12669，检索日期：2019 年 9 月 1 日。

Item 5: Folk Songs of the Yi Nationality (Toasting Songs of the Yi Nationality)

Item Serial Number: 612	Item ID Number: Ⅱ-113	Released Date: 2008 (Batch 2)	Category: Traditional Music
Affiliated Province: Yunnan Province	Type: New Item	Application Province or Unit: Wuding County, Yunnan Province	

Toasting Songs of the Yi Nationality is an ancient folk song art of the Yi people, mainly circulated in Wuding County, Chuxiong Yi Autonomous Prefecture, Yunnan Province.

Toasting Songs of the Yi Nationality in Wuding can be divided into many types, including “Nuoyi”, “Daoga”, “Qichu Nuoyiba”, “Ming’ao”, “Qichu”, “Zaochu”, “Nanga” and “Suowen Qiedachu”. Among them, “Nuoyi” means listening to ancient songs, and its content is ancient, mostly with historical stories and legends as subject matter; “Daoga” means singing ditties in clear and plain language, with the content mostly being aphorisms and adages; “Qichu Nuoyiba” means combining “Jiadiao Tune” and “Nuoyi”, that is, perfectly integrating the mode of Gong (one of the five ancient Chinese musical notes equal to “Do” in western musical scale) and the mode of Shang (one of the five ancient Chinese musical notes equal to “Re” in western musical scale); in “Ming’ao”, “Ming” means a poem, and “ao” means seeing, therefore “Ming’ao” means that singing the lyrics is just like seeing them, with its content mostly being narrative poems; “Qichu” means “Jiadiao Tune”, with more than 140 tunes, whose lyrics are not fixed; “Zaochu” is eulogistic tunes, mostly expressing congratulations, praise, compliments, etc.; “Nan’ga” is performed in the form of antiphonal singing, and sometimes in the form of chorusing; and “Suowen Qiedachu” is a toasting tune for important figures, represented by “A Song of Toast”, “A Guest-welcoming Tune”. **Toasting songs of the Yi Nationality** are generally performed without the accompaniment of musical instruments. The Sacrificial Toasting Song is performed to the accompaniment of leaves, the Sheepskin Drum and Faling Bell (a kind of shaking and percussion instrument). On the solemn occasion of welcoming guests, they are performed to the accompaniment of musical instruments of Yueqin (a four-stringed plucked musical instrument with a full-moon-shaped sound box), Big Sanxian (a three-stringed plucked musical instrument), tubas, Ditong (a single-reed blowing musical instrument), etc.

布朗族弹唱表演
the Performance of Playing and Singing of the Bulang Nationality

第 6 项：布朗族民歌

（布朗族弹唱）

项目序号：613	项目编号：Ⅱ-114	公布时间：2008（第二批）	类别：传统音乐
所属地区：云南省	类型：新增项目	申报地区或单位：云南省勐海县	

布朗族弹唱源于布朗族先民的歌唱，是在布朗族民间音乐基础上吸收傣族音乐形成的，流行于西双版纳傣族自治州勐海县的布朗山乡、西定乡、打洛镇、勐满镇等布朗族聚居区。

布朗族弹唱有“索”“甚”“拽”“宰”“团曼”五种基本曲调，其中以“索”调最为丰富多彩，它包括五个调子，或欢快跳跃，或舒缓深沉，风格各异。因“索”调使用布朗族传统乐器四弦琴伴奏，故称“布朗族弹唱”。“索”调的“索克里克罗”是有关爱情的曲调，多用来歌唱热烈的爱情，表达青年男女对未来美好生活的向往。布朗族弹唱一般为男女对唱，男子边唱边弹奏四弦琴，女子则以相应的词句回应，唱腔圆润委婉，旋律清甜优美，歌词多反映男女恋慕之情。布朗族弹唱常见于重大节庆、婚丧嫁娶等场合，演唱内容包括本民族迁徙历史、生产知识、祭祀等，此外也会唱一些山歌、情歌、劳动生活和儿歌等。近年来，布朗族弹唱的题材范围大大拓宽，增添了表现社会进步、新人新事不断涌现的内容。[①]

① 《布朗族民歌（布朗族弹唱）》，中国非物质文化遗产网，http://www.ihchina.cn/Article/Index/detail?id=12671，检索日期：2019 年 9 月 1 日。

Item 6: Folk Songs of the Bulang Nationality (Playing and Singing of the Bulang Nationality)

Item Serial Number: 613	Item ID Number: Ⅱ-114	Released Date: 2008 (Batch 2)	Category: Traditional Music
Affiliated Province: Yunnan Province	Type: New Item	Application Province or Unit: Menghai County, Yunnan Province	

Playing and Singing of the Bulang Nationality originated from the singing of the Bulang ancestors, which was formed by absorbing the music of the Dai nationality on the basis of the folk music of the Bulang nationality. It is popular in areas inhabited by the Bulang nationality, such as Bulangshan Township, Xiding Township, Daluo Township and Mengman Township in Menghai County, Xishuangbanna Dai Autonomous Prefecture.

Playing and Singing of the Bulang Nationality has five basic tunes: "Suo", "Shen", "Dragging", "Zai" and "Tuanman". Among them, the tune of "Suo" is the most colorful. It includes five sub-tunes, some being happy and lively, and some being soothing and deep, with varied styles. Because the tune of "Suo" is accompanied by Sixianqin (a four-stringed lute), a traditional musical instrument of the Bulang nationality, it is called "**Playing and Singing of the Bulang Nationality**". The sub-tune of "Suoke Likeluo" in the tune of "Suo" is a tune of love, which is mostly performed to sing in praise of passionate love and to express young men and women's yearings for a better life in the future. **Playing and Singing of the Bulang Nationality** is usually performed by men and women in the form of antiphonal singing, with men singing while playing Sixianqin (a four-stringed lute), and women singing corresponding lyrics in response. The singing is round and gentle, the melody is sweet and elegant, and the lyrics mostly reflect the love of men and women. **Playing and Singing of the Bulang Nationality** is mainly for the occasions of grand festival celebrations, weddings, funerals, etc. Its singing involves the content of the migration history, production knowledge, sacrifices, etc. of the Bulang nationality. In addition, it also involves some mountain songs, love songs, songs of labor life, children's songs, etc. In recent years, the subject matter of **Playing and Singing of the Bulang Nationality** has been greatly expanded, and the content that expresses social progress and the continuous emergence of new people and new things has been added.

妙善学女子洞经音乐演出
the Performance of Miaoshanxue Maiden Dongjing Music

第 7 项：洞经音乐

（妙善学女子洞经音乐）

项目序号：627	项目编号：Ⅱ-128	公布时间：2008（第二批）	类别：传统音乐
所属地区：云南省	类型：新增项目	申报地区或单位：云南省通海县	

洞经音乐主要流行于云南省的汉族、白族、纳西族群众中，原是一种道教礼仪音乐，因以诵唱《大洞仙经》经文为主要内容而得名。其音乐曲调十分丰富，每个流传地区都有独立成套的各类曲调。

云南现有的几百支洞经演奏队伍中，以通海妙善学女子洞经（古乐）班的表现最为突出。通海妙善学女子洞经（古乐）班成立于 1943 年，全班由 18 位少女组成，经过两年的学习，掌握了工尺谱和简谱，能熟练演奏 40 多首曲牌。1947 年，她们在三元宫弹演洞经后，创新性地将这一弹演活动带入民间礼佛仪式，其后相沿成俗，至今已有 60 多年的历史。女子洞经会的演奏曲目有【小开门】、【阴阳调】、【鹧鸪天】、【叠落金钱】等 39 首，可分为古典音乐、江南丝竹音乐和民间音乐几种主要类型。妙善学女子洞经音乐在传承通海音乐演奏传统的基础上，充分展示出女子演奏所特有的魅力：在为宗教仪式伴奏时严肃不失热情，虔诚中显出慈善；演唱时激昂中别见清脆，舒缓中透着甜润；演奏时则以纤巧细腻、缠绵婉转的艺术风格取胜。作为云南省唯一的女子洞经组织，妙善学女子洞经会开创了女性弹演洞经的先例，最完整地保留了洞经弹演的程序和内容。①

① 《洞经音乐（妙善学女子洞经音乐）》，中国非物质文化遗产网，http://www.ihchina.cn/Article/Index/detail?id=12726，检索日期：2019 年 8 月 11 日。

Item 7: Dongjing Music (Miaoshanxue Maiden Dongjing Music)

Item Serial Number: 627	Item ID Number: Ⅱ-128	Released Date: 2008 (Batch 2)	Category: Traditional Music
Affiliated Province: Yunnan Province	Type: New Item	Application Province or Unit: Tonghai County, Yunnan Province	

Dongjing Music is mainly popular among the Han, Bai and Naxi people in Yunnan Province. It was originally a Taoist ritual music, and got such a name because it took the recitation and singing of Dadong Immortals' Scriptures as the main content. It is very rich in tunes, and in each area where it is circulated, there are independent sets of various tunes.

Among the existing hundreds of performing teams of Dongjing in Yunnan Province, Miaoshanxue Maiden Dongjing (Ancient Music) Troupe in Tonghai County is the most prominent. This troupe was established in 1943, consisted of 18 girls. After two years of study, they have mastered Gongchi musical notation and numbered musical notation, and can skillfully play more than 40 pieces of Qupai (the tune name of a melody). In 1947, after they performed Dongjing in the Three Yuan Palace, they innovatively introduced this performance activity into folk Buddha-worship rituals. Later, it has become a common custom, with a history of more than 60 years up to now. The tunes performed by the Maiden Dongjing Society include 39 pieces, such as Xiaokaimen, Yingyang Tune, Zhegu Sky and Dieluo Jinqian (Fallen Money), which can be divided into several main types, such as classical music, Jiangnan Sizhu music (the one performed by using traditional stringed and woodwind instruments) and folk music. On the basis of inheriting the tradition of performing Tonghai Music, **Miaoshanxue Maiden Dongjing Music** fully demonstrates the unique charm of women's performance. When it is performed to accompany religious ceremonies, it is solemn and enthusiastic, showing charity in piety. When it is sung, the music is exciting, crisp, soothing and sweet. When it is performed, it's featured by a delicate, lingering and graceful artistic style. As the only organization of Maiden Dongjing in Yunnan Province, Miaoshanxue Maiden Dongjing Society has pioneered women's performance of Dongjing, retaining the most complete procedures and content of performing Dongjing.

第 8 项：弥渡民歌

弥渡民歌国家级传承人李彩凤
Li Caifeng, the State-level Inheritor of Midu Folk Songs

项目序号：1075	项目编号：Ⅱ-145	公布时间：2011（第三批）	类别：传统音乐
所属地区：云南省	类型：新增项目	申报地区或单位：云南省弥渡县	

弥渡民歌是指流传于云南省弥渡县境内的汉族和少数民族民歌，流传历史悠久。20 世纪 50 年代以来，随着《小河淌水》《十大姐》《绣荷包》《弥渡山歌》等一批弥渡传统民歌、改编民歌在国内外广为传播，“弥渡民歌”逐渐在全国产生广泛影响，成为我国知名度很高的民歌品类。

弥渡民歌内容丰富，形式多样，真实反映了人民群众的生产生活和思想情感。以民族分类，弥渡民歌可分为汉族民歌和少数民族民歌两类；以音乐体裁分类，弥渡民歌可分为山歌、小调、舞蹈歌、风俗歌等类型。其曲调极为丰富，旋律婉转悠扬。代表性曲调，山歌类有《小河淌水》《弥渡山歌》《埂子调》《密滴调》《密祉调》《放羊调》《过山调》等；小调有《赶马调》《绣荷包》《绣香袋》等；舞蹈歌有《十大姐》和多种《打歌调》；风俗歌有《迎亲调》《送亲调》《哭亡调》《指路歌》《祭祀歌》等。弥渡民歌的传承方式包括师传、家传和自学。①

Item 8: Midu Folk Songs

Item Serial Number: 1075	Item ID Number: Ⅱ-145	Released Date: 2011 (Batch 3)	Category: Traditional Music
Affiliated Province: Yunnan Province	Type: New Item	Application Province or Unit: Midu County, Yunnan Province	

① 《弥渡民歌》，中国非物质文化遗产网，http://www.ihchina.cn/Article/Index/detail?id=12781，检索日期：2019 年 9 月 1 日。

Midu Folk Songs refer to the folk songs of the Han nationality and ethnic minorities that are prevalent in Midu County, Yunnan Province, with a long history of inheritance. Since the 1950s, with the wide spread of a batch of traditional and adapted Midu folk songs at home and abroad, such as “Small River Flowing”, “Ten Elder Sisters”, “Embroidering Pouches” and “Midu Mountain Songs”, **Midu Folk Songs** have gradually exerted an extensive influence throughout China and become a very well-known folk song category in China.

Midu Folk Songs are rich in content and diverse in form, which truly reflect the masses’ production, life, thoughts and emotions. According to ethnicity, **Midu Folk Songs** can be divided into two types: folk songs of the Han nationality and folk songs of ethnic minorities. According to music genres, **Midu Folk Songs** can be divided into mountain songs, ditties, dancing songs, folk custom songs, etc. Their tunes are extremely rich and their melodies are gentle and melodious. Among the representative tunes, mountain songs include “Small River Flowing”, “Midu Mountain Songs”, “Gengzi Tune”, “Midi Tune”, “Mizhi Tune”, “A Sheep-herding Tune” and “A Mountain-crossing Tune”; ditties include “Horse-riding Tunes”, “Embroidering Pouches” and “Embroidering Fragrant Bags”; dancing songs include “Ten Elder Sisters” and a variety of “Dage Tunes”; and folk custom songs include “A Tune of Welcoming the Bride”, “A Tune of Seeing off the Bride”, “A Tune of Crying for the Dead”, “A Road-guiding Song” and “A Song for Offering Sacrifices”. The ways of inheriting **Midu Folk Songs** are masters’ instruction, family members’ instruction and self-study.

第 9 项：纳西族白沙细乐

纳西族白沙细乐国家级传承人和凛毅

He Linyi, the State-level Inheritor of Baisha Orchestral Music of the Naxi Nationality

项目序号：1082	项目编号：Ⅱ-152	公布时间：2011（第三批）	类别：传统音乐
所属地区：云南省	类型：新增项目	申报地区或单位：云南省丽江市古城区	

纳西族白沙细乐是纳西先民创制的一部器乐、声乐及舞蹈相结合的古典音乐套曲，流传于丽江市古城区和玉龙纳西族自治县。主要表现的是生离死别、怀恋缱绻的感情。

相传白沙细乐有十个调，现存八个调，分别是“笃”“一封书”“三思及”“美丽的白云”“公主哭”“跺蹉”“南曲”和“北曲”。赤足舞“跺蹉”、云雀舞“劳马蹉”、弓矢舞“抗蹉”、白鹤舞“夸蹉”等在送葬时奏跳。“跺蹉”“劳马蹉”“抗蹉”“夸蹉”均为纳西语，是舞蹈土生于民间的标记，从生离死别中还可佐证送魂路线等纳西史实。乐器有横笛、直笛、芦管、苏古笃、小曲项琵琶、古筝、二簧和胡琴，演奏至少要有八人，并以合奏为主，同时也伴歌舞。乐器中的苏古笃、芦管与元朝宴乐之器“火不思”“波伯”有异曲同工之妙。白沙细乐是元明遗音与纳西民间音乐的美满结合，是经过相当长的时间才逐步形成的套曲，构思独到，器乐兼歌并舞，曲调抒情，旋律委婉流畅。①

Item 9: Baisha Orchestral Music of the Naxi Nationality

Item Serial Number: 1082	Item ID Number: Ⅱ-152	Released Date: 2011 (Batch 3)	Category: Traditional Music
Affiliated Province: Yunnan Province	Type: New Item	Application Province or Unit: Ancient City District, Lijiang City, Yunnan Province	

① 《纳西族白沙细乐》，中国非物质文化遗产网，http://www.ihchina.cn/Article/Index/detail?id=12788，检索日期：2019 年 9 月 2 日。

Baisha Orchestral Music of the Naxi Nationality is a set of classical music integrating instrumental music, vocal music and dances, created by the Naxi ancestors, and spread in Ancient City District of Lijiang City and Yulong Naxi Autonomous County. It mainly reflects the feelings of parting for ever, nostalgia and deep attachment.

It's said that there were originally ten tunes in **Baisha Orchestral Music**, but only eight tunes are in existence at present, including "Du", "A Letter", "Sansiji", "Beautiful White Clouds", "The Princess' Crying", "Duocuo", "Southern Tunes" and "Northern Tunes". The Barefoot Dance of "Duocuo", the Skylark Dance of "Laomacuo", the Bow and Arrow Dance of "Kangcuo", and the White Crane Dance of "Kuacuo" are performed at funerals. "Duocuo", "Laomacuo", "Kangcuo" and "Kuacuo" are all transliteration of the Naxi language, being a sign that dances originate from the folk. From the separation between loved ones in life or death, historical facts of the Naxi nationality, such as the route of seeing off souls, can also be confirmed. The musical instruments include transverse flutes, vertical flutes, Luguan (a traditional Chinese oboe instrument), Sugudu (a stringed instrument of the Naxi nationality), Small Quxiang Pipa (a plucked string instrument with a fretted fingerboard), Guzheng (a Chinese zither), Erhuang (a bow-drawn stringed musical instrument of the Naxi nationality) and Huqin Musical Instrument. The performance of **Baisha Orchestral Music** needs at least 8 musicians, with the ensemble as the main, accompanied by singing and dancing at the same time. Among the musical instruments, Sugudu (a stringed instrument of the Naxi nationality) and Luguan (a traditional Chinese oboe instrument) are similar to the Banquet Musical Instruments of "Huobusi" and "Bobo" in the Yuan Dynasty. **Baisha Orchestral Music** is a perfect combination of the remaining music of the Yuan and Ming dynasties and the folk music of the Naxi nationality. It is a set of music gradually formed after a long period of time, unique in composition. The instrumental music is combined with songs and dances, the tunes are lyrical and the melodies are graceful and smooth.

第10项：剑川白曲

剑川白曲演奏
the Performance of Bai Melody of Jianchuan

项目序号：1258	项目编号：Ⅱ-164	公布时间：2014（第四批）	类别：传统音乐
所属地区：云南省	类型：新增项目	申报地区或单位：云南省大理白族自治州	

剑川白曲是白族地区流传较广、历史悠久的古老音乐品种，已有一千多年的历史。

剑川白曲具有叙事和抒情的功能，音乐表现力极强，其内容丰富、题材广泛，主要有创世古歌、祭祀歌、礼俗歌、劳动歌、情歌、一字歌、反意歌、咏物歌、寓意歌、生活歌和儿歌等。其表演形式有三种：（1）由一人怀抱龙头三弦，自弹自唱；（2）由一人伴奏，一人唱；（3）一人伴奏，男女对唱。其歌词结构为“七七七五”式，即第一、二、三句为七个字，第四句为五个字，俗称“山花体”。四句为一段，若干段为一首。根据篇幅长度，剑川白曲可分为短调和长歌两类，二者均采用“山花体”。短调最常见的为八句一首，常在山间、湖畔、田边、地头及石宝山歌会、火把节等民族节日里即兴对唱；长歌最长的达3000多行，多数有故事情节，但不复杂，以抒情为主。[①]

Item 10: Bai Melody of Jianchuan

Item Serial Number: 1258	Item ID Number: II-164	Released Date: 2014 (Batch 4)	Category: Traditional Music
Affiliated Province: Yunnan Province	Type: New Item	Application Province or Unit: Dali Bai Autonomous Prefecture, Yunnan Province	

① 张文、杨万涛，《剑川白曲：醉美白曲乡音》，载《大理日报》，2017年6月7日第3版。

Bai Melody of Jianchuan is an ancient variety of music widely spread in areas inhabited by the Bai nationality, with a history of more than a thousand years.

It has narrative and lyrical functions, and its musical expressive power is extremely great. It's rich in content and extensive in subject matter, mainly including ancient songs of creating the world, sacrificial songs, songs of etiquette and custom, labor songs, love songs, songs containing the Chinese character of "一", ironic songs, songs of praising things, allegorical songs, life songs and children's songs. There are three forms of performance for **Bai Melody of Jianchuan**: (1) One singer plays Dragon-head Sanxian (a three-stringed plucked musical instrument) and sings by himself/ herself; (2) One singer sings it, accompanied by one instrument player; (3)Male and female singers perform antiphonal singing, accompanied by one instrument player. The structure of its lyrics is "seven-seven-seven-five", that is, there are seven characters respectively in the first, second and third sentences, and five characters in the fourth sentence, commonly known as "Shanhua Style". Four sentences compose one stanza, and several stanzas compose a tune. According to lengths, **Bai Melody of Jianchuan** can be divided into two types: short tunes and long songs, both of which adopt "Shanhua Style". A short tune most commonly consists of eight sentences, which is often performed through impromptu antiphonal singing in the mountains, by the lakeside, beside the fields, at the edge of farming land, as well as at the ethnic festivals, such as the Singing Festival of the Shibao Mountain and the Torch Festival. The longest song can reach more than 3,000 lines, mostly with stories. But the stories are not complicated, they are primarily lyrical.

第三章 传统舞蹈

Chapter Three Traditional Dance

第1项：锅庄舞（迪庆锅庄舞）

迪庆锅庄舞表演

the Performance of Diqing Guozhuang Dance

项目序号：123	项目编号：Ⅲ-20	公布时间：2006（第一批）	类别：传统舞蹈
所属地区：云南省	类型：新增项目	申报地区或单位：云南省迪庆藏族自治州	

锅庄舞是藏族三大民间舞蹈之一，主要有用于大型宗教祭祀活动的“大锅庄”、用于民间传统节日的“中锅庄”和用于亲朋聚会的“小锅庄”三种类型。舞蹈时，一般男女各排半圆拉手成圈，一人领头，分男女一问一答，反复对唱，无乐器伴奏。整个舞蹈由先慢后快的两段舞组成，基本动作有“悠颤跨腿”“趋步辗转”“跨腿踏步蹲”等，舞者手臂以撩、甩、晃为主变换舞姿，队形按顺时针行进。

迪庆藏族锅庄舞主要分布在云南迪庆藏族自治州中，以德钦县奔子栏镇和香格里拉市沾塘镇、小中甸镇的最有代表性。奔子栏在待客时以锅庄歌舞形式表现系列礼仪程序，有“祝福锅庄”“逐客锅庄”“赞颂锅庄”“相会锅庄”“辞别锅庄”“挽留锅庄”“送别锅庄”“祈福锅庄”等种类，在全国各藏族聚居地十分罕见。其曲调分“吆”“卓金”“霞卓”“卓草”四个部分。香格里拉锅庄分古、新两种，“擦尼”是古锅庄，歌词内容、舞步形式都较古老，具有浓厚的祭祀性质，有专门的动作和歌词，多为宗教界和老年人喜爱；“擦司”是新舞，系随着不同时代而新编的歌舞。迪庆藏族锅庄的歌、舞、词都很丰富，唱词以三句为一段。凡遇喜庆佳节、新居落成、婚嫁喜事，人们不分男女老幼都要聚集在一起跳个通宵，表示欢庆和祈福。①

Item 1: Guozhuang Dance (Diqing Guozhuang Dance)

Item Serial Number: 123	Item ID Number: Ⅲ-20	Released Date: 2006 (Batch 1)	Category: Traditional Dance
Affiliated Province: Yunnan Province	Type: New Item	Application Province or Unit: Diqing Zang Autonomous Prefecture, Yunnan Province	

Guozhuang Dance is one of the three major folk dances of the Zang nationality. There are mainly thrcc typcs: “Big Guozhuang Dance” used for large-scale religious sacrificial activities, “Medium Guozhuang Dance” used for traditional folk festivals, and “Small Guozhuang Dance” used for gatherings of relatives and friends. When dancing, men and women generally form a semi-circle respectively to hold hands and form a circle, with one person serving as the leader. The dance is performed by two sides, the male and the female, with one side asking questions and the other giving answers. Such an antiphonal singing is repeated, without instrumental accompaniment. The whole dance consists of two sections, a slow one and then a fast one. Basic movements include “stretching legs while trembling”, “stepping and turning”, “stretching legs, stepping and squatting”, etc. Dancers’ arms change mainly by fluttering, swinging and shaking, and the formation moves clockwise.

Diqing Guozhuang Dance of the Zang nationality is mainly distributed in Diqing Zang Autonomous Prefecture, Yunnan Province, with dances in Benzilan Township

① 《锅庄舞（迪庆锅庄舞）》，中国非物质文化遗产网，http://www.ihchina.cn/Article/Index/detail?id=12932，检索日期：2019 年 9 月 1 日。

in Deqin County, as well as Zhantang Township and Xiaozhongxun Township in Shangri-La City being the most representative. When welcoming guests, people in Benzilan Township present a series of etiquette procedures in the form of Guozhuang singing and dancing, including "Guozhuang Dance of Blessings", "Guozhuang Dance of Expelling Guests", "Guozhuang Dance of Eulogizing", "Guozhuang Dance of Gatherings", "Guozhuang Dance of Bidding Farewell", "Guozhuang Dance of Detaining Guests", "Guozhuang Dance of Seeing Off Guests" and "Guozhuang Dance of Praying for Blessings", which are very rare in all areas inhabited by the Zang nationality across the country. The tune is divided into four parts: "Yao", "Zhuojin", "Xiazhuo" and "Zhuocao". Shangri-La Guozhuang Dance is divided into the ancient type and the new type. "Cani" is the ancient type. Its content of lyrics and forms of dance steps are relatively age-old, with a strong sacrificial nature. There are specialized movements and lyrics, which are mostly loved by religious circles and the elderly. "Casi" is the new type, which is the song and dance newly composed with the changing of times. The songs, dances and lyrics of Diqing Guozhuang Dance of the Zang nationality are very rich, with one passage of the lyric composed of three sentences. Whenever there is a festival, the completion of a new house, or weddings, people regardless of men and women, old and young, will gather together and dance all night to express joy and blessings.

第 2 项：木鼓舞

（沧源佤族木鼓舞）

沧源佤族木鼓舞比赛
the Competition of Cangyuan Wooden-drum Dance of the Wa Nationality

项目序号：128	项目编号：Ⅲ-25	公布时间：2006（第一批）	类别：传统舞蹈
所属地区：云南省	类型：新增项目	申报地区或单位：云南省沧源佤族自治县	

木鼓舞是流传在西南苗族、彝族和佤族人民中以敲击木鼓起舞祭祀的民间舞蹈。一般来说，木鼓舞为族群全体参与的大型祭祀活动的一部分，木鼓被视为族群的象征，以敲木鼓、跳木鼓为核心的祭祀活动充满着强烈的祖先崇拜、自然崇拜的寓意。沧源佤族木鼓舞主要分布在云南省临沧市沧源佤族自治县的岩帅、单甲、糯良、勐来、勐角和班洪等乡镇。

沧源佤族木鼓舞由拉木鼓、进木鼓房、敲木鼓和祭木鼓四部分组成。每逢年节庆典，佤族男女老少穿戴一新，在木鼓的敲击下围绕木鼓房，携手成圈蹁跹起舞。他们以屈膝、弓腰表示对木鼓的敬仰，按逆时针方向围圈缓慢移动，动作以甩手、走步和跺脚为主。第一拍右脚向右斜前方上一步，双手曲肘举至头斜上方，身体后仰；第二拍左脚跟踏一步，双手甩至身后斜下方，身躯前倾。如此循环反复。木鼓舞贯穿于木鼓祭祀活动全过程，舞蹈以敲打木鼓者的领唱和众人踏节而歌为伴奏，其他伴奏乐器还有铓锣、铜鼓和葫芦笙等，歌词多涉及民族历史、祭祀、劳动生产及生活等内容。跳木鼓舞时鼓声震天，舞者秀发飞扬，动作粗犷奔放，表现了佤族人勤劳勇敢的性格。[①]

① 《木鼓舞（沧源佤族木鼓舞）》，中国非物质文化遗产网，http://www.ihchina.cn/Article/Index/detail?id=12965，检索日期：2019 年 8 月 21 日。

Item 2: the Wooden-drum Dance (Cangyuan Wooden-drum Dance of the Wa Nationality)

Item Serial Number: 128	Item ID Number: Ⅲ-25	Released Date: 2006 (Batch 1)	Category: Traditional Dance
Affiliated Province: Yunnan Province	Type: New Item	Application Province or Unit: Cangyuan Wa Autonomous County, Yunnan Province	

The Wooden-drum Dance is a folk dance that is prevalent among the Miao, Yi and Wa people in Southwest China who offer sacrifices through beating the Wooden Drum and dancing. Generally, **the Wooden-drum Dance** is one part of the large-scale sacrificial activities participated by all members of one ethnic group. The Wooden Drum is regarded as a symbol of an ethnic group. The sacrificial activities centered on beating the Wooden Drum and performing **the Wooden-drum Dance** have the strong implications of ancestor worship and nature worship. **Cangyuan Wooden-drum Dance of the Wa Nationality** are mainly distributed in townships of Yanshuai, Danjia, Nuoliang, Menglai, Mengjiao, Banhong, etc. of Cangyuan Wa Autonomous County, Lincang City, Yunnan Province.

Cangyuan Wooden-drum Dance of the Wa Nationality consists of four parts: pulling the Wooden Drum, entering the Wooden Drum House, beating the Wooden Drum and offering sacrifices to the Wooden Drum. On each celebration of the Spring Festival or other festivals, the Wa people, men and women, old and young, wear new clothes and dance in a circle around the Wooden Drum House to the beat of the Wooden Drum. They bend their knees and bow their waists to express their respect for the Wooden Drum, moving slowly in a counterclockwise circle. Their movements are mainly swinging hands, walking and stamping. In the first beat, dancers take a step forward with the right foot diagonally to the right, their both hands with flexed elbows are raised to the oblique above of the head, and their bodies lean back. In the second beat, dancers take a step with the left heel and swing both hands to the oblique lower part of the back, with their bodies leaning forward. These movements are repeated over and over again. **The Wooden-drum Dance** is performed throughout the whole activity of offering sacrifices to **the Wooden Drum**. Its dance is performed to the accompaniment of the leading singing of the Wooden Drum beater and many people's singing to the beat. Other accompaniment instruments include Mangluo (a copper percussion instrument used by the ethnic minorities in Yunnan Province), the Bronze Drum and Hulusheng (a gourd-made musical instrument). The lyrics are mostly concerned with the ethnic history, sacrifices, labor production, life, etc. When performing **the Wooden-drum Dance**, the sound of beating drums is extremely loud, and the female dancers' hairs fly with the dance. Their movements are wild and unrestrained, showing the diligent and brave characters of the Wa people.

第 3 项：文山壮族、彝族铜鼓舞

文山州富宁县彝族白倮支系的铜鼓舞
the Bronze-drum Dance of the Bailuo Branch of the Yi Nationality in Wenshan Prefecture

项目序号：129	项目编号：Ⅲ-26	公布时间：2006（第一批）	类别：传统舞蹈
所属地区：云南省	类型：新增项目	申报地区或单位：云南省文山壮族苗族自治州	

铜鼓舞是云南省文山壮族苗族自治州壮族、彝族民众中流传最广、影响最大的古老舞种之一，分布于广南、麻栗坡、富宁、西畴、马关和邱北等县的壮族、彝族村寨，尤以广南县壮、彝族和麻栗坡县新寨乡和富宁县木央乡几个彝族白倮支系的铜鼓舞最具代表性。

铜鼓舞始于文山壮族、彝族先民的自然崇拜和祖先崇拜。彝族认为铜鼓是万物之灵，通过敲铜鼓、跳舞，可以向上苍和祖先传递人们的意愿。壮族则认为敲铜鼓跳舞，可以为村寨降妖驱邪，祈求平安。铜鼓舞属族群性的集体舞蹈。舞者围成圆圈，踏着鼓声节奏沿逆时针方向起舞，跳完一组舞蹈动作再跳另一组，内容都是壮族、彝族农耕生产生活的反映。广南县那洒镇马贵村壮族的铜鼓舞完整保留了十二套舞蹈动作，反映了一年四季十二个月不同的生产内容。麻栗坡、富宁等县的几个村寨中的铜鼓舞，主要用于祈雨、求丰收和老人丧葬等民俗活动。壮族铜鼓舞表演时，一人敲铜鼓，另一人以木盒辅助形成共鸣滑音，这在其他音乐演奏中是找不到的。彝族的铜鼓演奏则是一种专门技巧，一人演奏公、母两面铜鼓，能够呈现十二种音调组合，简称十二调。据称公鼓代表太阳，母鼓代表月亮，十二调代表一年十二个月，因此彝族的铜鼓舞还包含着本民族的历法文化内容。①

① 《铜鼓舞（文山壮族、彝族铜鼓舞）》，中国非物质文化遗产网，http://www.ihchina.cn/Article/Index/detail?id=12966，检索日期：2019 年 9 月 1 日。

Item 3: the Bronze-drum Dance of the Zhuang and Yi Nationalities of Wenshan Prefecture

Item Serial Number: 129	Item ID Number: Ⅲ-26	Released Date: 2006 (Batch 1)	Category: Traditional Dance
Affiliated Province: Yunnan Province	Type: New Item	Application Province or Unit: Wenshan Zhuang and Miao Autonomous Prefecture, Yunnan Province	

The Bronze-drum Dance is one of the most widespread and influential ancient dance types among the Zhuang and Yi people in Wenshan Zhuang and Miao Autonomous Prefecture, Yunnan Province. It is distributed in the stockaded villages inhabited by the Zhuang and Yi nationalities in counties of Guangnan, Malipo, Funing, Xichou, Maguan, Qiubei, etc. **The Bronze-drum Dance of the Zhuang and Yi nationalities** in Guangnan County, and that of the Bailuo Branch of the Yi nationality in Xinzhai Township of Malipo County and Muyang Township of Funing County are the most representative.

The Bronze-drum Dance began with the worship of nature and ancestors of the Zhuang and Yi ancestors in Wenshan. The Yi people believe that the Bronze Drum is the spirit of all things. By playing the Bronze Drum and dancing, they can convey their wishes to Heaven and their ancestors. The Zhuang people believe that dancing when beating the Bronze Drum can help subdue demons, exorcise evil spirits and pray for peace for the villages. **The Bronze-drum Dance** is an ethnic collective dance. Dancers form a circle and dance in a counterclockwise direction to the beat of the drum. After one set of dance moves, they begin another set. The content is a reflection of the farming, production and life of the Zhuang and Yi nationalities. **The Bronze-drum Dance of the Zhuang Nationality** in Magui Village, Nasa Township, Guangnan County has retained twelve sets of dance moves, reflecting the different production content of twelve months throughout the year. **The Bronze-drum Dance** in several villages of Malipo and Funing counties, etc. is mainly used in the folk activities of praying for rain and a good harvest, funerals for the elderly, etc. During the performance of **the Bronze-drum Dance of the Zhuang Nationality**, one participant beats the Bronze Drum, and the other uses a wooden box to assist in forming a resonance glide, which can't be found in other musical performances.

The performance of **the Bronze-drum Dance of the Yi Nationality** is a specialized technique. By playing two drums, one male and the other female, one person can produce twelve tonal combinations, which is referred to as the Twelve Tunes. It's said that the male drum represents the sun, the female drum represents the moon, and the Twelve Tunes represent the twelve months in one year. Therefore, **the Bronze-drum Dance of the Yi Nationality** also contains the calendar culture of this nationality.

第 4 项：傣族孔雀舞

傣族孔雀舞表演
the Performance of the Peacock Dance of the Dai Nationality

项目序号：130	项目编号：Ⅲ-27	公布时间：2006（第一批）	类别：传统舞蹈
所属地区：云南省	类型：新增项目	申报地区或单位：云南省瑞丽市	

傣族孔雀舞是我国傣族民间舞中最负盛名的传统表演性舞蹈，流传于云南省德宏傣族景颇族自治州的瑞丽市、芒市及西双版纳、孟定、孟达、景谷、沧源等傣族聚居区，其中以瑞丽市的孔雀舞最具代表性。相传一千多年前傣族领袖召麻栗杰数模仿孔雀的优美姿态而学舞，后经历代民间艺人不断完善，流传下来，形成孔雀舞。

在傣族人民心目中，“圣鸟”孔雀是幸福吉祥的象征。孔雀舞是傣族人们最喜爱的民间舞蹈，在傣族聚居的坝区，几乎月月有“摆”（节日），年年有歌舞。在傣族一年一度的“泼水节”“关门节”“开门节”“赶摆”等民俗节日，只要是尽兴欢乐的场所，傣族人都会聚集在一起，敲响大锣，打起象脚鼓，跳起姿态优美的“孔雀舞”，歌舞声中呈现出丰收的喜庆气氛和民族团结的美好景象。瑞丽傣族孔雀舞以单人舞为主，也有双人孔雀舞。舞者以男性居多。孔雀舞有丰富多样的手形动作和跳、转等技巧，四肢和躯干的各个关节要重拍向下屈伸，全身均匀颤动，形成优美的“三道弯”舞姿。架子孔雀舞的舞蹈语汇尤为丰富，有“飞跑下山”“林中窥看”“漫步森林”“抖翅”“点水”等惟妙惟肖模拟孔雀神态的动作。孔雀舞风格轻盈灵秀，情感表达细腻，舞姿婀娜优美，是傣族最有文化认同感的舞蹈。①

① 《傣族孔雀舞》，中国非物质文化遗产网，http://www.ihchina.cn/Article/Index/detail?id=12970，检索日期：2019 年 9 月 1 日。

Item 4: the Peacock Dance of the Dai Nationality

Item Serial Number: 130	Item ID Number: Ⅲ-27	Released Date: 2006 (Batch 1)	Category: Traditional Dance
Affiliated Province: Yunnan Province	Type: New Item	Application Province or Unit: Ruili City, Yunnan Province	

The Peacock Dance of the Dai Nationality is the most prestigious traditional performing dance among the folk dances of the Dai nationality in China. It is prevalent in areas inhabited by the Dai nationality in Ruili and Mangshi cities of Dehong Dai and Jingpo Autonomous Prefecture, as well as Xishuangbanna Prefecture, Mengding Township, Mengda Township, Jinggu County and Cangyuan County in Yunnan Province, with the Peacock Dance in Ruili City being the most representative. According to legend, more than a thousand years ago, the leader of the Dai nationality, called Zhaoma Lijieshu, imitated the graceful postures of a peacock and learned to dance. Later, after generations of folk artists made constant improvement, the Peacock Dance took shape and has been passed down up to now.

In the minds of the Dai people, peacocks, "the holy bird", are a symbol of happiness and auspiciousness. **The Peacock Dance** is the most favorite folk dance of the Dai people. In the areas where the Dai people live, there is "Bai activity" (festival) almost every month, as well as songs and dances every year. During the folk festivals, such as "the Water-splashing Festival", "the Door-closing Festival", "the Door-opening Festival" and "Ganbai (going to a fair)", which are held annually, in the place where the Dai people can have fun, they will gather together, beat the big gong and the Elephant-foot Drum, and perform the graceful Peacock Dance. The song and dance present a festive atmosphere of a good harvest and a beautiful scene of national unity. **Ruili Peacock Dance of the Dai Nationality** is mainly performed by a single dancer. There is also the Double-dancer Peacock Dance. The majority of dancers are male. **The Peacock Dance** has a variety of hand movements and techniques of jumping, turning, etc. The joints of the four limbs and the torso are flexed downwards, with the whole body trembling evenly and forming a beautiful "three-bend" dancing posture. The dance vocabulary of Jiazi Peacock Dance (a dance performed with the racks of peacock wings) is particularly rich, which includes the movements that vividly imitate a peacock's demeanor, such as "flying down the mountain", "peeping in the forest", "wandering in the forest", "flapping wings" and "poking at water". The style of **the Peacock Dance** is light and graceful, with delicate emotional expression and graceful postures. It is the most culturally recognizable dance of the Dai nationality.

叶枝傈僳族阿尺木刮表演
the Performance of Achi Mugua Dance of the Lisu Nationality in Yezhi Township

第 5 项：傈僳族阿尺木刮

项目序号：138	项目编号：Ⅲ-35	公布时间：2006（第一批）	类别：传统舞蹈
所属地区：云南省	类型：新增项目	申报地区或单位：云南省维西傈僳族自治县	

傈僳族阿尺木刮意为“山羊的歌舞”或“学山羊叫的歌调”，流传于云南省迪庆藏族自治州维西傈僳族自治县叶枝镇的同乐村、新乐村一带，是当地传统的自娱性民间歌舞。舞蹈形式热烈奔放，是维西傈僳人传统生产生活和思想感情的生动表现。

维西县历史上交通闭塞，傈僳族很少与外界往来，生产方式基本处于半农半牧阶段。山羊是家家必养的牲畜，在生产生活中，维西傈僳族人与山羊结下了深厚感情，由模仿山羊叫、模仿山羊跳而产生了歌舞阿尺木刮。[①] 阿尺木刮无乐器伴奏，曲调可缓可急，音符的跳动较为频繁，且跳动幅度大，唱时多颤音，以模拟山羊叫声为基调。唱词多涉及天文地理、栽种收割、悲欢离合的内容，舞者自始至终随歌声的节奏而踏步。舞者一般在五人以上，多时可达上百人。现今流传的跳法有十种，包括舞圆环、进退舞步、三步跺脚、跳山羊、对脚板、龙盘旋、舞旋风、磨盘旋转、迎宾客、寻求爱侣等。队形变化有大圆圈、半圆弧、直纵队、穿插式等。脚步动作主要包括跳摆和搓蹂。歌舞时的服饰为自己缝制刺绣的生活装。维西傈僳族人在春节、火把节、婚嫁、祭祀、迎宾接客以及喜庆之事时都要跳阿尺木刮。[②]

① 《傈僳族阿尺木刮》，中国非物质文化遗产网，http://www.ihchina.cn/Article/Index/detail?id=12979，检索日期：2019 年 9 月 1 日。

② 《叶枝镇傈僳族阿尺木刮歌舞之乡》，云南非物质文化遗产保护网，http://www.ynich.cn/view.php?id=1209&cat_id=11111，检索日期：2019 年 8 月 31 日。

Item 5: Achi Mugua Dance of the Lisu Nationality

Item Serial Number: 138	Item ID Number: Ⅲ-35	Released Date: 2006 (Batch 1)	Category: Traditional Dance
Affiliated Province: Yunnan Province	Type: New Item	Application Province or Unit: Weixi Lisu Autonomous County, Yunnan Province	

Achi Mugua Dance of the Lisu Nationality means "the singing and dancing of goats" or "the tunes imitating the bleating of goats". It is circulated in Tongle Village and Xinle Village of Yezhi Township, Weixi Lisu Autonomous County, Diqing Zang Autonomous Prefecture, Yunnan Province. It is a kind of traditional local folk singing and dancing for self-entertainment. Its dancing style is enthusiastic and wild, which is a vivid expression of the traditional production, life, thoughts and emotions of the Lisu people in Weixi Lisu Autonomous County.

In the history, Weixi County was very hard to get to, so the Lisu nationality had little contact with the outside world. Its way of production is basically at the stage of half-agriculture and half-husbandry. Goats are indispensable livestock for every family. In their production and life, the Lisu people in Weixi County have formed a close emotional bond with goats. By imitating goats' bleating and jumping, they created Achi Mugua Dance. There is no instrumental accompaniment for its performance. Its tunes can be slow or fast, the beating of its notes is frequent, with a large beating amplitude. There are many tremolos in singing, and its basic tone is to imitate the bleating of goats. Its lyrics are mostly related to astronomy and geography, planting and harvesting, as well as joys and sorrows. Dancers dance to the rhythm of the song from beginning to end. There are generally more than five dancers, and sometimes the number can reach to more than one hundred. There are ten popular dance methods nowadays, including circling dance, forward-and-backward dance steps, three-step stamping, goat jumping, dance with two soles in opposition, dragon circling, whirlwind dancing, millstone rotating, guest welcoming and lover seeking. The changes of dance formations include large circles, semi-circular arcs, straight columns and interspersed styles. The dance steps are mainly jumping, swaying and rubbing. The costumes for singing and dancing are the clothing for everyday wear made and embroidered by dancers themselves. The Lisu people in Weixi Lisu Autonomous County perform **Achi Mugua Dance** on the occasions of the Spring Festival, the Torch Festival, weddings, sacrificial ceremonies, welcoming guests and festive events.

第 6 项：彝族葫芦笙舞

花倮彝族葫芦笙舞
Hulusheng Dance of the Hualuo Branch of the Yi Nationality

项目序号：139	项目编号：Ⅲ-36	公布时间：2006（第一批）	类别：传统舞蹈
所属地区：云南省	类型：新增项目	申报地区或单位：云南省文山壮族苗族自治州	

彝族葫芦笙舞流传于云南省文山壮族苗族自治州西畴县鸡街乡曼竜村。曼竜村是彝族花倮人聚居的自然村。

花倮人的葫芦笙舞是一种古老的彝族民间舞蹈，以躯体“S”形前后曲动的典型舞姿而独树一帜，体现了古代滇人葫芦笙舞的遗韵。在开化古铜鼓图饰上，有四个头戴羽冠、衣着羽衣、吹葫芦笙翩翩起舞的舞人饰纹，舞姿正是一个典型的“S”形前后曲动的造型动作，这表明古滇先民跳葫芦笙舞时头戴羽冠、手执羽毛、身穿羽衣、屈肢顿足而周旋飞舞。今天曼竜村花倮妇女的头饰和服饰仍保留了“羽冠”和“羽衣”的痕迹，说明曼竜村花倮人的葫芦笙舞是由古滇先民舞蹈传承而来。[①] 在花倮人的重要节日，全村男女老幼欢聚于场院，妇女身穿节日盛装，在葫芦笙的伴奏下，围成圆圈翩翩起舞。舞蹈主要表现生产劳动的内容，如种棉、收棉、纺棉和织布等过程，节奏沉缓，动作简朴。葫芦笙舞有七套不同的舞蹈动作：站着跳、起步跳、移步翻身、走圆圈、穿花、对点头和前跳又后跳。七套动作配合不同的葫芦笙曲调，音乐十分丰富。葫芦笙是舞蹈的主要伴奏乐器。[②]

---

① 《彝族葫芦笙舞》，中国非物质文化遗产网，http://www.ihchina.cn/Article/Index/detail?id=12980，检索日期：2019 年 9 月 1 日。

② 《彝族葫芦笙舞》，云南非物质文化遗产保护网，http://www.ynich.cn/view.php?id=1236&cat_id=11110，检索日期：2019 年 9 月 1 日。

Item 6: Hulusheng Dance of the Yi Nationality

Item Serial Number: 139	Item ID Number: Ⅲ-36	Released Date: 2006 (Batch 1)	Category: Traditional Dance
Affiliated Province: Yunnan Province	Type: New Item	Application Province or Unit: Wenshan Zhuang and Miao Autonomous Prefecture, Yunnan Province	

Hulusheng Dance of the Yi Nationality is prevalent in Manlong Village, Jijie Township, Xichou County, Wenshan Zhuang and Miao Autonomous Prefecture, Yunnan Province. Manlong Village is a natural village inhabited by the Hualuo people of the Yi nationality.

Hulusheng Dance of the Hualuo people is an ancient folk dance of the Yi nationality. It is unique with the typical dancing posture of the "S" shape of the body moving back and forth, which demonstrates the lingering charm of **Hulusheng Dance** of the ancient Yunnan people. On the decoration of the ancient Kaihua Bronze Drum, there are decorated patterns of four dancers wearing feather crowns on their heads and feather clothes, and dancing while playing Hulusheng (a gourd-made musical instrument). The postures of the dancers are the typical styling of moving forward and backward in the shape of "S", which shows that when performing **Hulusheng Dance**, ancestors of ancient Yunnan wore feather crowns on their heads and feather clothes, held feathers in their hands, bent their limbs, stamped their feet and flew around. Today, the headwear and costumes of the Hualuo women in Manlong Village still retain the traces of "feather crowns" and "feather clothes", indicating that **Hulusheng Dance** of the Hualuo people in Manlong Village has been passed down from the dances of ancient Yunnan ancestors. At the important festivals of the Hualuo people, men and women, old and young, in the whole village gather together in the yard. Women dress in festive costumes, and dance in a circle to the accompaniment of Hulusheng (a gourd-made musical instrument). The dance mainly expresses the content of production and labor, such as the processes of planting cotton, harvesting cotton, spinning cotton and weaving cloth, with a slow rhythm and simple movements. There are seven sets of different dance movements for **Hulusheng Dance**: jumping while standing, jumping while stamping, moving and turning, walking in a circle, wearing flowers, nodding to each other, as well as jumping forward and then backward. For these seven sets of dance movements, there are different Hulusheng tunes, which are very rich in music. Hulusheng (a gourd-made musical instrument) is the main accompaniment instrument of the dance.

第 7 项：彝族烟盒舞

石屏彝族烟盒舞
the Cigarette-box Dance of the Yi Nationality in Shiping County

项目序号：140	项目编号：Ⅲ-37	公布时间：2006（第一批）	类别：传统舞蹈
所属地区：云南省	类型：新增项目	申报地区或单位：云南省红河哈尼族彝族自治州	

彝族烟盒舞，又称“跳弦”，流传于云南省红河哈尼族彝族自治州石屏县的彝族村寨。

彝族烟盒舞包括正弦和杂弦两部分，形成了山区和坝区两种风格和多种流派，舞蹈套数多达 220 套，目前仅搜集整理 117 套，其中正弦 62 套，杂弦 55 套。舞蹈形式有双人舞、三人舞和群舞。舞者手持旧时盛火草烟的圆形木制烟盒，在四弦乐器的伴奏下，弹击盒底击节作舞。石屏彝族烟盒舞个性鲜明，技巧多样，著名的技巧动作有“仙人搭桥”“蚂蚁搬家”“倒挂金钩”等。彝族烟盒舞既可健身又可怡情，动作流畅潇洒，极富艺术感染力，现已发展为集歌、舞、乐、竞技于一体的综合性舞蹈艺术。烟盒舞通过头、脚、身、手、腰等部位的巧妙运用，以优美的舞姿生动地表达了彝族特有的审美趣味，其中下腰连环翻滚的舞蹈动作难度极高，展现了高超的舞蹈技能。[①]

① 《彝族烟盒舞》，中国非物质文化遗产网，http://www.ihchina.cn/Article/Index/detail?id=12981，检索日期：2019 年 9 月 1 日。

Item 7: the Cigarette-box Dance of the Yi Nationality

Item Serial Number: 140	Item ID Number: Ⅲ-37	Released Date: 2006 (Batch 1)	Category: Traditional Dance
Affiliated Province: Yunnan Province	Type: New Item	Application Province or Unit: Honghe Hani and Yi Autonomous Prefecture, Yunnan Province	

The Cigarette-box Dance of the Yi Nationality, also known as "String Dancing", is circulated in the stockaded villages of the Yi nationality in Shiping County, Honghe Hani and Yi Autonomous Prefecture, Yunnan Province.

The Cigarette-box Dance of the Yi Nationality consists of two parts, main and miscellaneous strings, forming two styles of the mountainous area and the plain area, as well as multiple genres. There are as many as 220 sets of dances. Currently, only 117 sets are collected, of which 62 are main strings and 55 are miscellaneous strings. The dance forms include two-person dance, three-person dance and group dance. The dancers hold a round wooden cigarette box used to contain cigarette in old days, and dance to the accompaniment of Sixian (a four-stringed plucked musical instrument) while tapping the bottom of box. **The Cigarette-box Dance of the Yi Nationality** in Shiping County has a distinctive feature with diverse skills. The famous skills of movements are "immortals building bridges", "ants moving house", "hanging upside down", etc. **The Cigarette-box Dance of the Yi Nationality** can serve for both fitness and delight. Its motion is smooth and unrestrained, full of artistic appeal. At present, it has developed into a comprehensive dance art integrating songs, dances, music and competition. Through the ingenious use of the head, feet, the body, hands, the waist and other parts, **the Cigarette Box Dance** vividly expresses the unique aesthetic taste of the Yi nationality by means of graceful dancing postures. Among them, the dance movements of back bend and continuous somersaults are extremely difficult, which reflect superb dancing skills.

第 8 项：基诺大鼓舞

基诺大鼓舞表演
the Performance of the Big Drum Dance of the Jinuo Nationality

项目序号：141	项目编号：Ⅲ-38	公布时间：2006（第一批）	类别：传统舞蹈
所属地区：云南省	类型：新增项目	申报地区或单位：云南省景洪市	

大鼓舞，基诺语称“司土锅”，“司土”为“大鼓”，“锅”为“跳”，流传于云南省西双版纳傣族自治州景洪市基诺山基诺族乡的基诺族村寨。

基诺族跳大鼓舞是为了感谢传说中用大鼓拯救了基诺人的创世女神阿嫫腰白。跳大鼓舞在过特懋克节时最为隆重，时间是在立春后三天。跳大鼓舞有一套完整的仪式：舞蹈开始前，寨老们要先杀一头乳猪、一只鸡，供于鼓前，由七位长老磕头拜祭，其中一位长老念诵祭词，祈祷大鼓给人们带来吉祥平安。祭祀结束后，由一人双手执鼓槌边击边舞，另有若干击镲、伴舞伴歌者，跳大鼓舞时的唱词多为基诺人的历史、道德和习惯等内容，舞蹈动作有“拜神灵”“欢乐跳”和“过年调”等。大鼓是基诺族的礼器、重器和神物，只能挂在卓巴（寨老）家的神柱上，制造大鼓要遵循很严格的程序。①

Item 8: the Big Drum Dance of the Jinuo Nationality

Item Serial Number: 141	Item ID Number: Ⅲ-38	Released Date: 2006 (Batch 1)	Category: Traditional Dance
Affiliated Province: Yunnan Province	Type: New Item	Application Province or Unit: Jinghong City, Yunnan Province	

① 《基诺大鼓舞》，中国非物质文化遗产网，http://www.ihchina.cn/Article/Index/detail?id=12982，检索日期：2019 年 9 月 1 日。

The Big Drum Dance is called "Situguo" in the Jinuo language, with "Situ" meaning "the Big Drum" and "guo" meaning "dance". It is spread in the stockaded villages of the Jinuo nationality in Jinuo Township on the Jinuo Mountain in Jinghong City, Xishuangbanna Dai Autonomous Prefecture, Yunnan Province.

The performance of **the Big Drum Dance of the Jinuo Nationality** is to express gratitude to the legendary figure, Amo Yaobai, the Goddess of the Creation, who saved the Jinuo people with the Big Drum. The grandest occasion of performing **the Big Drum Dance** is at the Temaoke Festival, three days after the Beginning of Spring. There is a complete set of rituals for its performance: Before the dance, Zhailao (a head of a stockaded village) must kill one suckling pig and one chicken, and offer them as sacrifices in front of the drum. Then, seven seniors kowtow to worship it, with one of them reciting the sacrificial words and praying that the Big Drum brings auspiciousness and peace to people. After the sacrificial activity, one person holds the drumsticks with both hands, beating and dancing. There are also a number of people who play the small cymbals, dance and sing to act as accompaniments. The lyrics sung when **the Big Drum Dance** is performed are mostly related to the history, morals and habits of the Jinuo people. The dance movements include "worshipping the deity", "jumping happily" and "the tune of celebrating the New Year". The Big Drum is a sacrificial vessel, a treasured vessel and a sacred object of the Jinuo people. It can only be hung on the sacred pillar in the house of Zhuoba or Zhailao (a head of a stockaded village). The making of the Big Drum must follow very strict procedures.

第 9 项：傣族象脚鼓舞

傣族象脚鼓舞表演
the Performance of the Elephant-foot Drum Dance of the Dai Nationality

项目序号：658	项目编号：Ⅲ-61	公布时间：2008（第二批）	类别：传统舞蹈
所属地区：云南省	类型：新增项目	申报地区或单位：云南省潞西市；云南省西双版纳傣族自治州	

象脚鼓舞是傣族流行最广泛、表演水平最高、最具代表性的一种传统民族舞蹈，主要流传于国内的傣族、德昂族、景颇族、阿昌族等少数民族以及东南亚的许多国家。

傣族象脚鼓舞的表演目的是为祭祀神灵、驱灾避邪和庆贺丰年。表演类型有两种：一是击鼓而舞，有单人舞、双人舞、对舞、群舞等形式；二是跟鼓而舞，其中的“三道弯”源于早期人类采摘树上果实的动作，表演时，舞者的手臂要做出后抡翻腕、向前掏转的动作，这是傣族先民从背箩里取种、撒种的形象反映。表演傣族象脚鼓舞时，舞者以左肩背鼓、鼓面对前、鼓尾向下，以右手击鼓为主，左手配合，一般用拳、掌、指敲打鼓面，有时也用肘、膝、脚跟、脚趾等敲打，手敲鼓，膝即弯曲，抬手肘即站立。步伐有前点半步蹲、后点半步蹲、踏步全蹲、八字步半蹲，还有悠腿、抬腿、踢脚、吸腿跳等动作。根据鼓的长、中、小形状有三种跳法：长象脚鼓舞、中象脚鼓舞和小象脚鼓舞。由于鼓身长对人体运动的限制，舞蹈动作以下半身为主，有时配以身体轻微闪动的动作。傣族象脚鼓舞是一种既可自娱也可表演的男子舞蹈，是傣族人抒发欢乐情绪的手段，有怡情悦性、强健身心、以舞会友的功能。[①]

Item 9: the Elephant-foot Drum Dance of the Dai Nationality

Item Serial Number: 658	Item ID Number: Ⅲ-61	Released Date: 2008 (Batch 2)	Category: Traditional Dance
Affiliated Province: Yunnan Province	Type: New Item	Application Province or Unit: Luxi City, Yunnan Province; Xishuangbanna Dai Autonomous Prefecture, Yunnan Province	

The Elephant-foot Drum Dance is a traditional ethnic dance of the Dai nationality that is circulated in the widest area and the most representative with the highest level of performance. It is mainly spread among the Dai, De'ang, Jingpo, Achang and other ethnic minorities in China, as well as many countries in Southeast Asia.

The purpose of performing **the Elephant-foot Drum Dance of the Dai Nationality** is to offer sacrifices to gods, dispel disasters and avoid evil spirits, as well as celebrate good harvests. There are two types of performances: the first one is dancing while beating the drum, which includes the forms of single-person dance, two-person dance, contra dance, group dance, etc.; and the second one is dancing while following the drum, among which the "three-bend" dancing posture originated from early humans' picking fruits from trees. During the performance, dancers' arms make the movements of flinging backward and flipping over wrists as well as fishing out and turning forward, which is a vivid reflection of the ancestors of the Dai people taking seeds out of their back baskets and sowing seeds. When performing **the Elephant-foot Drum Dance of the Dai Nationality**, dancers use their left shoulders to carry the drums, with the drumheads facing forward and the drum tails facing downward. The right hand is mainly used to beat the drum, with the left one cooperating. Generally, fists, palms and fingers are used to beat the drumhead. Sometimes, elbows, knees, heels, toes, etc. are also used to beat the drumhead. When dancers' hands beat the drums, their knees will be bent; and when

---

① 《傣族象脚鼓舞》，中国非物质文化遗产网，http://www.ihchina.cn/Article/Index/detail?id=13047，检索日期：2019 年 9 月 1 日。

their elbows are raised, they will stand. The steps include moving half step forward and squatting, moving half step backward and squatting, stepping and full squatting, splayfooted half squatting, as well as the movements of swinging legs leisurely, raising legs, kicking feet, knee-lift jumping, etc. According to the length of the drum, the dancing methods are divided into three kinds: long Elephant-foot Drum Dance, medium Elephant-foot Drum Dance and short Elephant-foot Drum Dance. Due to the limitation of the length of the drum on the movement of the human body, the dance movements mainly focus on the lower part of the body, sometimes accompanied by its slightly flickering movements. **The Elephant-foot Drum Dance of the Dai Nationality** is a male dance that can be used for both self-entertainment and performance. It is a means for the Dai people to express their happy emotions, having the functions of cheering the heart and pleasing the feelings, strengthening their bodies and minds, and making friends through dancing.

第10项：彝族打歌

彝族打歌
Dage Dance of the Yi Nationality

项目序号：667	项目编号：Ⅲ-70	公布时间：2008（第二批）	类别：传统舞蹈
所属地区：云南省	类型：新增项目	申报地区或单位：云南省巍山彝族回族自治县	

彝族打歌也称“踏歌”，是云南省巍山县影响最大、最普及的一种自娱性民族民间舞蹈。每逢春节、小年（农历正月十五）、火把节或婚嫁、聚会，彝族人都会彻夜踏跳。

彝族打歌多在晚上进行，开始时先在舞场中央点燃篝火，人们以火为圆心，围成一圈或数圈，踏地为节，舞蹈歌唱。若在白天打歌，则无需点火。芦笙和笛子是打歌不可缺少的乐器，活动进行时，圈内一人或数人吹奏芦笙，称为“歌头”；另有一人吹奏笛子，1～2人舞刀弄棍。除芦笙和笛子以外，有的地方还以三弦和月琴作为陪衬乐器。在巍山县，西山一带的打歌多为男半圈女半圈，如此一圈一圈层层围拢，展开活动；东山一带则多为男一对女一对，如此数十对逆时针舞动，边唱边跳，逐渐形成圆圈。舞蹈动作以腰、腿为律动，队形变化不多，人数只能成双，手扣手，肩搭肩。彝族打歌的曲调主要有喜事打歌调、节日打歌调、忧事打歌调、善事庙会打歌调和平常打歌调等。一首曲调可根据舞者情绪的变化和需要，可快可慢，反复加花使用。其歌词形式有四句式、六句式、八句式、十句式、十二句式和奇数式等。彝族打歌是巍山当地彝族传统节日及婚丧嫁娶、飘梁竖柱等重大活动中不可缺少的内容。①

① 《彝族打歌》，中国非物质文化遗产网，http://www.ihchina.cn/Article/Index/detail?id=13056，检索日期：2019年9月1日。

Item 10: Dage Dance of the Yi Nationality

Item Serial Number: 667	Item ID Number: Ⅲ-70	Released Date: 2008 (Batch 2)	Category: Traditional Dance
Affiliated Province: Yunnan Province	Type: New Item	Application Province or Unit: Weishan Yi and Hui Autonomous Prefecture, Yunnan Province	

Dage Dance of the Yi Nationality, also called "Tage", is the most influential and most popular self-entertaining folk dance in Weishan County, Yunnan Province. Whenever it is at the Spring Festival, the Minor New Year (the 15th day of the first month of the lunar calendar), the Torch Festival, weddings and gatherings, the Yi people will dance all through the night.

Dage Dance of the Yi Nationality is mostly performed at night. At the beginning, a bonfire is lit in the center of the dancing square. With the bonfire as the center, people form a circle or several circles, and step on the ground to produce beats, dancing and singing. If it is performed in the daytime, there is no need to light the bonfire. Lusheng Musical Instruments and flutes are indispensable musical instruments for its performance. When the activity is in progress, one or several persons in the circle play Lusheng Musical Instruments, which is called "leader(s) of the song". Another plays the flute, and 1-2 people wield the knives and sticks. In addition to Lusheng Musical Instruments and flutes, Sanxian (a three-stringed plucked musical instrument) and Yueqin (a four-stringed plucked musical instrument with a full-moon-shaped sound box) are also used as accompaniment musical instruments in some places. In Weishan County, **Dage Dance** in the area of Xishan is performed with mostly men's half-circle and women's half-circle. Surrounded in circles and layers, dancers carry on this activity. In the area of Dongshan, mostly pairs of men and pairs of women dance together, dozens of pairs dancing counterclockwise, singing and dancing, and gradually forming a circle. The dance movements are the rhythmed movements of the waist and legs, and the formation does not change too much. The number of dancers can only be even. They perform the dance with one hand clasping the hand of the dancer after him/her and the other hand placed on the shoulder of the dancer before him/her. The tunes of **Dage Dance of the Yi Nationality** mainly include Dage Tune of Happy Events, Dage Tune of Festivals, Dage Tune of Worries, Dage Tune of Good Deeds of the Temple Fair and Dage Tune of Daily Life. A tune can be quickened or slowed according to dancers' emotional changes and needs, and can be added with flowers repeatedly. The forms of lyrics include four-sentence, six-sentence, eight-sentence, ten-sentence, twelve-sentence and odd-numbered forms. **Dage Dance of the Yi Nationality** is an indispensable part of the important activities of the local Yi nationality in Weishan County, such as the traditional festivals, weddings and funerals, as well as placing the beams and erecting the pillars.

第 11 项：彝族跳菜

彝族跳菜表演
the Performance of Tiaocai Dance of the Yi Nationality

项目序号：668	项目编号：Ⅲ-71	公布时间：2008（第二批）	类别：传统舞蹈
所属地区：云南省	类型：新增项目	申报地区或单位：云南省南涧彝族自治县	

彝族跳菜，又名“抬菜舞”，起源于古老的祭祀，是云南省南涧彝族自治县境内流传的一种礼节性风俗舞蹈。

彝族民间办宴席上菜时，为了表示对宾客的尊重和增加喜庆气氛，往往要跳这种舞蹈。彝族跳菜主要有“席间跳菜”和“表演跳菜”两大类。“表演跳菜”以“席间跳菜”为基础，以南涧境内流传的多种打歌步伐为主要舞步。按不同的抬菜方式，“席间跳菜”分为“头功跳菜”“口功跳菜”和“手功跳菜”三种。按不同的表演风格，“表演跳菜”分为“无量山系黑彝跳菜”“哀牢山系黑彝跳菜”和“无量乡红星村白彝跳菜”三种；按不同的表演场地，“表演跳菜”又分为“舞台跳菜”和“广场跳菜”两种。“舞台跳菜”在舞台上表演，演员通常在 20 人左右，舞蹈动作粗犷豪放、刚健有力，声音高亢嘹亮；“广场跳菜”演出场地宽广，演员少则数十人，多则数百人，呈现出一种气势恢宏、整齐和谐的艺术效果。彝族跳菜反映了彝族人民对丰收的喜悦和对美好生活的憧憬，展现出他们善良淳朴、热情好客的特点。①

① 《彝族跳菜》，中国非物质文化遗产网，http://www.ihchina.cn/Article/Index/detail?id=13057，检索日期：2019 年 9 月 1 日。

Item 11: Tiaocai Dance of the Yi Nationality

Item Serial Number: 668	Item ID Number: Ⅲ-71	Released Date: 2008 (Batch 2)	Category: Traditional Dance
Affiliated Province: Yunnan Province	Type: New Item	Application Province or Unit: Nanjian Yi Autonomous County, Yunnan Province	

Tiaocai Dance of the Yi Nationality, also known as "dish-serving dance", originates from ancient sacrificial rites. It is a kind of etiquette folk dance spread in Nanjian Yi Autonomous County, Yunnan Province.

When serving dishes at a banquet, to show respect for guests and to enhance the festive atmosphere, the Yi people often perform this dance. It is mainly divided into two categories, "Tiaocai Dance at the Banquet" and "Tiaocai Dance for Performance". The latter is based on the former, with the multiple steps of Dage Dance that are spread in Nanjian County as major dance steps. According to different ways of serving dishes, "Tiaocai Dance at the Banquet" is divided into three types, "Tiaocai Dance of Serving Dishes with Heads", "Tiaocai Dance of Serving Dishes with Mouths", and "Tiaocai Dance of Serving Dishes with Hands". According to different performance styles, "Tiaocai Dance for Performance" can be divided into three types: "the Black Yi Tiaocai Dance in the Wuliang Mountain", "the Black Yi Tiaocai Dance in the Ailao Mountain", and "the White Yi Tiaocai Dance in Hongxing Village of Wuliang Township". According to different performance venues, "Tiaocai Dance for Performance" is divided into "Stage Tiaocai Dance" and "Square Tiaocai Dance". "Stage Tiaocai Dance" is performed on the stage with usually about 20 dancers. The dance movements are rough, bold, vigorous and powerful with loud and clear sound. "Square Tiaocai Dance" is performed at a wide venue, with performers ranging from dozens to hundreds, presenting a magnificent, uniform and harmonious artistic effect. **Tiaocai Dance of the Yi Nationality** reflects the Yi people's joy of a bumper harvest and their longing for a better life, showing their characteristics of kindness, simplicity, warm-heartedness and hospitality.

第12项：彝族老虎笙

彝族老虎笙表演
the Performance of the Tiger Sheng Dance of the Yi Nationality

项目序号：669	项目编号：Ⅲ-72	公布时间：2008（第二批）	类别：传统舞蹈
所属地区：云南省	类型：新增项目	申报地区或单位：云南省双柏县	

彝族老虎笙是一种兼具祭祀性和自娱性的舞蹈，流传于云南省楚雄彝族自治州双柏县。

彝族先民认为虎尸分解创造了万物，他们崇虎、敬虎，以虎为祖先，自称为“虎族”。双柏县法脿镇的小麦地冲是老虎笙的发源地，居住于此的彝族每年正月初八到正月十五有历时八天的“虎节”，其间会举行“祭虎”“接虎”“跳虎”和“送虎”等活动。表演者以黑毡捆扎成虎皮的样子，在身体裸露部位用颜料画上虎的花纹，整个人装扮成老虎的模样。跳老虎笙一般需要十六人，分别装扮成八头虎、两只猫、两位山神、一个道人，此外还有两个击鼓者和一个敲锣者。舞者排列成一列纵队，按逆时针方向行进。老虎笙的舞蹈动作十分丰富，既有老虎亲嘴、老虎搭桥、老虎擦屁股等模仿老虎习性的动作，也有送肥、犁田、耕地、撒秧、栽种、拔秧和收割等模拟农事活动的动作，展现了山地民族的刚强性格，表达了彝族人对虎的崇拜。彝族老虎笙生动体现了彝族先民的崇虎观及人与自然和谐相处的发展观，承载着许多彝族的历史文化信息和原始记忆。①

① 《彝族老虎笙》，中国非物质文化遗产网，http://www.ihchina.cn/Article/Index/detail?id=13058，检索日期：2019年9月1日。

Item 12: the Tiger Sheng Dance of the Yi Nationality

Item Serial Number: 669	Item ID Number: Ⅲ-72	Released Date: 2008 (Batch 2)	Category: Traditional Dance
Affiliated Province: Yunnan Province	Type: New Item	Application Province or Unit: Shuangbai County, Yunnan Province	

The Tiger Sheng Dance of the Yi Nationality is a kind of dance for both sacrificial and self-entertaining purposes, which is spread in Shuangbai County, Chuxiong Yi Autonomous Prefecture, Yunnan Province.

The ancestors of the Yi nationality believed that the decomposition of tiger carcasses created all things. Thus, they worshipped and respected tigers, regarding the tiger as their ancestor, and call themselves "the nationality of the tiger". The village of Small Maidichong in Fabiao Township, Shuangbai County is the birthplace of **the Tiger Sheng Dance**. The Yi people living here have "the Tiger Festival" that lasts 8 days from the 8th to the 15th days of the first lunar month every year, during which the activities of "offering sacrifices to tigers", "receiving tigers", "performing the Tiger Dance", "seeing off tigers", etc. will be held. The performers of **the Tiger Sheng Dance** tie up black felt in the shape of a tiger skin, and paint tiger patterns on the exposed parts of their bodies by using pigments, dressing up themselves as tigers. The performance of **the Tiger Sheng Dance** generally requires 16 people, with eight people dressed as tigers, two people as cats, two people as mountain gods, and one as a Taoist, as well as two drummers and one gong beater. The dancers line up in a column and march counterclockwise. The movements of **the Tiger Sheng Dance** are very rich. There are not only actions that imitate the habits of tigers, such as tigers' kissing, tigers' building a bridge and tigers' wiping the butts, but also the actions imitating agricultural activities, such as sending fertilizers, plowing the field, plowing the land, sowing rice seedlings, planting, pulling rice seedlings and harvesting. It shows the tough character of the people living in the mountain area, and expresses the Yi people's worship of the tiger. **The Tiger Sheng Dance** vividly embodies the Yi ancestors' concept of worshipping the tiger and the development concept of the harmonious coexistence between man and nature, and carries much historical and cultural information as well as primitive memories of the Yi nationality.

第13项：彝族左脚舞

彝族左脚舞表演
the Performance of the Left Foot Dance of the Yi Nationality

项目序号：670	项目编号：Ⅲ-73	公布时间：2008（第二批）	类别：传统舞蹈
所属地区：云南省	类型：新增项目	申报地区或单位：云南省牟定县	

彝族左脚舞，是彝族在长期的刀耕火种生活中逐渐形成的一种代表性的传统舞蹈，歌、舞、乐合一，以娱人、交往、健身为目的。主要流传于云南省楚雄彝族自治州牟定县，对牟定县彝族人民乃至全县的政治、经济、文化都有着重要的影响。

跳彝族左脚舞的音乐是左脚调，有情歌类、颂歌类、叙事歌类、讽刺类、诙谐幽默类、劝世类、教育类和酒歌等八个类别，近三百多首曲目。彝族左脚舞表演时，唱腔多样，舞姿起时先起左脚，垫三脚踢一脚，基本步法有直脚、甩脚和垫脚等，特殊动作为串花、翻身等。小伙子们弹起龙头四弦，拉起小二胡，姑娘们唱左脚调，共跳左脚舞，少则十余人，多则成百上千人，气势恢宏。舞蹈随意性较强，不限人数，不分男女老幼，不限时间、地点，内容涉及彝族文化、生产、生活方方面面，节奏明快、通俗易懂、表现力丰富。彝族左脚舞记录着彝族人民对天、地、日、月、火、虎、自然等的原始崇拜，反映了他们在漫长的历史发展过程中团结奋进、勇于创造的民族精神，包含了彝族民风民俗、传统工艺、民族服饰等诸多文化内容。①

① 《彝族左脚舞》，中国非物质文化遗产网，http://www.ihchina.cn/Article/Index/detail?id=13059，检索日期：2019年9月1日。

Item 13: the Left Foot Dance of the Yi Nationality

Item Serial Number: 670	Item ID Number: Ⅲ-73	Released Date: 2008 (Batch 2)	Category: Traditional Dance
Affiliated Province: Yunnan Province	Type: New Item	Application Province or Unit: Mouding County, Yunnan Province	

The Left Foot Dance of the Yi Nationality is a representative traditional dance gradually formed in the long-term slash-and-burn cultivation life of the Yi nationality, which integrates singing, dancing and music, with the purposes of entertaining people, fostering social interaction and body building. It is mainly spread in Mouding County, Chuxiong Yi Autonomous Prefecture, Yunnan Province, and has an important influence on the Yi people in Mouding County as well as the politics, economy and culture of the whole county.

The music of performing **the Left Foot Dance of the Yi Nationality** is the Left Foot Tune, which is divided into eight categories, including love songs, songs of praising, narrative songs, satirical songs, witty and humorous songs, admonishing songs, educational songs and Toasting Songs, with nearly over 300 songs. For the performance of **the Left Foot Dance of the Yi Nationality**, the singing tones are diverse. When the posture starts, the left foot is raised first. After stepping three times, dancers kick one time. The basic footwork includes straight feet, swinging feet and stepping. The special movements are stringing flowers, turning over, etc. The young men play Dragon-head Sixian (a four-stringed plucked musical instrument) and Small Erhu (a two-stringed bowed instrument). The girls sing the Left Foot Tune and perform **the Left Foot Dance**, with dancers ranging from more than a dozen to hundreds, or even thousands of people, which has magnificent momentum. The dance is highly random, with no limit on the number of people, performance time and locations, regardless of genders and ages. Its content involves all aspects of the culture, production and life of the Yi nationality. The dance has a bright rhythm and rich expressiveness, which is easy to understand. **The Left Foot Dance of the Yi Nationality** records the Yi people's primitive worship of the sky, the earth, the sun, the moon, fire, the tiger, nature, etc. It reflects their national spirit of unity, forging ahead and boldness in making innovations in the long historical development process, and contains much cultural content, such as folk customs, traditional crafts and ethnic costumes of the Yi nationality.

第14项：乐作舞

乐作舞表演
the Performance of Lezuo Dance

项目序号：671	项目编号：Ⅲ-74	公布时间：2008（第二批）	类别：传统舞蹈
所属地区：云南省	类型：新增项目	申报地区或单位：云南省红河县	

乐作舞是哈尼族和彝族共有的一种歌、舞、乐一体的古老民间舞蹈，流传于云南省红河哈尼族彝族自治州红河县的哈尼族、彝族村寨。

根据哈尼语音译，“乐”是大家之意，“作”是玩跳之意，“乐作”就是大家来跳乐。在彝族中，“乐作”这一名称是石屏、建水人称红河南岸彝族舞蹈的别称。经近百年的演变，“乐作”在哈尼族、彝族群众中已成为广为接受的舞蹈名称。① 跳乐作舞不受时间、地点、人数和形式的限制，但一般以偶数男女搭配围成圆圈来跳。伴奏乐器有笛子、巴乌、二胡、三弦、四弦、草杆和树叶等，配以手掌拍打节奏。目前已收集表现劳动和生活内容的十二套舞蹈：舍咔、踩荞、撵调、三步弦、斗脚、经线、找对象、擦背、游调、摸螺蛳、翻身和作瑟。舞蹈以踩荞步法、撵调步法为基础，贯穿十二套舞，每套变化不同。踩荞步法为逆时针或顺时针的进三步退一步，舞姿轻盈舒展；撵调步法在前行或后退一步时有一个小垫步，轻快敏捷。独特的舞步加上乐声伴奏和人声伴唱，韵味独特。②

① 《乐作舞》，中国非物质文化遗产网，http://www.ihchina.cn/Article/Index/detail?id=13060，检索日期：2019年9月1日。

② 《红河县乐作舞之乡》，云南非物质文化遗产保护网，http://www.ynich.cn/view.php?id=1217&cat_id=11111，检索日期：2019年9月1日。

Item 14: Lezuo Dance

Item Serial Number: 671	Item ID Number: Ⅲ-74	Released Date: 2008 (Batch 2)	Category: Traditional Dance
Affiliated Province: Yunnan Province	Type: New Item	Application Province or Unit: Honghe County, Yunnan Province	

Lezuo Dance is an ancient folk dance, which integrates singing, dancing and music, shared by the Hani and Yi nationalities. It is spread in the stockaded villages of the Hani and Yi nationalities in Honghe County, Honghe Hani and Yi Autonomous Prefecture, Yunnan Province.

Transliterated from the Hani language, "Le" means everyone, and "zuo" means playing and dancing. Thus, "Lezuo" means that everyone comes to have fun, playing and dancing. Among the Yi people, "Lezuo" is another name for the dance of the Yi nationality on the south bank of the Red River called by people living in Shiping and Jianshui counties. After nearly a hundred years of evolution, "Lezuo" has become another name for dance widely accepted by the Hani and Yi people. For the performance of **Lezuo Dance**, there is no limitation on time, dancing place, number of dancers and dancing form, but the number of men and women pairs must be even, and they form a circle when dancing. Accompaniment instruments include flutes, Bawu (a reed-pipe musical instrument), Erhu (a two-stringed bowed instrument), Sanxian (a three-stringed plucked musical instrument), Sixian (a four-stringed plucked musical instrument), straws and leaves, accompanied by palm-clapping to produce rhythms. At present, twelve sets of dances showing the content of labor and life have been collected: Shechi, Stepping on Buckwheat, Catching-up Tune, Three Step String, Doujiao, Jingxian, Looking for a Mate, Scrubbing the Back, Youdiao, Fumbling Spiral Shells, Turning Over and Zuose. The dance is based on the footwork of Stepping on Buckwheat and that of Catching-up Tune, which run through the twelve sets of dances, with each varying. The footwork of Stepping on Buckwheat is a counterclockwise or clockwise motion, with three steps forward and then one step backward, the posture of which is light and stretching. The footwork of Catching-up Tune is to make an appel after a forward or backward step, which is brisk and agile. The unique dance steps, together with musical accompaniment and vocal accompaniment, make the charm of this dance unique.

第15项：彝族三弦舞（阿细跳月）

阿细跳月表演
the Performance of Axi Dance in the Moonlight

项目序号：672	项目编号：Ⅲ-75	公布时间：2008（第二批）	类别：传统舞蹈
所属地区：云南省	类型：新增项目	申报地区或单位：云南省弥勒县	

彝族三弦舞是彝族人代代相传的一种民间舞蹈，不同地区和不同彝族支系对三弦舞称谓各不相同，流传于阿细彝区的三弦舞被称为“阿细跳月”，流传于撒尼彝区的三弦舞被称为“撒尼大三弦”。阿细跳月，意为“欢乐跳”，是彝族阿细人最具代表性的民族舞蹈，源于阿细人古朴的“阿细跳乐”，因多在月光下的篝火旁起舞，故名“阿细跳月”，流传于云南省红河哈尼族彝族自治州弥勒县彝族阿细人聚居的村寨。

阿细跳月参加者少则十几人，多则上千人，多在祭祀、节日、盛典时表演，具有很强的自发性、自娱性和群众性。它集歌、舞、乐于一体，有规范的舞步和套路。其舞蹈可分为老人舞和青年舞；舞步包括踹脚跳、鹤步单腿跳、弹跳步、跑步跳、转身跳、拍掌跳等形式；音乐为宫调式大三度五拍节。主要以大三弦、大中小竹笛、小三弦、三胡、月琴、唢呐和哨子等阿细民间自制乐器伴奏。其节奏热烈欢快，动作豪放粗犷，舞姿矫健飘逸，韵律强劲，具有强烈的感召力。①

Item 15: Sanxian Dance of the Yi Nationality (Axi Dance in the Moonlight)

Item Serial Number: 672	Item ID Number: Ⅲ-75	Released Date: 2008 (Batch 2)	Category: Traditional Dance

① 《彝族三弦舞（阿细跳月）》，中国非物质文化遗产网，http://www.ihchina.cn/Article/Index/detail?id=13062，检索日期：2019年9月1日。

Affiliated Province: Yunnan Province	Type: New Item	Application Province or Unit: Mile County, Yunnan Province

Sanxian Dance of the Yi Nationality is a folk dance passed down by the Yi people from generation to generation. In different regions and branches of the Yi nationality, **Sanxian Dance** is called differently. **Sanxian Dance** spread in areas inhabited by the Axi branch of the Yi nationality is called "**Axi Dance in the Moonlight**", and that circulated in areas inhabited by the Sani branch of the Yi nationality is called "Sani Big Sanxian Dance". "**Axi Dance in the Moonlight**", meaning "happy dance", is the most representative folk dance of the Axi people of the Yi nationality, which originates from their simple and unsophisticated "Axi Dance to Music". This dance is usually performed in the moonlight around the bonfire, hence the name "**Axi Dance in the Moonlight**". It is circulated in the stockaded villages inhabited by the Axi people of the Yi nationality in Mile County, Honghe Hani and Yi Autonomous Prefecture, Yunnan Province.

Performers of **Axi Dance in the Moonlight** can range from a dozen to a thousand. It is mostly performed at sacrificial ceremonies, festivals and grand ceremonies, having a strong nature of spontaneity, self-entertainment and mass character. Integrating singing, dancing and music into one, this dance has normative dance steps and dance routines. It can be divided into the dance of the old and the dance of the young. Its dance steps include kicking jump, the crane-step single leg jump, bounce step, running jump, turn-around jump, clapping jump and others; and its music is the mode of Gong (one of the five ancient Chinese musical notes equal to "Do" in western musical scale), major third, and five beats. It is mainly performed to the accompaniment of the musical instruments made by the Axi people themselves, such as Big Sanxian (a three-stringed plucked musical instrument); large-, medium- and small-sized bamboo flutes; Small Sanxian (a three-stringed plucked musical instrument); Sanhu(a three-stringed bowed instrument); Yueqin (a four-stringed plucked musical instrument with a full-moon-shaped sound box); Suona Horn (a woodwind instrument) and whistles. Its rhythms are warm and cheerful, its movements are bold and rough, and its dancing postures are vigorous and elegant, with a strong rhythm and powerful appeal.

撒尼大三弦表演
the Performance of Sani Big Sanxian Dance

第16项：彝族三弦舞（撒尼大三弦）

项目序号：672	项目编号：Ⅲ-75	公布时间：2008（第二批）	类别：传统舞蹈
所属地区：云南省	类型：新增项目	申报地区或单位：云南省石林彝族自治县	

“撒尼大三弦”是指流传于撒尼彝区的三弦舞，主要流传于云南省石林彝族自治县的撒尼彝族人中。

大三弦是撒尼人娱乐、抒情的主要乐器。“大三弦舞”是撒尼人借鉴阿细跳月发展起来的一种民间集体舞蹈，其舞步以三步一踢脚为基本步伐，舞蹈时即按此步伐变化队形，称为“快三步”。跳快三步时，青年男子手操大三弦，以中笛、小笛和哨子伴奏。笛声一响，男青年边弹边跳，女青年则手牵着手，踏着乐声的节拍呈一字形横排急步向男青年跳过来，双方皆三步一踢脚，拍着巴掌欢快起舞。女青年三步后一般都会转身360度，因运动量较大，每次跳四五分钟即需休息片刻。快三步舞节奏明快，情绪热烈奔放，比较适合青年人，故称“青年舞”，也叫“跳大三弦”。每到夜晚，哨声脆响，金笛齐鸣，紧凑而急迫的弦声粗犷、整齐地响起，青年男女合着“1、3、5”的旋律对面而舞，踏三步起一脚，同时伴之以歌唱和“哦哦”的呼声，与弦声、掌声一起汇成欢快、激昂的声浪。石林一带的撒尼族家家都有大三弦，人人会跳大三弦舞。①

Item 16: Sanxian Dance of the Yi Nationality (Sani Big Sanxian Dance)

Item Serial Number: 672	Item ID Number: Ⅲ-75	Released Date: 2008 (Batch 2)	Category: Traditional Dance

① 《彝族三弦舞（撒尼大三弦）》，中国非物质文化遗产网，http://www.ihchina.cn/Article/Index/detail?id=13061，检索日期：2019年9月1日。

Affiliated Province: Yunnan Province	Type: New Item	Application Province or Unit: Shilin Yi Autonomous County, Yunnan Province

"Sani Big Sanxian Dance" refers to the Sanxian Dance spread in areas inhabited by the Sani branch of the Yi nationality, which is mainly circulated among the Sani people of the Yi nationality in Shilin Yi Autonomous County of Yunnan Province.

Big Sanxian (a three-stringed plucked musical instrument) is the main musical instrument for Sani people's entertainment and emotional expression. "**Big Sanxian Dance**" is a kind of collective folk dance developed by the Sani people, who borrow from **Axi Dance in the Moonlight**. Its dance steps take three steps and one kick as the basic footwork, according to which dancers change the formation when dancing. This is called "the Fast Three-step Dance". When performing "the Fast Three-step Dance", young men hold Big Sanxian (a three-stringed plucked musical instrument) in their hands, to the accompaniment of medium flutes, small flutes and whistles. As soon as flutes sound, young men will play Big Sanxian (a three-stringed plucked musical instrument) while dancing, and young women will hold hands together, dance to the beat of the music, and leap towards young men with rapid strides in a horizontal line. Both parties dance three steps and kick once, clapping their hands while dancing happily. Young women usually turn around 360 degrees after dancing three steps. Due to a large amount of exercise, they need to have a short rest after dancing four or five minutes each time. The rhythm of "the Fast Three-step Dance" is bright, expressing passionate and unrestrained emotions, which is more suitable for young people, so it is called "the Youth's Dance", also known as "Performing Big Sanxian Dance". Every night, when whistles sound crisply, golden flutes ring in unison, and the tight and urgent strings sound in a bold and unconstrained manner in unison, young men and women will dance to the melody of "1, 3, 5", facing each other. They dance three steps and kick once, accompanied by singing and the cries of "oh, oh", which merge into a joyful and passionate wave of sound together with the sounds of strings and applause. In Shilin Yi Autonomous County, there is Big Sanxian (a three-stringed plucked musical instrument) in each Sani family, and everyone can perform **Big Sanxian Dance**.

第17项：纳西族热美蹉

纳西族热美蹉表演
the Performance of Remeicuo Dance of the Naxi Nationality

项目序号：673	项目编号：Ⅲ-76	公布时间：2008（第二批）	类别：传统舞蹈
所属地区：云南省	类型：新增项目	申报地区或单位：云南省丽江市古城区	

纳西族热美蹉是纳西族历经数千年传承至今的一种原始集体歌舞，流传于云南省丽江市古城区坝子东北的大东乡，包括玉龙雪山以东、金沙江以西的崇山峻岭和沿江小片河谷地带。

“热美蹉”是纳西语的汉字记音。纳西族热美蹉将诗、歌、舞融为一体，完整成套，表演时男女混唱，集体舞蹈，不用任何道具，人数也无限制，参加者少则十余人，多则数百人。男女老少手拉手围着火堆按顺时针方向边唱边跳，舞蹈动作古朴自然，唱腔几近呼喊，但每位参与者必须在歌舞中和其他人节拍一致，达到和谐。热美蹉的舞蹈动作毫无装饰，音乐是发自胸喉的天籁之声，故不可能准确记录以供学习，纳西人须从年幼时开始通过长辈的口传心授和长时期的实践参与习得热美蹉技巧，并在场景激发下即兴发挥。纳西族热美蹉历史悠久，内涵丰富，对丽江古乐和纳西古典音乐套曲《白沙细乐》都产生过明显的影响。[①]

① 《纳西族热美蹉》，中国非物质文化遗产网，http://www.ihchina.cn/Article/Index/detail?id=13063，检索日期：2019年9月1日。

Item 17: Remeicuo Dance of the Naxi Nationality

Item Serial Number: 673	Item ID Number: Ⅲ-76	Released Date: 2008 (Batch 2)	Category: Traditional Dance
Affiliated Province: Yunnan Province	Type: New Item	Application Province or Unit: Ancient City District, Lijiang City, Yunnan Province	

Remeicuo Dance of the Naxi Nationality is a primitive collective song and dance passed down by the Naxi people for thousands of years. It is spread in Dadong Township, the northeast of Bazi, Ancient City District, Lijiang City, Yunnan Province, which includes the high mountains and lofty hills east of the Yulong Snow Mountain and west of the Jinsha River, as well as the small valley areas along the river.

"Remeicuo" is the Chinese transliteration of the Naxi language. **Remeicuo Dance of the Naxi Nationality** integrates poems, songs and dances into one, forming complete sets. When performing it, men and women sing in a mixed manner, dancing collectively without using any props. There is no limitation on the number of participants, with as little as more than ten and as many as hundreds. Men and women, young and old, hold hands around the bonfire, singing and dancing in a clockwise direction. Its dance moves are simple, unsophisticated, and natural. Its singing is almost like shouting, but each participant must be consistent with others in beats to achieve harmony when singing and dancing. The moves of **Remeicuo Dance** are undecorated, and its music is the sound of nature from the chest and the throat, so it is impossible to record accurately for learning. The Naxi people must acquire the skills of performing **Remeicuo Dance** from their young age through the oral instruction of the elders and the long-term participation and practice, and perform it extemporaneously under the inspiration of the scene. With a long history and rich connotation, **Remeicuo Dance of the Naxi Nationality** has had a significant influence on both Lijiang ancient music and Baisha Orchestral Music, a song cycle of Naxi classical music.

第18项：布朗族蜂桶鼓舞

布朗族蜂桶鼓舞表演
the Performance of the Bee-barrel Drum Dance of the Bulang Nationality

项目序号：674	项目编号：Ⅲ-77	公布时间：2008（第二批）	类别：传统舞蹈
所属地区：云南省	类型：新增项目	申报地区或单位：云南省双江拉祜族佤族布朗族傣族自治县	

布朗族蜂桶鼓舞是布朗族跳鼓的总称，起源于布朗族的创世传说和祭祀活动，在云南省临沧市双江拉祜族佤族布朗族傣族自治县邦丙乡、大文乡等的布朗族村寨中流传。

布朗族蜂桶鼓舞以蜂桶鼓为主要打击乐器，同时需要象脚鼓、金芒、锣和镲等打击乐器配合演奏，主要由跳蜂桶鼓、跳象脚鼓和跳甩手巾三部分组成。有五种套路，三步和五步两种基本步伐。其中，“三步舞”动作优柔缓慢，“五步舞”动作激越刚健。蜂桶鼓舞既适合广场演出，也适合舞台演出，人数不限，参与的布朗族群众往往排成单行或双行，在寨子里的道路或广场上轻松起舞。参与者分为男、女两队，男队身背蜂桶鼓边舞边敲，女队手拿毛巾，随着鼓点的节奏边舞边甩。整个舞蹈场面壮观，姿态优美，有很强的感染力，表达了布朗人祈求美好生活的愿望。① 表演布朗族蜂桶鼓舞，须身着布朗族传统服饰，布朗族崇尚黑色，因此服饰多以黑色为主色调。

① 《布朗族蜂桶鼓舞》，中国非物质文化遗产网，http://www.ihchina.cn/Article/Index/detail?id=13064，检索日期：2019 年 9 月 1 日。

Item 18: the Bee-barrel Drum Dance of the Bulang Nationality

Item Serial Number: 674	Item ID Number: Ⅲ-77	Released Date: 2008 (Batch 2)	Category: Traditional Dance
Affiliated Province: Yunnan Province	Type: New Item	Application Province or Unit: Shuangjiang Lahu, Wa, Bulang and Dai Autonomous County, Yunnan Province	

The Bee-barrel Drum Dance of the Bulang Nationality is the general name for the Drum Dance of the Bulang nationality, originating from the creation legends and sacrificial activities of the Bulang people. It is circulated in stockaded villages inhabited by the Bulang people in Bangbing Township, Dawen Township, etc. of Shuangjiang Lahu, Wa, Bulang and Dai Autonomous County, Lincang City, Yunnan Province.

For the performance of **the Bee-barrel Drum Dance of the Bulang Nationality**, the Bee-barrel Drum is the main percussion instrument, accompanied by other percussion instruments, such as the Elephant-foot Drum, Golden Mang Musical Instrument, gongs and cymbals. It mainly consists of three parts: performing the Bee-barrel Drum Dance, performing the Elephant-foot Drum Dance and performing the Towel-shaking Dance. There are five kinds of routines, as well as two kinds of basic footwork of three steps and five steps. Among them, the movements of "the Three-step Dance" are soft and slow, and those of "the Five-step Dance" are exciting and vigorous. **The Bee-barrel Drum Dance** is suitable for both square and stage performances. There is no limit to the number of performers. The participants usually line up in single or double rows and dance with ease on the roads or squares in the stockaded villages. They are divided into two teams, the male team and the female team. The male dancers carry the Bee-barrel Drums on their backs, beating them while dancing; and the female dancers hold towels in their hands, dancing to the beats of the drums while shaking towels. The entire scene is spectacular, with graceful postures and powerful appeal, expressing the Bulang people's desire for a better life. When performing **the Bee-barrel Drum Dance of the Bulang Nationality**, dancers must wear traditional costumes of the Bulang nationality. The Bulang people revere the black color, so black is the main color of their costumes.

第19项：普米族搓蹉

普米族搓蹉表演
the Performance of Cuocuo Dance of the Pumi Nationality

项目序号：675	项目编号：Ⅲ-78	公布时间：2008（第二批）	类别：传统舞蹈
所属地区：云南省	类型：新增项目	申报地区或单位：云南省兰坪白族普米族自治县	

搓蹉，又称“四弦舞”“羊皮舞”，是普米族的一种民间舞蹈，以四弦的“比柏”伴奏，以羊皮鼓击节。主要流传于怒江傈僳族自治州兰坪县的通甸、河西、啦井、金顶及石登等乡镇普米族聚居的村寨。

表演时，人们围成一圈或数圈，在四弦和羊皮鼓所奏音乐的引导下欢快起舞。舞蹈中舞步变化丰富，舞者在舞曲变换的间隙放声歌唱，一领众和。普米族搓蹉有开放式搓蹉和封闭式搓蹉两种。其中，开放式搓蹉属自娱性舞蹈，是普米族民众日常自娱自乐的重要形式，在普米族交际、喜庆之类大型活动中不可或缺。其表演不受时间、地点和人数限制，参加者可随时加入舞蹈。舞者可以依次开始，也可以部分人舞蹈，部分人边走边唱，唱完后再行起舞。跳舞过程中，退步时身体前偏，上身和下身方向相反；上前时身体后仰，上下身方向亦相反。舞蹈速度一般为中速。速度慢时，舞步轻盈飘洒；速度加快时，舞步粗犷有力。开放式搓蹉有十二套舞步，队形包括单圆圈、双圆圈和半圆圈，一般以逆时针方向跳，也可按顺时针方向跳，多用于各种自娱、喜庆和健身活动。①

① 《普米族搓蹉》，中国非物质文化遗产网，http://www.ihchina.cn/Article/Index/detail?id=13065，检索日期：2019年9月1日。

Item 19: Cuocuo Dance of the Pumi Nationality

Item Serial Number: 675	Item ID Number: Ⅲ-78	Released Date: 2008 (Batch 2)	Category: Traditional Dance
Affiliated Province: Yunnan Province	Type: New Item	Application Province or Unit: Lanping Bai and Pumi Autonomous County, Yunnan Province	

Cuocuo Dance, also known as "Sixian Dance" and "the Sheep-skin Dance", is a folk dance of the Pumi nationality. It is performed to the accompaniment of Sixian (a four-stringed plucked musical instrument), called "Bibo" by the Pumi people, with the Sheepskin Drum producing beats. It is primarily spread in the stockaded villages inhabited by the Pumi people in Tongdian, Hexi, Lajing, Jinding, Shideng, etc. townships of Lanping County, Nujiang Lisu Autonomous Prefecture.

When performing this dance, people form a circle or several circles, and dance happily to the rhythm of the music played by Sixian (a four-stringed plucked musical instrument) and the Sheepskin Drum. During the performance, the dance steps are varied, and dancers sing aloud at the interval when the dance music changes, with one leading the singing and all others singing in chorus. **Cuocuo Dance of the Pumi Nationality** is divided into two types, the open Cuocuo Dance and the enclosed Cuocuo Dance. Among them, the open Cuocuo Dance is a self-entertaining dance, an important form for the Pumi people to entertain themselves in daily life, which is indispensable in the large-scale communicative and festive activities of the Pumi nationality. Its performance is not restricted by time, place and the number of people, and participants can join the dance at any time. The dancers can start dancing one after another, or some people dance first, while others sing while walking. After they finish singing, they can join the dancing. In the process of dancing, dancers lean forward when stepping backward, with their upper and lower bodies in the opposite direction. When stepping forward, they lean back, with their upper and lower bodies also in the opposite direction. Usually, it is performed at a medium speed. When the speed is low, the dance steps are light and elegant. When the speed is quickened, the dance steps are rough and powerful. There are twelve sets of dance steps for the open Cuocuo Dance. Its formation includes a single circle, a double circle and a half circle. It is generally performed in a counterclockwise direction, and can also be performed clockwise, mostly used in various self-entertaining, festive and fitness activities.

第20项：拉祜族芦笙舞

拉祜族芦笙舞表演
the Performance of Lusheng Dance of the Lahu Nationality

项目序号：676	项目编号：Ⅲ-79	公布时间：2008（第二批）	类别：传统舞蹈
所属地区：云南省	类型：新增项目	申报地区或单位：云南省澜沧拉祜族自治县	

拉祜族芦笙舞是拉祜族具有代表性的民间舞蹈，流行于全国唯一的拉祜族自治县——云南省普洱市澜沧县。

拉祜族芦笙舞由最初的娱神祈福仪式演化而来，内容以表现拉祜族原始的宗教礼仪、生产生活、模拟动物，展现人的欢乐情绪等为主。拉祜族崇拜葫芦，把葫芦视作祖先诞生的母体。拉祜族人在葫芦上插上五根竹管制成芦笙，每年尝新节和春节跳起芦笙舞，表现对祖先的敬仰和对来年幸福生活的祈盼。芦笙舞经过数百代拉祜族群众和民间艺人的加工锤炼，现已形成一百多个套路。每逢拉祜族传统节日、原始宗教活动或农闲时节，人们都会兴致盎然地聚在一起，按一定程序通宵达旦地跳起芦笙舞，以庆祝丰收，感谢神灵护佑，祝愿来年平安幸福。在澜沧县，芦笙舞已成为全民性的社会活动，男子人人会吹芦笙、跳芦笙舞。拉祜族芦笙舞表演时，男子吹起葫芦笙，围圈而舞，女子牵手在外围伴舞。舞步主要有正步、踏步、蹉步和绕步；舞者的身段以俯、仰、摆、转等为主要特点；舞蹈节奏有张有弛，表现手法时而夸张洒脱，时而逼真细腻。整个舞蹈动作简练，曲调优美，风格深沉坚毅，具有古朴的韵味。①

Item 20: Lusheng Dance of the Lahu Nationality

Item Serial Number: 676	Item ID Number: Ⅲ-79	Released Date: 2008 (Batch 2)	Category: Traditional Dance

① 《拉祜族芦笙舞》，中国非物质文化遗产网，http://www.ihchina.cn/Article/Index/detail?id=13066，检索日期：2019年9月1日。

Affiliated Province: Yunnan Province	Type: New Item	Application Province or Unit: Lancang Lahu Autonomous County, Yunnan Province

Lusheng Dance of the Lahu Nationality is a representative folk dance of the Lahu people, popular in Lancang County, Pu'er City, Yunnan Province, the only Lahu Autonomous County in China.

Lusheng Dance of the Lahu Nationality evolved from the original ceremony of entertaining gods and praying for blessings, the content of which focuses on expressing the primitive religious etiquette, production and life, and the imitation of animals of the Lahu nationality, as well as showing people's happy emotions, etc. The Lahu people worship the gourd and regard it as the maternal body from which their ancestors were born. They insert five bamboo tubes in the gourd to make Lusheng Musical Instruments. At the New Rice-tasting Festival and the Spring Festival every year, they will perform Lusheng Dance to show their respect for their ancestors and hope for a happy life in the coming year. After hundreds of generations' improvement of the Lahu people and folk artists, Lusheng Dance has formed more than 100 sets of routines. Every time during the traditional festivals, primitive religious activities or agricultural slack seasons of the Lahu nationality, people will gather together in great interest and perform Lusheng Dance throughout the night according to certain procedures to celebrate the harvest, thank the gods for protection, and pray for peace and happiness in the coming year. In Lancang County, Lusheng Dance has become a social activity of all the people, and all men can play Lusheng Musical Instruments and perform Lusheng Dance. When performing **Lusheng Dance of the Lahu Nationality**, men play Hulusheng (a gourd-made musical instrument), forming a circle to dance, while women hold hands to accompany the dance on the periphery. Its dance steps mainly include parade steps, stepping, Cuobu steps (dance steps where two feet alternately wipe the ground and move forward) and coiling steps; dancers' bodies are mainly characterized by stooping, tilting upward, swinging, turning, etc.; its dance rhythm is both relaxing and intense; and its performance techniques are sometimes exaggerated, free and easy, while sometimes lifelike and delicate. The whole dance movements are concise, its tune is beautiful, and its style is deep and firm, which has a charm of primitive simplicity.

第21项：棕扇舞

棕扇舞表演
the Performance of the Palm-leaf Fan Dance

项目序号：1092	项目编号：Ⅲ-103	公布时间：2011（第三批）	类别：传统舞蹈
所属地区：云南省	类型：新增项目	申报地区或单位：云南省元江哈尼族彝族傣族自治县	

棕扇舞是哈尼族集歌、舞、乐和仿生表演于一体的传统舞蹈，流传于云南省红河与元江两县交界的哈尼族村寨。[①]

棕扇舞最初主要用于祭祀活动，每个动作均有象征性，男性模拟动物或鸟类，女性手持棕扇模拟白鹇鸟动作，各自起舞，表示对死者的尊敬和怀念。随着社会发展，棕扇舞的祭祀色彩逐渐减弱，发展为既可用于祭祀又可自娱的舞蹈，不仅在祭祀、丧葬时歌舞，逢年过节、农事休闲时亦歌亦舞。棕扇舞有六十多种套路。舞蹈前，要先由长者领跳并吟唱古歌和祝词。参与者自由形成圆圈，男里女外，长者先跳，小辈跟进；舞至酣畅，争相进入圈内展示舞蹈技艺。主要伴奏乐器有铓、鼓、钹和唢呐等。道具由内装谷子、包谷、荞子、银链和铜币的一对竹筒及若干松枝组成。棕扇为女子专用道具。舞蹈有一定技巧性，动作多用脚步颤动，起伏开跨及大小手臂的甩转。主要舞蹈动作有“老熊洗脸”“猴子作揖”“猴子抱瓜”“老鹰叼小鸡”“老熊穿裤”“猴子搂腰”“公鸡斗架”“猴子掰包谷”“老鹰拍翅膀”和“老熊走路”等，形态逼真。主要传承方式为师传，由师傅向徒弟传授舞蹈的主要动作和基本技法。[②]

---

① 《棕扇舞》，中国非物质文化遗产网，http://www.ihchina.cn/Article/Index/detail?id=13103，检索日期：2019年9月1日。

② 《哈尼族棕扇舞》，云南非物质文化遗产保护网，http://www.ynich.cn/view.php?id=1131&cat_id=11111，检索日期：2019年9月1日。

Item 21: the Palm-leaf Fan Dance

Item Serial Number: 1092	Item ID Number: Ⅲ-103	Released Date: 2011 (Batch 3)	Category: Traditional Dance
Affiliated Province: Yunnan Province	Type: New Item	Application Province or Unit: Yuanjiang Hani, Yi and Dai Autonomous County, Yunnan Province	

The Palm-leaf Fan Dance is a traditional dance of the Hani nationality that integrates singing, dancing, music, and biomimetic performance. It is prevalent in the stockaded villages of the Hani nationality at the juncture of Honghe and Yuanjiang counties in Yunnan Province.

The Palm-leaf Fan Dance was mainly used for sacrificial activities at first. Each movement is symbolic. Male dancers imitate animals or birds, and female dancers hold the Palm-leaf Fans to imitate the movements of silver pheasants. They dance respectively to express their respect for and remembrance of the dead. With the development of the society, the sacrificial element of **the Palm-leaf Fan Dance** has been gradually diluted, and it has developed into a dance that can be used for both sacrificial activity and self-entertainment, which is performed not only during sacrifices and funerals, but also at festivals and agricultural slack seasons. There are more than 60 sets of routines for **the Palm-leaf Fan Dance**. Before the dance, a venerable elder leads the dance, sings ancient songs and delivers a congratulatory speech at first. Participants form circles freely, with the male inside and the female outside. The elders dance first, and the juniors follow. When they dance to a climax, dancers compete to enter the circle to show their dance skills. The main accompaniment instruments are Mang (a folk copper percussion instrument), drums, cymbals, Suona Horn (a woodwind instrument), etc. The props are a pair of bamboo tubes containing millet, corns, buckwheat, silver chains and copper coins, as well as several pine branches. The Palm-leaf Fan is a specialized prop for women. This dance has a certain degree of skills, and its movements are mostly trembling foot steps, undulating strides, as well as swinging and rotating upper arms and forearms. The main dance movements are "An Old Bear Washing Face", "A Monkey Bowing", "A Monkey Hugging a Melon", "An Eagle Holding a Chick in Its Beak", "An Old Bear Wearing Trousers", "A Monkey Cuddling the Waist", "Roosters Fighting", "A Monkey Breaking off Corns with Hands", "An Eagle Flapping Wings", "An Old Bear Walking", etc., which are performed vividly. The main way of inheritance is masters' impartation, with masters teaching their disciples the main dance movements and basic techniques.

第22项：耳子歌

耳子歌表演
the Performance of Erzige Dance

项目序号：1279	项目编号：Ⅲ-126	公布时间：2014（第四批）	类别：传统舞蹈
所属地区：云南省	类型：新增项目	申报地区或单位：云南省大理白族自治州	

耳子歌是白语汉译，白语“耳子”意为“憨子”，“歌”意为“舞”。耳子歌属于民间傩仪文化表演，起源于云南省大理白族自治州云龙县检槽乡的白族聚居区，至今当地农村办婚事时都要表演耳子歌。

其表演一般由耳子三人、耳子媳妇三人，老倌、老妈、厨官、春官和江湖郎中等角色组成。伴奏以打击乐和唢呐为主。表演时耳子全身用棕皮包裹，非人非兽，既有灵性的一面，暗示可以通天；又有憨傻的一面，以示无知无畏。腰部棕皮系有麻绳，悬挂着大铃铛和猪尿泡（喻男性生殖器），手上分别拿笊篱、杵棒、锄头、连枷和荨麻等工具。表演中，耳子朝东南西北“跳四方”，挥舞荨麻四下抽打，以示驱邪逐秽；在席间穿梭跳唱、打诨逗乐，示痴傻状；在与父亲角色的问答过程中，巧妙地用道具和对白来表现家庭生活、野外劳作和男女交媾等内容。[①] 耳子歌傩祭仪式的重要目的是驱鬼逐疫，祈求人丁繁衍兴旺、家族发达、农业丰收。此外，该仪式还承载着道德教化功能，通过“春官审案”的表演来告诫人们要积德行善、不能坑蒙拐骗，传达了善恶相报的思想。

① 《[非遗故事]神秘的白族傩仪——“耳子歌”》，中国·云龙网，http://www.yunlong.yn.cn/c/2017-06-02/1802500.shtml，检索日期：2019年10月10日。

Item22: Erzige Dance

Item Serial Number: 1279	Item ID Number: Ⅲ-126	Released Date: 2014 (Batch 4)	Category: Traditional Dance
Affiliated Province: Yunnan Province	Type: New Item	Application Province or Unit: Dali Bai Autonomous Prefecture, Yunnan Province	

Erzige Dance is a Chinese translation of the Bai language, with "Erzi" meaning fools and "ge" meaning "dance", which belongs to the performance of folk Nuo ritual culture. It originated in areas inhabited by the Bai nationality in Jiancao Township, Yunlong County, Dali Bai Autonomous Prefecture, Yunnan Province. Up to now, when marriage ceremony is held in local villages, **Erzige Dance** is still performed.

The roles for the performance of **Erzige Dance** consist of three Erzi (fools), three wives of Erzi (fools), an old man, an old woman, a chef, a Spring Official, a quack, etc. Its accompaniment is mainly percussion instruments and Suona Horn (a woodwind instrument). During the performance, the roles of Erzi (fools) are all wrapped in barks of palm tree. They are neither human nor beasts. They not only have the aspect of spirituality, suggesting that they can communicate with the heaven; but also have a silly aspect, showing ignorance and fearlessness. A hemp rope is tied on the palm bark around their waists, with a big bell and a pig bladder (symbolizing the male genitalia) hanging on it. They hold tools of sieves, pestles, hoes, flails, nettles, etc. in hands respectively. In the performance, the roles of Erzi (fools) perform "Sifang Dance" eastward, southward, westward and northward, brandishing nettles and lashing around to drive out evil spirits and filth; shuttling between seats and singing, making fun to show foolishness. In the process of asking and answering questions between Erzi (fools) and the role of father, he cleverly uses props and dialogues to express the family life, field labor, the sexual intercourse between men and women, etc. The important purpose of the Nuo sacrificial ritual of **Erzige Dance** is to expel the ghosts, get rid of plagues, as well as pray for the prosperity of the people and the family, and a good harvest. In addition, this ritual also has the function of moral education. The performance of the Spring Official's Trial of a Case warns people to accumulate virtuous deeds, do good deeds and not to commit swindling, bluffing, cheating or lying, which conveys the idea of karma and comeuppance.

第23项：
铓鼓舞

铓鼓舞表演
the Performance of Manggu Drum Dance

项目序号：1280	项目编号：Ⅲ-127	公布时间：2014（第四批）	类别：传统舞蹈
所属地区：云南省	类型：新增项目	申报地区或单位：云南省建水县	

铓鼓舞是流传于云南省建水县哈尼族中的一种祭祀舞蹈，在哈尼族的传统祭祖节“昂玛突”期间表演。

铓鼓舞表达了哈尼人祈祷风调雨顺、庄稼饱满、粮食丰收的愿望。其动作源于哈尼人的田间劳作，表现的是哈尼人的农耕劳作，如“赶牛犁田”“糊田埂”“撒谷种”“插秧苗”“踩肥料”等。表演时，舞者围成圆圈，舞铓者在圆心，代表“昂玛”神树；舞鼓者在外，以舞铓者为中心，听其号令，围圈而舞。[①] 其形式以一人舞铓，四人击鼓，或者两人舞铓，八人击鼓为主。[②] 铓鼓舞中，舞铓者多为年长者，左手持铓，右手用槌抵住铓乳中部，双手持铓在身体两旁推划横“8”字舞动，后退或前进时铓在身体正前由上往下推划弧圈舞动，身体随铓左右拧动，稍前俯。舞铓者时而双腿朝天做神树状，时而摹拟仪式的祭拜动作。舞鼓者时而双腿跪地，身体左右摆动；时而腾空而起，潇洒击鼓；时而对击，对舞。[③] 铓鼓舞的舞蹈动作展现了哈尼族先民远古农耕生活的图景，表现了哈尼族男子坚韧的精神、强健的体魄以及哈尼族博大精深的农耕文化。

① 建水县文化和旅游局，《建水县非物质文化遗产保护名录》，昆明：云南人民出版社，2019 年，第 9 页。

② 汪致敏、侯健，《哈尼族铓鼓舞源流新探》，载《民族艺术研究》，1993 年第 3 期，第 73-78 页。

③ 曹天明，《铓鼓舞》，载《民族艺术》，1993 年第 1 期，第 136-141 页。

Item 23: Manggu Drum Dance

Item Serial Number: 1280	Item ID Number: Ⅲ-127	Released Date: 2014 (Batch 4)	Category: Traditional Dance
Affiliated Province: Yunnan Province	Type: New Item	Application Province or Unit: Jianshui County, Yunnan Province	

Manggu Drum Dance is a kind of sacrificial dance spread among the Hani people in Jianshui County, Yunnan Province, which is performed during the traditional ancestor worship festival, “Angmatu”, of the Hani nationality.

This dance expresses the Hani people’ wishes for timely wind and rain, full crops, and a bumper harvest. Its dance movements originated from the Hani people’s field labor, such as “driving cattle to plow fields”, “plastering field ridges with mud”, “scattering grain seeds”, “transplanting rice seedlings” and “stepping on fertilizers”, which express the farming labor of the Hani people. When performing it, dancers form a circle, and the performers of Mang (a folk copper percussion instrument) stand in the center of the circle, representing the divine tree of “Angma”; and the drummers stand outside the circle, centering on Mang performers, following their orders and dancing in a circle. The main forms are one Mang performer and four drummers, or two Mang performers and eight drummers. In **Manggu Drum Dance**, most Mang performers are seniors, with left hands holding the instruments, and right hands pressing the mallets against their middle parts. They hold Mang (a folk copper percussion instrument) in both hands to make the movements of pushing and pulling and produce the horizontal “8” on both sides of the body to dance. When stepping backward or forward, they push and pull Mang (a folk copper percussion instrument) in front of their bodies from top to bottom, and make an arc, with their bodies twisting from left to right with Mang (a folk copper percussion instrument) and leaning forward slightly. Mang performers sometimes have their legs up to the sky in the form of a divine tree, and sometimes imitate the worshipping actions in rituals. Drum performers sometimes kneel on the ground, swinging their bodies from side to side; sometimes they rise up into the air, beating the drums elegantly; and sometimes they beat the drums and dance face to face. The dance movements of **Manggu Drum Dance** show the farming life scenes of the ancestors of the Hani nationality, reflecting the tough spirit and strong body of the Hani men, as well as the extensive and profound farming culture of the Hani nationality.

德昂族水鼓舞表演
the Performance of the Water Drum Dance of the De'ang Nationality

第24项：水鼓舞

项目序号：1281	项目编号：Ⅲ-128	公布时间：2014（第四批）	类别：传统舞蹈
所属地区：云南省	类型：新增项目	申报地区或单位：云南省瑞丽市	

水鼓舞是德昂族民众中流行的一种以祭祀祖先、祈求风调雨顺和村寨平安的水、鼓、舞相结合的群众舞蹈，流传于德宏傣族景颇族自治州。

水鼓是德昂族的主要打击乐器。根据形状和个头，水鼓分为大、小两种，两者的跳法和打法各不相同。[①]跳小水鼓舞时，由一男子将鼓横挎于腹前，其打法是右手持鼓槌敲大头，左手用手掌拍打小头，另两名男子各持镲和大铓，同时击乐，构成交错重叠的节奏，边敲边跳相互交换位置。其余人众围绕成圆圈，踩着鼓点载歌载舞。舞步以"单脚提步绕"为主，动作有"单双蹉步""踢脚转圈""绕鼓尾""崴鼓""公鸡打架""蹲跳""对蹬"等。大水鼓则是用固定的鼓架架住鼓身，敲鼓人可正面敲打，或者转身背身敲打，旁边另以镲、铓和小象脚鼓围绕伴奏，众人随鼓声而舞。舞步有"单步踢脚""原地跨步转圈""对跳"，手自然向上翻腕绕花。水鼓舞展现了德昂人从播种、耕耘到收割的农事过程。瑞丽市德昂族主要使用的就是大水鼓。[②]

① 孙家显，《论德昂族"水鼓"和"水鼓舞"文化》，载《民族音乐》，2014 年第 2 期，第 61-62 页。

② 《水鼓舞》，瑞丽市门户网，http://www.ruili.gov.cn/dmrl/fwyc/content-188-493-1.html，检索日期：2019 年 12 月 13 日。

Item 24: the Water Drum Dance

Item Serial Number: 1281	Item ID Number: Ⅲ-128	Released Date: 2014 (Batch 4)	Category: Traditional Dance
Affiliated Province: Yunnan Province	Type: New Item	Application Province or Unit: Ruili City, Yunnan Province	

The Water Drum Dance is a popular folk dance among the De'ang people that combines water, drums and dances to worship ancestors and to pray for timely wind and rain as well as village safety. It is circulated in Dehong Dai and Jingpo Autonomous Prefecture.

The Water Drum is the main percussion instrument of the De'ang nationality. According to the shape and the size, the Water Drum is divided into two types: large and small, each having different methods of dancing and playing. When performing the small Water Drum Dance, a man slungs the drum in front of his abdomen, with his right hand holding the drumstick to hit the big end of the drum and his left hand slapping its small end with the palm. Two other men hold a small cymbal and a Big Mang (a folk copper percussion instrument) respectively, and beat them at the same time, creating a staggered and overlapping rhythm. They exchange their positions with each other while beating and dancing. The rest of the people form a circle, singing and dancing to the beats of the drum. The dance steps are mainly "single foot-lifting and winding", and the movements include "single and double Cuobu steps (dance steps where two feet alternately wipe the ground and move forward)", "kicking and twirling in circles", "circling the drum tail", "twisting the drum", "roosters fighting", "squat jump" and "pedaling face to face". The large Water Drum is fixed on a stand to support it. The drummer can beat it in the front, or turn around to beat it, accompanied by the small cymbal, Mang (a folk copper percussion instrument) and the small Elephant-foot Drum. Everyone dances to the beats of the drum. The dance steps include "single-step kicking", "stepping and circling in place" and "dancing face to face". Dancers' hands naturally supinate upwards and circle into flowers. **The Water Drum Dance** shows the farming process of the De'ang people from sowing, tilling, to harvesting. The De'ang people in Ruili City mainly play the large Water Drum.

第25项：怒族达比亚舞

怒族达比亚舞表演
the Performance of Dabiya Dance of the Nu Nationality

项目序号：1282	项目编号：Ⅲ-129	公布时间：2014（第四批）	类别：传统舞蹈
所属地区：云南省	类型：新增项目	申报地区或单位：云南省福贡县	

怒族达比亚舞是怒族具有代表性的舞种之一，流传于云南省怒江傈僳族自治州福贡县的各怒族村寨。

“达比亚”是怒族的传统弹拨乐器，外形似琵琶、三弦。舞者手持达比亚，边弹边舞，有近百个套路，表现题材十分广泛：有反映怒族祖先不断迁徙的《第一、二、三次找土地舞》；有保卫家园的《古战争》；有反映性崇拜及生殖崇拜的《掰胯舞》和《生育舞》；有表现动物形态的《江边阳雀舞》《乌鸦喝水舞》和《鸡刨食舞》；有表现男女爱情的《窝得得》《双人达比亚舞》《找情人舞》和《情人相约逃婚舞》；有反映生产生活的《找野菜舞》《割小米舞》《狩猎舞》和《母鸡下蛋舞》等。[①]达比亚舞的上身弹奏姿态丰富，有左右高弹、平弹、低弹、背弹和反弹等。下身舞步主要风格有两种：（1）双膝屈伸带送胯动律的踏、点、刨、磋、勾，其屈伸较为明显；（2）双膝屈伸带转身韵律的踏、点、刨、磋、勾，磋、屈伸较小。左右送胯、左右转身、屈伸颤动是形成达比亚舞特有韵律的三个因素。[②]达比亚舞在内容和舞步上，各村基本相同，个别村寨在有的舞蹈后加有结尾动作组合。该舞蹈既要弹弦，又要跳舞，技术难度较大。

① 《怒族达比亚舞》，云南非物质文化遗产保护网，http://www.ynich.cn/view.php?id=1133&cat_id=11111，检索日期：2019年9月1日。

② 《怒族“达比亚舞”》，中国民族建筑研究会中国民族建筑网，http://yn.naic.org.cn/2018/0423/202644.html，检索日期：2020年7月20日。

Item 25: Dabiya Dance of the Nu Nationality

Item Serial Number: 1282	Item ID Number: Ⅲ-129	Released Date: 2014 (Batch 4)	Category: Traditional Dance
Affiliated Province: Yunnan Province	Type: New Item	Application Province or Unit: Fugong County, Yunnan Province	

Dabiya Dance of the Nu Nationality is one of the representative dances of the Nu people, spread in various Nu stockaded villages in Fugong County, Nujiang Lisu Autonomous Prefecture, Yunnan Province.

"Dabiya" is a traditional plucked instrument of the Nu nationality, resembling a Pipa (a plucked string instrument with a fretted fingerboard) or Sanxian (a three-stringed plucked musical instrument) in form. Dancers hold Dabiya (a traditional plucked instrument of the Nu nationality) in their hands, dancing and playing. There are nearly a hundred sets of routines, with a very wide range of themes: there is the dance reflecting the constant migration of the ancestors of the Nu people, namely the First, Second and Third Land-seeking Dance; there is the dance reflecting the safeguarding of the homeland, namely the Ancient War Dance; there are the dances reflecting their sexual and reproductive worship, such as the Crotch Dance and the Reproduction Dance; there are the dances imitating animals' behaviors, such as the Riverside Cuckoo Dance, the Dance of Crow Drinking Water and the Dance of Chicken Searching Food; there are the dances expressing the love of men and women, such as Wodede Dance, the Double-person Dabiya Dance, the Lover-seeking Dance and the Dance of Lovers' Appointment to Escape Marriage; and there are the dances showcasing the production and life, such as the Dance of Looking for Wild Vegetables, the Millet-harvesting Dance, the Hunting Dance and the Dance of the Hen's Laying Eggs. The postures of the upper body for playing Dabiya (a traditional plucked instrument of the Nu nationality) are rich, including left-and-right high playing, flat playing, low playing, playing at the back and playing reversely. There are two main styles of the dance steps of the lower body: (1) the treading, pointing, planing, rubbing and hooking steps, together with the obvious movements of the double-knee flexion and stretching with the rhythm of moving crotches; (2) the treading, pointing, planing, rubbing and hooking steps, together with the movements of the double-knee flexion and stretching with the rhythm of turning around, in which the movements of rubbing, flexion and stretching are smaller. Moving the crotch left and right, turning around left and right, as well as flexion, stretching and trembling are the three factors that form the unique rhythm of Dabiya Dance. The content and dance steps of Dabiya Dance are basically the same in each village, and a combination of ending moves is added to the end of the dance performed in individual villages. This dance involves both playing the strings and dancing, which is technically difficult.

第26项：热巴舞

热巴舞表演
the Performance of Reba Dance

项目序号：124	项目编号：Ⅲ-21	公布时间：2014（第四批）	类别：传统舞蹈
所属地区：云南省	类型：扩展项目	申报地区或单位：云南省迪庆藏族自治州	

热巴舞是一门融铃鼓舞、杂剧、哑剧、寓言、歌舞、说唱、杂技、小戏和弦子舞等为一体的综合表演艺术，是藏族古代灿烂文化艺术中的奇葩。流传于云南省迪庆藏族自治州。

相传，热巴舞由藏传佛教噶举派的第二代祖师米拉日巴开创的。约在公元 11 世纪中后期，藏传佛教噶举派传入云南省迪庆藏族自治州，热巴舞蹈随之在迪庆流行起来。随后，迪庆州境内的热巴舞不仅由藏族传承，还被傈僳族和纳西族学习并传承下来，在迪庆各地域传承的过程中融入了本民族和地域的文化，形成了迪庆热巴舞。最初，热巴舞只在寺院跳，用于祭祀和宣扬弘法，后来流传到民间，形成多种流派和风格的热巴舞，即祭祀热巴、流浪热巴、商贸热巴和傈僳族肋巴舞、纳西族勒巴舞等。如德钦县云岭乡的“斯农藏族热巴舞”以及香格里拉县五境乡的“子母雄热巴”和“傈僳族热巴舞”均属于流浪热巴；维西县的“塔城藏族神川热巴”，香格里拉县上江乡的“巴迪、木高傈僳族肋巴舞”和金江镇的“下所邑、上所邑纳西族勒巴舞”等属于祭祀热巴。[①]

① 《热巴舞》，迪庆非物质文化遗产保护网，http://www.dqich.cn/baohuminglu/detail/16/64，检索日期：2019 年 8 月 31 日。

Item 26: Reba Dance

Item Serial Number: 124	Item ID Number: Ⅲ-21	Released Date: 2014 (Batch 4)	Category: Traditional Dance
Affiliated Province: Yunnan Province	Type: Extended Item	Application Province or Unit: Diqing Zang Autonomous Prefecture, Yunnan Province	

Reba Dance is a comprehensive performing art integrating the Bell Drum Dance, Zaju Opera, dumb shows, fables, songs and dances, talking and singing, acrobatics, short plays, the String Dance, etc. It is a wonderful work in the splendid ancient culture and art of the Zang nationality, spread in Diqing Zang Autonomous Prefecture in Yunnan Province.

Legend has it that it was created by Milarepa, the second-generation patriarch of the Kagyu School of Tibetan Buddhism. Around the middle and late 11th century, the Kagyu School of Tibetan Buddhism was introduced to Diqing Zang Autonomous Prefecture in Yunnan Province, and **Reba Dance** became popular in Diqing. Subsequently, **Reba Dance** in Diqing Prefecture has been not only inherited by the Zang nationality, but also learned and passed down by the Lisu and Naxi nationalities. In the process of its inheritance in the various regions of Diqing Prefecture, **Reba Dance** has been integrated into the local culture of this nationality and this region, forming **Diqing Reba Dance**. In the beginning, **Reba Dance** was only performed in monasteries for sacrifices and the publicity of Buddhism. Later, it has been spread among the people, forming Reba Dances with a variety of genres and styles, namely, Reba Dance of Offering Sacrifices, the Wandering Reba Dance, the Trade Reba Dance, Leba Dance of the Lisu Nationality, Leba Dance of the Naxi Nationality, etc. For example, “Sinong Reba Dance of the Zang Nationality” in Yunling Township of Deqin County, as well as “Zimuxiong Reba Dance” and “Reba Dance of the Lisu Nationality” in Wujing Township of Shangri-La County belong to the Wandering Reba Dance. “Tacheng Shenchuan Reba Dance of the Zang Nationality” in Weixi County, “Badi and Mugao Leba Dance of the Lisu Nationality” in Shangjiang Township of Shangri-La County, as well as “Xiasuoyi and Shangsuoyi Leba Dance of the Naxi Nationality” in Jinjiang Township belong to Reba Dance of Offering Sacrifices.

第四章 传统戏剧

Chapter Four **Traditional Opera**

第 1 项：花灯戏（玉溪花灯戏）

玉溪花灯戏《莫愁女》剧照

a Stage Photo of "A Girl with No Worries", a Yuxi Lantern Opera

项目序号：222	项目编号：Ⅳ-78	公布时间：2006（第一批）	类别：传统戏剧
所属地区：云南省	类型：新增项目	申报地区或单位：云南省玉溪市	

玉溪花灯戏是云南玉溪市的主要地方剧种，是云南花灯戏的三大支系之一，属于传统民间艺术，主要流行于玉溪市所辖红塔区、澄江市、华宁县、易门县和通海县，以红塔区最盛。

玉溪花灯戏随屯军玉溪的明军而传入，当时以演唱江南小曲为主。这种民歌演唱与当地土主神（土地神）祭祀结合，逐渐演变成当地"社火"活动的主要内容。玉溪花灯戏以新灯戏而出名。玉溪花灯戏艺人从滇戏中汲取养分，对老灯戏进行改造，创作出一大批新花灯戏剧目，把老灯戏由乡间的团场歌舞推向舞台，并将新灯戏推广至省城昆明，形成专业性质卖票演出，随之出现了一批知名的新灯戏艺人。至此，新灯戏完全取代老灯戏，正式成为一个剧种，风靡全滇。玉溪新灯戏的发展以剧目为中心，带动了舞台艺术的发展，在表演上，行当的划分由简单渐趋复杂。新灯戏艺人逐渐专业化，有些在艺术上独具特色，较有声望的有余四（佘永宁）、申六（申国文）等。玉溪新灯戏的曲调以“道情”“走板”“虞美情”“全十字”“五里塘”五大调为主。代表性剧目有《双接妹》《出门走厂》《新彩礼》《莫愁女》等。玉溪花灯戏在 300 余年的发展中早已与玉溪的文化融为一体，成为与玉溪人的精神世界血脉相联的文化现象。①

Item 1: the Lantern Opera (Yuxi Lantern Opera)

Item Serial Number: 222	Item ID Number: Ⅳ-78	Released Date: 2006 (Batch 1)	Category: Traditional Opera
Affiliated Province: Yunnan Province	Type: New Item	Application Province or Unit: Yuxi City, Yunnan Province	

Yuxi Lantern Opera is the main local opera in Yuxi City, Yunnan Province, which is one of the three branches of Yunnan Lantern Opera. It belongs to traditional folk art and is mainly popular in Hongta District, Chengjiang City, Huaning County, Yimen County and Tonghai County that are under the jurisdiction of Yuxi City, with the one in Hongta District being the most popular.

Yuxi Lantern Opera was introduced along with the Ming army garrisoned inYuxi, with the singing of Jiangnan ditties in the majority at that time. This kind of folk song singing was integrated with the local activity of offering sacrifices to the god of the land owner (the god of land), and gradually evolved into the main content of the local “Shehuo” activity. **Yuxi Lantern Opera** is famous for the New Lantern Opera. Its artists have drawn nutrients from Yunnan Opera, transforming the Old Lantern Opera and creating a large number of plays of the New Lantern Opera. They

① 额瑜婷，《玉溪花灯是民族杂居区文化交融的结晶》，载《玉溪师范学院学报》，2010 年第 2 期，第 58-62 页。

have promoted the Old Lantern Opera from rural group singing and dancing to stage, and have spread the New Lantern Opera to the provincial capital, Kunming City. It became specialized and formed a system of selling tickets for the performance. Subsequently, there appeared a group of well-known artists of the New Lantern Opera. At this point, the New Lantern Opera completely replaced the Old Lantern Opera and formally became an opera category, popular all over Yunnan Province. The development of new **Yuxi Lantern Opera** focuses on the repertoire, which has promoted the development of stage art. In terms of the performance, the division of the types of roles has changed from simple to complex. The artists of the New Lantern Opera have gradually become professional, and some of them have unique features in art. The rather renowned ones are She Si (She Yongning), Shen Liu (Shen Guowen), etc. The tunes of new **Yuxi Lantern Opera** are mainly the five major tunes of “Daoqing”, “Zouban”, “Yumeiqing”, “Quanshizi” and “Wulitang”. Representative plays include “Picking Up the Sister Twice”, “Going Out of the Factory”, “New Betrothal Gifts” and “A Girl with No Worries”. **Yuxi Lantern Opera** has long been integrated with the Yuxi culture in its development of more than 300 years, and has become a cultural phenomenon connected with the spiritual world of the Yuxi people.

第 2 项：花灯戏

云南省花灯剧团的花灯戏《探干妹》演出
"Visiting the Beloved Girl", Performed by the Lantern Opera Troupe of Yunnan Province

<table>
<tr><td>项目序号：222</td><td>项目编号：Ⅳ-78</td><td>公布时间：2008（第二批）</td><td>类别：传统戏剧</td></tr>
<tr><td>所属地区：云南省</td><td>类型：扩展项目</td><td colspan="2">申报地区或单位：云南省花灯剧团、弥渡县、姚安县、元谋县</td></tr>
</table>

云南花灯戏源于民间花灯歌舞，是清末民初形成流行于云南的地方戏曲。流行过程中因受各地语音、民歌小曲和习俗影响而形成不同的演唱和表演风格。云南花灯戏有昆明花灯戏、姚安花灯戏和玉溪花灯戏三大支系。其中，昆明花灯戏保留明清小曲及明清剧目最多，伴奏乐器以胡琴为主；姚安花灯戏民歌色彩浓重，主要用笛子、梆子伴奏；玉溪花灯戏革新最早，被称为“新灯”，其剧目及演出形式受滇剧影响较大。此外，小支派名目繁多，文山、曲靖、楚雄、弥渡、罗平、元谋、禄丰、建水、蒙自等地都有自己的花灯戏。

云南花灯戏最初演出的是歌舞成分很重的花灯小戏，后受滇戏等剧种影响，出现了情节较为曲折复杂的剧目，同时吸收其他剧种的曲调加以变化、拓展、翻新，形成了花灯戏新调。① 新编的灯调采用曲调连接的编曲方式，具有板腔音乐的特点，适合演出传统大戏。花灯戏演出很注重舞蹈，云南花灯舞蹈的基本特征是“崴”，“崴步”都有手部动作配合，手中的道具和扇子的“手中花”及“扇花”的种种变化是其具体表现。花灯戏表演时艺人手不离扇、帕，载歌载舞。云南花灯戏最繁荣的时期是 20 世纪五六十年代，此时不仅涌现了史宝凤、熊介臣和袁留安等一批著名花灯戏演员，还出现了《探干妹》《闹渡》《刘成看菜》《三访亲》等优秀剧目。熊介臣是最早把农村晒场演出的“簸箕灯”搬上舞台的前辈艺人之一，他擅演小生，以演《山伯访友》中的

① 《花灯戏》，中国非物质文化遗产网，http://www.ihchina.cn/Article/Index/detail?id=13342，检索日期：2019 年 9 月 1 日。

梁山伯、《白蛇传》中的许仙闻名。①

Item 2: the Lantern Opera

Item Serial Number: 222	Item ID Number: Ⅳ-78	Released Date: 2008 (Batch 2)	Category: Traditional Opera
Affiliated Province: Yunnan Province	Type: Extended Item	Application Province or Unit: the Lantern Opera Troupe, Midu County, Yao'an County and Yuanmou County of Yunnan Province	

Yunnan Lantern Opera originated from folk lantern singing and dancing, which was a local opera that was formed and became popular in Yunnan in the late Qing Dynasty and the early Republic of China. In the process of circulation, influenced by the speech sounds, folk ditties and customs of various localities, it has formed different singing and performance styles. **Yunnan Lantern Opera** has three branches: **Kunming Lantern Opera**, **Yao'an Lantern Opera** and **Yuxi Lantern Opera**. Among them, **Kunming Lantern Opera** retains the largest number of the ditties and plays of the Ming and Qing dynasties. The accompaniment instrument is mainly Huqin Musical Instrument. **Yao'an Lantern Opera** has a strong color of folk songs, mainly using flutes and clappers as accompaniment instruments. **Yuxi Lantern Opera** underwent the earliest innovation, thus known as "**the New Lantern Opera**". Its plays and performance form have been greatly influenced by Yunnan Opera. In addition, it has many sub-branches, with such places as Wenshan, Qujing, Chuxiong, Midu, Luoping, Yuanmou, Lufeng, Jianshui and Mengzi having their own lantern operas.

For **Yunnan Lantern Opera**, the originally-performed one was the small-scale Lantern Opera which had a high proportion of singing and dancing. Later, influenced by Yunnan Opera and other operas, there appeared the plays with more complex plots. At the same time, it absorbed the tunes of other operas, and then underwent changes, expansion and renovations, forming a new tune of **the Lantern Opera**. The newly adapted tunes of **the Lantern Opera** adopt the arrangement method of tune

① 《花灯戏（玉溪花灯戏）》，中国非物质文化遗产网，http://www.ihchina.cn/Article/Index/detail?id=13340，检索日期：2019 年 8 月 12 日。

connection, which has the feature of Banqiang music and is suitable for performing traditional big operas. The performance of **the Lantern Opera** lays emphasis on dancing. The basic feature of the dances of **Yunnan Lantern Opera** is "Wai (twisted dance steps)", and all twisted dance steps are matched with hand movements, which are demonstrated by the various changes in "the Hand Flower" and "the Fan Flower" of the props and fans in hand. When performing it, artists hold fans and kerchiefs in hands, singing and dancing. The boom periods of **Yunnan Lantern Opera** were in the 1950s and 1960s. At that time, there appeared not only a number of renowned actors of **the Lantern Opera**, such as Shi Baofeng, Xiong Jiechen and Yuan Liu'an, but also excellent plays, such as "Visiting the Beloved Girl", "Stirring Up Trouble in a Ferry Crossing", "Liu Cheng Guards Vegetables" and "Visiting the Relative Three Times". Xiong Jiechen is one of the earliest senior artists who have brought "the Dustpan Lantern" performed on rural threshing ground onto the stage. He is good at playing the role of Xiaosheng (the young man's role), famous for acting Liang Shanbo in "Shanbo Visits His Friend" and Xu Xian in "The Legend of the White Snake".

傣剧《娥并与桑洛》剧照
the Stage Photo of Dai Opera of "Ebing and Sangluo"

第 3 项：傣剧

项目序号：230	项目编号：Ⅳ-86	公布时间：2006（第一批）	类别：传统戏剧
所属地区：云南省	类型：新增项目	申报地区或单位：云南省德宏傣族景颇族自治州	

傣剧是云南独具特色的少数民族戏曲剧种之一，流传于云南省德宏傣族景颇族自治州的傣族聚居区。每逢传统佳节、农闲、婚庆等场合都有傣剧演出。

傣剧发源于有一定人物情节的傣族歌舞表演及佛经讲唱，后吸收滇剧、皮影戏的艺术营养，逐步形成较完整的戏曲形式。起初，傣剧中由男性穿傣族女装扮演女性角色，男性角色的装扮及男女角色的动作套路与滇剧和京剧相仿。表演时，演员上前三步演唱或做动作，再退后三步听场边人提词，唱段之间以锣鼓等打击乐伴奏。后来唱腔经逐步发展形成【喊混】（男腔）和【喊朗】（女腔）两个基本腔调。演出中着傣装，表演动作中融入傣族民间舞蹈步态，伴奏方面增加了葫芦丝、二胡及象脚鼓等乐器，民族风格更加浓郁。傣剧传统剧目有的源自傣族民间故事、叙事长诗或佛经故事，如《相勐》《千瓣莲花》《朗推罕》；有的翻译移植自汉族剧目，如《庄子试妻》《甘露寺》《杨门女将》。20 世纪 60 年代以来，傣剧改编和创作了《娥并与桑洛》《海罕》《竹楼情深》等大批剧目，其中《娥并与桑洛》被誉为“东南亚的明珠”。除德宏州傣剧团专业团体外，较大的傣族村落都有业余演出队伍。①

Item 3: Dai Opera

Item Serial Number: 230	Item ID Number: Ⅳ-86	Released Date: 2006 (Batch 1)	Category: Traditional Opera

① 《傣剧》，中国非物质文化遗产网，http://www.ihchina.cn/Article/Index/detail?id=13369，检索日期：2019 年 8 月 31 日。

Affiliated Province: Yunnan Province	Type: New Item	Application Province or Unit: Dehong Dai and Jingpo Autonomous Prefecture, Yunnan Province

Dai Opera is one of the unique ethnic opera types in Yunnan Province. It is spread in areas inhabited by the Dai nationality in Dehong Dai and Jingpo Autonomous Prefecture, Yunnan Province. **Dai Opera** is performed on every occasion of traditional festivals, slack seasons, weddings, etc.

Dai Opera originated from the singing and dancing performances of the Dai nationality containing certain characters and plots, as well as the recitation and singing of Buddhist scriptures, and later absorbed the artistic nutrients of Yunnan Opera and Shadow Play, gradually developing into a more complete opera form. At first, the female characters in **Dai Opera** were played by men wearing women's costumes. The costume and make-up of the male characters and the action routines of the male and female characters were similar to those of Yunnan Opera and Peking Opera. When performing it, actors go forward three steps to sing or perform, and then step back three steps to listen to the bystanders' prompting, with percussion accompaniments of gongs, drums, etc. played between two sections of librettos. Later, the singing tones have gradually developed into two basic tones, Hanhun (the male tone) and Hanlang (the female tone). In the performance, actors wear Dai costumes. They integrate the folk dance gait of the Dai nationality in their dance movements. In terms of accompaniments, the musical instruments of Hulusi (a wind instrument made of the gourd), Erhu (a two-stringed bowed instrument), the Elephant-foot Drum, etc. are added, which makes **Dai Opera** have more ethnic flavor. Some of the traditional plays of **Dai Opera** are derived from the folk tales and long narrative poems of the Dai nationality or Buddhist stories, such as "Xiang Meng, the Prince", "A Thousand-petal Lotus Flower" and "Langtuihan, the Peacock Princess"; and some are translated and borrowed from the Han operas, such as "Zhuangzi Tests His Wife", "Ganlu Temple" and "Women Generals of the Yang Family". Since the 1960s, **Dai Opera** has adapted and created a large number of plays, such as "Ebing and Sangluo", "Haihan, the Adopted Son" and "The Deep Love in the Bamboo House". Among them, "Ebing and Sangluo" has been acclaimed as "a Pearl of Southeast Asia". Besides **Dai Opera** Troupe of Dehong Prefecture, a professional organization, there are amateur performance teams in large villages inhabited by the Dai people.

第 4 项：滇剧

滇剧《白蛇传》选段《游湖》剧照
the Stage Photo of Yunnan Opera, the Selected Excerpt from *The Legend of the White Snake*, titled "A Tour on the Lake"

项目序号：733	项目编号：Ⅳ-132	公布时间：2008（第二批）	类别：传统戏剧
所属地区：云南省	类型：新增项目	申报地区或单位：云南省昆明市、云南省滇剧院、云南省玉溪市滇剧团	

滇剧是云南省主要的地方剧种，形成于清代道光年间，已有近 200 年的历史。光绪年间，滇剧演出活动在玉溪等地已经十分盛行。滇剧流行于云南全省及贵州、四川的部分地区，缅甸、泰国、新加坡、马来西亚等国家的一些地区也都有滇剧的演唱活动。

滇剧声腔独特，表现力强。其三大声腔，即丝弦腔、胡琴腔和襄阳腔分别源于秦腔、徽调和汉调等古老的声腔，同时又受到云南民族民间音乐的滋养。滇剧板式丰富多变，曲调自然流畅，能表演各种题材、样式、结构和情调的剧目，具有独特的艺术个性和风格，因而有"滇粹"之誉。滇剧传统剧目有 1000 多个，有秦腔路子、川路子、京路子和滇路子之分。秦腔路子剧目有《春秋配》《花田错》《高平关》等。川路子剧目来自川剧，如《黄袍记》（赵匡胤雪夜访普）、《青袍记》（梁灏八十中状元）、《白袍记》（尉迟恭访薛仁贵）、《绿袍记》（萧何月下追韩信）和《红袍记》（刘知远打天下）等。京路子剧目来自皮簧戏（徽、汉、京剧），如《打渔杀家》《坐宫》等。滇路子剧目有两种：一是云南作者或艺人编写的当地历史故事戏，如《薛尔望投潭》《逼死坡》《宁北妃》《陈圆圆出家》等；二是移植外地剧种的剧目，如《三国》《水浒》《红楼》等。历代艺人在排演传统剧目的同时，均能结合时代特点和云南当地状况编演反映边疆少数民族历史和现实生活的作品。①

① 《滇剧》，中国非物质文化遗产网，http://www.ihchina.cn/Article/Index/detail?id=13544，检索日期：2019 年 9 月 1 日。

Item 4: Yunnan Opera

Item Serial Number: 733	Item ID Number: Ⅳ-132	Released Date: 2008 (Batch 2)	Category: Traditional Opera
Affiliated Province: Yunnan Province	Type: New Item	Application Province or Unit: Kunming City, Yunan Province; Yunnan Opera Troupe of Yunnan Province; Yunnan Opera Troupe of Yuxi City, Yunnan Province	

Yunnan Opera is the main local opera in Yunnan Province. It was formed during the reign of Emperor Daoguang of the Qing Dynasty with a history of nearly 200 years. During the reign of Emperor Guangxu, the performances of **Yunnan Opera** have already been very popular in Yuxi and other places. **Yunnan Opera** is popular in the whole province of Yunnan and parts of Guizhou and Sichuan. It is also performed in some regions of such countries as Myanmar, Thailand, Singapore, and Malaysia.

Yunnan Opera is unique in singing tones, which is very expressive. Its three major tones, namely, Sixian tone, Huqin tone and Xiangyang tone, were derived from ancient tones of Qinqiang tone, Huidiao and Handiao respectively. At the same time, they were also nurtured by the ethnic folk music in Yunnan. **Yunnan Opera** has rich and varied styles, as well as natural and smooth tunes, and can perform plays of various themes, styles, structures and moods. It has a unique artistic personality and style, thus acclaimed as "the Essence of Yunnan". The traditional repertoire of **Yunnan Opera** reaches more than 1,000 works, which are divided into Qinqiang tone style, Sichuan style, Beijing style and Yunnan style. The repertoire of Qinqiang tone style includes "The Matching of Spring and Autumn", "Mistakes in Flower Field" and "Gaoping Pass". The repertoire of Sichuan style comes from Sichuan Opera, such as "Stories of the Imperial Robe" (Zhao Kuangyin Visits Zhao Pu on a Snowy Night), "Stories of the Cyan Robe" (Liang Hao Received Number One Scholar at the Age of Eighty), "Stories of the White Robe" (Yuchi Gong Visits Xue Rengui), "Stories of the Green Robe" (Xiao He Chases Han Xin in the Moonlight) and "Stories of the Red Robe" (Liu Zhiyuan Struggles to Seize State Power). The repertoire of Beijing style derives from Pihuang Operas (Anhui Opera, Han Opera and Peking Opera), such as "A Fisherman's Struggle" and "Sitting in the Palace". There are two types of repertoire of Yunnan style: the first type is the plays concerning local historical stories written by local authors or artists, such as “Xue Erwang Jumped into the Pool”, “The Death-forcing Slope”, “Ningbei Consort” and “Chen Yuanyuan Became a Nun”; and the second type is the plays transplanted from operas of other places, such as “The Three Kingdoms”, “The Water Margin” and “The Red Mansion”. While rehearsing and performing traditional repertoire, artists of each generation are able to combine the characteristics of the times and the local conditions of Yunnan to compose and perform works that reflect the history and real life of the ethnic minorities in the border areas.

第 5 项：佤族清戏

佤族清戏《安安送米》剧照
the Stage Photo of "An'an Delivers Rice", a Qing Opera of the Wa Nationality

项目序号：736	项目编号：Ⅳ-135	公布时间：2008（第二批）	类别：传统戏剧
所属地区：云南省	类型：新增项目	申报地区或单位：云南省腾冲县	

清戏，又叫湖北高腔。明末清初，湖北人根据古老的青阳腔创造出了清戏这种新的戏曲形式。清代咸丰年之前，过境的商贾军民将湖北清戏带到地处古丝路要冲的云南省腾冲县甘蔗寨，在甘蔗寨佤族民众中传播开来，逐渐演变成佤族清戏。

佤族清戏是腾冲县唯一被列入中国少数民族剧种的地方戏剧，至今仍保留着早期清戏原始古朴的特色，被誉为“珍贵的民族剧种”。[①] 其声腔包括“九腔十三板”，这些曲调抑扬顿挫，悦耳动听，既善叙事，又善抒情，具有较强的艺术表现力和感染力。佤族清戏文辞优美，故事感人，情节生动，人物性格鲜明。流传下来的常演剧目有《姜姑刁嫂》《逐赶庞氏》《芦林相会》《安安送米》等十数折，均取材于汉族民间故事《三孝记》和《白鹤传》。[②]

Item 5: Qing Opera of the Wa Nationality

Item Serial Number: 736	Item ID Number: Ⅳ-135	Released Date: 2008 (Batch 2)	Category: Traditional Opera
Affiliated Province: Yunnan Province	Type: New Item	Application Province or Unit: Tengchong County, Yunnan Province	

① 段应宗、杨占全、李绍伟，《腾冲举办佤族清戏骨干培训班》，http://www.ynich.cn/view.php?id=1939&cat_id=11411，检索日期：2019 年 9 月 1 日。

② 《佤族清戏》，中国非物质文化遗产网，http://www.ihchina.cn/Article/Index/detail?id=13549，检索日期：2019 年 8 月 31 日。

Qing Opera is also called Hubei High Tone. At the end of the Ming Dynasty and the beginning of the Qing Dynasty, Hubei people created **Qing Opera**, a new form of opera, based on the ancient Qingyang Tone. Before the reign of Emperor Xianfeng of the Qing Dynasty, merchants, soldiers and civilians passing through brought **Hubei Qing Opera** to Ganzhe Stockaded Village in Tengchong County, Yunnan Province, located in the vital communications hub of the ancient Silk Road. It has been spread among the Wa people in Ganzhe Stockaded Village and has gradually evolved into **Qing Opera of the Wa Nationality**.

Qing Opera of the Wa Nationality is the only local opera listed in Chinese Ethnic Minority Operas in Tengchong County. Up to now, it still retains the primitive and simple characteristics of the early Qing Opera, acclaimed as "a precious ethnic opera". Its singing tones include "Nine Tones and Thirteen Boards". These tunes rise and fall in cadence, mellow and pleasing to the ear. They are both narrative and lyrical, with strong artistic expression and appeal. **Qing Opera of the Wa Nationality** boasts graceful librettos, touching stories, vivid plots and distinctive characters. There are several dozens of plays that have been handed down and performed often, such as "Aunt Jiang and Tricky Sister-in-law", "Driving Away the Person Surnamed Pang", "Meeting in a Copse of Reeds" and "An'an Delivers Rice". They all originated from the folk tales of the Han nationality, such as "Records of Three Kinds of Filial Piety" and "A Biography of the White Crane".

第 6 项：彝剧

彝剧《疯娘》剧照
the Stage Photo of "The Mad Mother", a Yi Opera

项目序号：737	项目编号：Ⅳ-136	公布时间：2008（第二批）	类别：传统戏剧
所属地区：云南省	类型：新增项目	申报地区或单位：云南省大姚县	

彝剧是楚雄彝族特有的地方民族戏剧，起源于大姚县昙华乡，主要流传于云南省楚雄彝族自治州的彝族聚居区。

彝剧真实地表现了彝族的社会生活，展现出彝人的民族精神、宗教信仰和价值取向。[①] 目前，彝剧表演还未形成一套完整的程式，也无严格的行当分工。最初是模拟生活动作和动物特征的简单表演，后从毕摩（彝族祭司）祭祀和唱《梅葛》的动作、声调、表情中吸收一些表演技巧，再从“打跳”中提取某些身段、步伐，变成节奏性和舞蹈性较强的表演技巧，发展为以歌、舞、乐、剧结合的表现形式，具有鲜明的民族特点。演出道具均为当地彝族人民常用的劳动工具，服装、头饰是彝族妇女手工精制而成。彝剧音乐由彝族流行的山歌小调、舞曲和器乐曲结合形成唱腔，称为“山歌体”，尚未形成固定的板腔和联曲体。主要伴奏乐器有笛子、三弦（或月琴）和芦笙。彝剧剧目有近百个，多是反映现实生活的现代戏，代表性剧目有《半夜羊叫》《曼嫫与玛若》《歌场两家亲》《查德恩达》《银锁》《掌火人》等。[②]

① 《彝剧》，中国非物质文化遗产网，http://www.ihchina.cn/Article/Index/detail?id=13550，检索日期：2019 年 9 月 1 日。

② 《彝剧》，云南非物质文化遗产保护网，http://www.ynich.cn/view.php?id=1153&cat_id=11111，检索日期：2019 年 9 月 1 日。

Item 6: Yi Opera

Item Serial Number: 737	Item ID Number: Ⅳ-136	Released Date: 2008 (Batch 2)	Category: Traditional Opera
Affiliated Province: Yunnan Province	Type: New Item	Application Province or Unit: Dayao County, Yunnan Province	

Yi Opera is a local ethnic opera unique to the Yi nationality in Chuxiong, with Tanhua Township of Dayao County as its birthplace. It is mainly spread in areas inhabited by the Yi people in Chuxiong Yi Autonomous Prefecture of Yunnan Province.

Yi Opera truly expresses the social life of the Yi nationality, reflecting the national spirit, religious beliefs and value orientation of the Yi people. At present, its performance has not yet formed a complete set of procedure, and also has no strict division of the types of roles. At first, it was a simple performance that imitated daily life actions and animal features. Later, it has absorbed some performance skills from the movements, tones and expressions of the sacrificial ceremony presided over by Bimo (the priest of the Yi nationality) as well as the singing of *Meige Epic*, and then has extracted some postures and steps from "Datiao Dance", forming performance skills with more rhythmicity and dances. Then it has developed into a form of expression integrating singing, dancing, music and opera, with distinctive ethnic characteristics. All performance props are tools commonly used by the local Yi people, and the costumes and headwear are handmade exquisitely by the Yi women. The music of **Yi Opera** forms a singing tone by combining mountain-song ditties, dance music and instrumental music that are popular among the Yi people, known as "the mountain-song style", which has not yet formed a fixed Banqiang Tone or the joint-tune style. The main accompaniment instruments are flutes, Sanxian (a three-stringed plucked musical instrument) or Yueqin (a four-stringed plucked musical instrument with a full-moon-shaped sound box), and Lusheng Musical Instruments. There are nearly one hundred plays of **Yi Opera**, most of which are modern plays that reflect real life. Representative ones are "Sheep's Bleating in the Middle of the Night", "Manmo and Maruo", "Two Relatives by Marriage in the Song Field", "Chade Enda", "Silver Locks", "The Person in Charge of Fire", etc.

第 7 项：白剧

白剧《情暖苍山》剧照
the Stage Photo of "Warm Love in the Cangshan Mountain", a Bai Opera

项目序号：738	项目编号：Ⅳ-137	公布时间：2008（第二批）	类别：传统戏剧
所属地区：云南省	类型：新增项目	申报地区或单位：云南省大理白族自治州	

白剧是大理白族的一个古老剧种，吸收了京剧、滇剧、花灯和川剧等的表演手段及本民族和其他民族的舞蹈语汇，既保持古老剧种的民族特色，又注重戏曲的程式化、生活化，流传于大理白族自治州及丽江市部分白族聚居区。

白剧音乐包括唱腔音乐和伴奏音乐两部分。唱腔音乐由吹吹腔和大本曲两大类组成，同时还吸收改编了部分民间乐曲。伴奏音乐包括传统吹吹腔的唢呐曲牌、打击乐和大本曲的三弦曲牌，亦吸收了部分民间吹打乐和歌舞乐。白剧唱词多采用白族"山花体"格式，即"三七一五"或"七七一五"，人称"七句半"。用白语或汉语演唱，道白用"汉语白音"。角色按生、旦、净、丑行当扮演各种人物。白剧只用红、黑、白、蓝、紫五色的独特脸谱，以区分不同的人物性格。伴奏乐队除保留唢呐和三弦两种传统乐器外，现已发展为以民族乐器为主的中西混合乐队。白剧剧目丰富，目前收集到大约 400 多个，其中传统剧目 300 多个，改编剧目 130 余个。主要有袍带戏、生活剧、民间传说故事剧、新编历史剧和现代戏五类。代表剧目有《红色三弦》《苍山红梅》《望夫云》《阿盖公主》《情暖苍山》《苍山会盟》《白月亮白姐姐》等。[①]

Item 7: Bai Opera

Item Serial Number: 738	Item ID Number: Ⅳ-137	Released Date: 2008 (Batch 2)	Category: Traditional Opera
Affiliated Province: Yunnan Province	Type: New Item	Application Province or Unit: Dali Bai Autonomous Prefecture, Yunnan Province	

① 《白剧》，云南非物质文化遗产保护网，http://www.ynich.cn/view.php?id=1154&cat_id=11111，检索日期：2019 年 9 月 1 日。

Bai Opera is an ancient opera of the Bai nationality in Dali. It has absorbed the performance techniques of Peking Opera, Yunnan Opera, the Lantern Opera, Sichuan Opera, etc. as well as the dance vocabulary of the Bai nationality and other nationalities. It not only retains the ethnic characteristics of the ancient opera, but also pays attention to the stylization and secularization of the opera. It is spread in Dali Bai Autonomous Prefecture and some areas inhabited by the Bai nationality in Lijiang City.

The music of **Bai Opera** includes two parts: vocal music and accompaniment music. The vocal music includes two categories: Chuichui Tone and Daben Tune. At the same time, it has also absorbed and adapted part of folk music. The accompaniment music includes Suona Qupai (the tune name of a melody) of the traditional Chuichui Tone, percussion music and Sanxian Qupai (the tune name of a melody) of Daben Tune, which has also absorbed part of folk wind and percussion music as well as song-and-dance music. The librettos of **Bai Opera** mostly adopt the format of "the mountain-flower style" of the Bai nationality, that is, there are seven words in the first three lines respectively and five words in the fourth line, or there are seven words in the first seven lines respectively and five words in the eighth line, which is called "seven and a half sentences". **Bai Opera** is sung in the Bai language or Chinese, while Daobai (the spoken part in an opera) is performed in the Chinese versions of the Bai accents. Actors and actresses play the role of different characters according to the role types of Sheng Character (a male role in Chinese opera, usually referring to the role with a beard or a young man), Dan Character (a female role), Jing Character (a male role in Chinese opera, usually with rough and bold personalities) and Chou Character (a clown). **Bai Opera** only uses the unique facial makeup in five colors of red, black, white, blue and purple to distinguish different personalities of characters. In addition to retaining the two traditional instruments of Suona Horn (a woodwind instrument) and Sanxian (a three-stringed plucked musical instrument), the accompaniment band has developed into a mixed Chinese and Western band dominated by ethnic instruments up to now. The repertoire of **Bai Opera** is rich, and currently more than 400 plays have been collected, among which more than 300 are traditional plays and more than 130 are adapted ones. They are mainly divided into five types, Paodai operas (the operas in which performers wear the Python Robe and the Jade Belt), life operas, folktale operas, newly-adapted historical operas and modern operas. Representative ones are "The Red Sanxian (a three-stringed plucked musical instrument)", "The Red Plum Blossom in the Cangshan Mountain", "Wangfu Cloud", "Princess Agai", "Warm Love in the Cangshan Mountain", "The Alliance in the Cangshan Mountain", "The White Moon and the White Sister", etc.

云南壮剧剧照
the Stage Photo of Zhuang Opera in Yunnan Province

第 8 项：壮剧

项目序号：226	项目编号：Ⅳ-82	公布时间：2008（第二批）	类别：传统戏剧
所属地区：云南省	类型：扩展项目	申报地区或单位：云南省文山壮族苗族自治州	

壮剧流传于云南省文山壮族苗族自治州，主要有富宁土戏、广南沙戏和文山乐西土戏三个分支，各分支起源不尽相同。其中，富宁土戏形成最早，已有300多年的历史，云南壮剧最早的唱腔形式即源自富宁土戏；广南沙戏和文山乐西土戏均形成于清光绪年间。

壮剧在融汇壮族山歌、舞蹈、音乐、说唱和民间故事等艺术形式的基础上不断吸收外来戏剧的长处，经过长时间的发展，成为成熟的地方戏曲剧种。壮剧最初的形式是“单分”（念歌），后逐渐演变为“板凳戏”（几名歌手坐唱），后来演变为多幕戏。[①] 其伴奏乐器有土锣、土鼓、钹、土二胡、土三弦、笛子和唢呐等。在壮族最隆重的“陇端节”[②] 上，壮剧是必演节目。其剧目涉及当地壮族群众日常生活、节日庆典、婚丧嫁娶等方面的内容，体现了云南壮族人民的精神追求和理想信仰。[③] 代表性剧目有《螺蛳姑娘》《张四姐下凡》《宝葫芦》《红铜鼓》《金花和银花》《莫一大王》《百鸟衣》等。

① 《富宁县壮剧之乡》，云南非物质文化遗产保护网，http://www.ynich.cn/view-ml-11111-1210.html，检索日期：2024 年 3 月 13 日。

② “陇端节”被称为壮族传统的“情人节”。

③ 《壮剧》，中国非物质文化遗产网，http://www.ihchina.cn/Article/Index/detail?id=13363，检索日期：2019 年 9 月 1 日。

Item 8: Zhuang Opera

Item Serial Number: 226	Item ID Number: Ⅳ-82	Released Date: 2008 (Batch 2)	Category: Traditional Opera
Affiliated Province: Yunnan Province	Type: Extended Item	Application Province or Unit: Wenshan Zhuang and Miao Autonomous Prefecture, Yunnan Province	

Zhuang Opera is spread in Wenshan Zhuang and Miao Autonomous Prefecture of Yunnan Province, having three major branches of Funing Local Opera, Guangnan Shaxi Opera and Wenshan Lexi Local Opera, each of which has different origins. Among them, Funing Local Opera came into existence the earliest, with a history of more than 300 years. The earliest singing tone of **Zhuang Opera** in Yunnan Province originated from Funing Local Opera. Guangnan Shaxi Opera and Wenshan Lexi Local Opera both came into being during the reign of Emperor Guangxu of the Qing Dynasty.

Based on the integration of the artistic forms of the mountain songs, dances, music, talking and singing, folk tales, etc. of the Zhuang nationality, **Zhuang Opera** continues to absorb the strengths of other operas. After a long period of development, it has become a mature local opera. The original form of **Zhuang Opera** was "Danfen" (reciting lyrics). Later, it gradually evolved into "the Bench Opera" (with several singers sitting and singing), and then developed into a multi-act opera. Its accompaniment instruments include local gongs, local drums, cymbals, local Erhu (a two-stringed bowed instrument), local Sanxian (a three-stringed plucked musical instrument), flutes and Suona Horn (a woodwind instrument). At the grandest "Longduan Festival" of the Zhuang nationality, **Zhuang Opera** is a must program. Its repertoire involves the content of the daily life, festival celebrations, weddings and funerals of the local Zhuang people, reflecting the spiritual pursuit and ideal belief of the Zhuang People in Yunnan Province. Representative ones are "The Spiral Shell Girl", "The Fourth Sister of Zhang Descends to the World", "The Treasured Gourd", "The Red Bronze Drum", "The Golden Flower and the Silver Flower", "King Moyi", "Hundred-bird Clothes", etc.

第 9 项：关索戏

关索戏剧照
the Stage Photo of Guansuo Opera

项目序号：1113	项目编号：Ⅳ-151	公布时间：2011（第三批）	类别：传统戏剧
所属地区：云南省	类型：新增项目	申报地区或单位：云南省澄江县	

关索戏初为古代用以驱邪逐疫的傩祭仪式，后发展为娱神娱人的傩戏，常逢年过节演出，多是白天在广场、院坝表演。流行于云南省澄江县阳宗镇小屯村，已有 300 多年的历史。[①] 小屯原名先锋营，相传诸葛亮平定南中时，命关羽之子关索为先锋，后屯兵于小屯村。故有关索戏是随军传入澄江之说。

关索戏的行当只有生、旦、净三行，而旦角仅有两人（鲍三娘、百花公主），且为男扮女装，演员不用擦胭脂画脸谱，只戴面具。演出有一套完整的程序：演出前先到灵峰寺祭祀药王，然后进行踩村、踩街、踩家、点将和辞神等驱鬼逐疫、消灾祈神等傩祭仪式。关索戏专演三国故事，其中以演蜀汉人物刘备、孔明、关羽、张飞、关索和鲍三娘等角色为主，主要演员有 20 人，加上马童、龙套、锣鼓手等共有 36 人。演员扮演固定角色，实行父传子、子传孙的家庭传承方式。演戏时，演员把各人物的木制面具戴在头上，扮演不同角色。常见剧目有 20 多个，如《古城会》《战长沙》《长坂坡》《过五关斩六将》《三请孔明》《三战吕布》《收周仓》《夜战马超》《花关索战三娘》等。戏开场时，先由马童和小军出场表现剧情，有唱有打，唱中夹白。无弦乐，无伴唱，只用锣鼓伴奏。唱、白都用阳宗本地方言，音乐唱腔有五字板、七字板、十字板、大刀腔、哭板、长板、短板和流水板等，转板换调均用锣鼓指挥。关索戏有浓厚的古朴之风。[②]

① 《关索戏》，中国非物质文化遗产网，http://www.ihchina.cn/Article/Index/detail?id=13565，检索日期：2019 年 8 月 1 日。

② 《小屯村关索戏》，云南非物质文化遗产保护网，http://www.ynich.cn/view.php?id=1145&cat_id=11111，检索日期：2019 年 9 月 1 日。

Item 9: Guansuo Opera

Item Serial Number: 1113	Item ID Number: Ⅳ-151	Released Date: 2011 (Batch3)	Category: Traditional Opera
Affiliated Province: Yunnan Province	Type: New Item	Application Province or Unit: Chengjiang County, Yunnan Province	

Guansuo Opera was originally an ancient Nuo sacrificial ceremony used to drive away evil spirits and epidemics, and later developed into Nuo Opera to entertain the gods and people. It is often performed on New Year's Day or other festivals, mostly in squares and courtyards during the day. It is popular in Xiaotun Village, Yangzong Township, Chengjiang County, Yunnan Province, with a history of more than 300 years. Xiaotun was formerly called Vanguard Camp. Legend has it that when Zhuge Liang pacified Nanzhong, he ordered Guan Suo, the son of Guan Yu, to be the vanguard, who later was garrisoned in Xiaotun Village. Therefore, it is said that **Guansuo Opera** was introduced into Chengjiang with the army.

Guansuo Opera only has three types of roles, namely Sheng Character (a male role in Chinese opera, usually referring to the role with a beard or a young man), Dan Character (a female role) and Jing Character (a male role in Chinese opera, usually with rough and bold personalities). There are only two figures for Dan Character (a female role), that is, Bao Sanniang and Princess Baihua, who are usually acted by males. Actors don't need to wear facial makeup, but only wear masks. Its performance has a complete set of procedures: before the performance, actors first go to the Lingfeng Temple to offer sacrifices to the God of Medicine, and then carry out the Nuo sacrificial ceremonies of parading in the village, on the street and to each family, as well as appointing actors to particular roles and bidding farewell to the god in order to expel ghosts, get rid of plagues, dispel disasters and pray for the god. **Guansuo Opera** specializes in the performances of the stories in the Three Kingdoms. Among them, most are the performances of acting the characters in the Kingdom of Shu Han, such as Liu Bei, Kongming, Guan Yu, Zhang Fei, Guan Suo and Bao Sanniang. There are 20 major actors, plus stable boys, utility men, and gong-and-drums players etc., with a total of 36 ones. Actors play fixed roles and adopt the way of family inheritance, that is, passing from fathers on to sons and from sons on to grandsons. During the performance, actors wear wooden masks of various characters on their heads to play different roles. There are more than 20 pieces of frequently-performed repertoire, such as “Meeting in the Ancient City”, “Fighting in Changsha”, “Changban Slope”, “Surmounting Numerous Difficulties”, “Inviting Kongming Three Times”, “Fighting against Lü Bu Three Times”, “Accepting Zhoucang as a Follower”, “Fighting against Ma Chao at Night” and “Hua Guansuo Fights against Bao Sanniang”. At the beginning of the opera, the stable boys and junior soldiers first appear on the stage to show the plot, singing while fighting, with the speaking part interspersed in the singing. **Guansuo Opera** has no string music or backing vocals, only accompanied by gongs and drums. Its singing and speaking parts are both performed in the local dialect of Yangzong Township, and its musical singing tones include five-character style, seven-character style, ten-character style, Dadao tone, the Crying Board, the Long Board, the Short Board and the Water-flowing Board. The conversion of tunes and tones is directed by means of gongs and drums. **Guansuo Opera** has a style of strong primitive simplicity.

腾冲皮影戏《西游记》
Tengchong Shadow Play of "The Journey to the West"

第 10 项：皮影戏（腾冲皮影戏）

项目序号：235	项目编号：Ⅳ-91	公布时间：2011（第三批）	类别：传统戏剧
所属地区：云南省	类型：扩展项目	申报地区或单位：云南省腾冲县	

腾冲皮影戏是一种云南腾冲民间喜闻乐见的传统艺术形式，至今有六七百年历史，相传明初由来自江南、湖广和四川等地屯军边疆的移民带到腾冲，主要流传于云南省腾冲县一带，当地人又称"灯影子""皮人戏""土电影"。

影人多用牛皮制成，形体较大，高约 50 厘米，造型朴实。受地域和语言差异的影响，腾冲皮影戏分为"东腔"和"西腔"两个流派："东腔"出自腾越镇洞山村和勐连村一带，以图像高大、旋律优雅、气氛庄重闻名；"西腔"出自固东镇、明光镇和瑞滇乡一带，以图像精巧、节奏明快，情绪昂扬著称。[①] 腾冲皮影戏的唱腔有男腔、女腔、走马腔、碱云腔和悲板等。其剧目丰富，多取材于传奇、演义及民间故事等，尤以三国戏、列国戏、封神戏、水浒戏、西游戏、说唐、说岳、薛家将和杨家将等居多。著名剧目有《封神演义》《三国演义》《说唐》《杨门女将》《西游记》等。腾冲皮影戏的演出组织以村为单位，叫作"堂"，相当于一个村寨的皮影戏组，影响力最大的是固东镇刘家寨的皮影班子。

① 《皮影戏（腾冲皮影戏）》，中国非物质文化遗产网，http://www.ihchina.cn/Article/Index/detail?id=13424，检索日期：2019 年 8 月 31 日。

Item 10: the Shadow Play (Tengchong Shadow Play)

Item Serial Number: 235	Item ID Number: Ⅳ-91	Released Date: 2011 (Batch 3)	Category: Traditional Opera
Affiliated Province: Yunnan Province	Type: Extended Item	Application Province or Unit: Tengchong County, Yunnan Province	

Tengchong Shadow Play is a traditional art form popular among the people of Tengchong County, Yunnan Province, with a history of six to seven hundred years up to now. According to legend, it was introduced to Tengchong by soldiers who migrated from regions south of the Yangtze River, Hubei and Hunan provinces, as well as Sichuan, and were garrisoned in the border areas in the early Ming Dynasty. It is mainly circulated in Tengchong County, Yunnan Province, also called "the Lamp Shadow", "the Leather-figure Opera" and "the Indigenous Movie" by local people.

The shadow figures are mostly made of cowhide. They are large in physique and simple in modelling, about 50 cm high. Affected by regional and linguistic differences, **Tengchong Shadow Play** can be divided into two schools: "the East Tone" and "the West Tone". "The East Tone", coming from Dongshan Village and Menglian Village of Tengyue Township, is famous for its tall images, elegant melody and solemn atmosphere. "The West Tone", coming from Gudong, Mingguang and Ruidian townships, is famous for its exquisite images, lively rhythm and high spirits. The singing tones of **Tengchong Shadow Play** include male tone, female tone, Zouma tone, Jianyun tone and Beiban tone. Its repertoire is rich, mostly based on legends, historical romances, folk tales, etc., especially operas of the Three Kingdoms, operas of various states, operas of the Legend of Deification, operas of the Water Margin, operas of the Journey to the West, Comments on the Tang Dynasty, Comments on Yue Fei, Generals of the Xue Family and Generals of the Yang Family being in the majority. The famous ones are "The Legend of Deification", "The Romance of the Three Kingdoms", "Comments on the Tang Dynasty", "Female Generals of the Yang Family", "The Journey to the West", etc. The unit of performing **Tengchong Shadow Play** is villages, known as "Tang", which is equal to a shadow-play team of one stockaded village. The most influential one is the shadow-play troupe in Liujia Stockaded Village of Gudong Township.

第五章 曲艺

Chapter Five

Quyi (a general term for all Chinese talking-and-singing art forms)

第 1 项：傣族章哈

傣族章哈《乌莎巴罗》剧照

the Stage Photo of "Wusha Baluo", Zhangha of the Dai Nationality

项目序号：280	项目编号：Ⅴ-44	公布时间：2006（第一批）	类别：曲艺
所属地区：云南省	类型：新增项目	申报地区或单位：云南省西双版纳傣族自治州	

傣族章哈是傣族传统的曲艺表演形式，主要流传于云南省西双版纳傣族自治州及思茅市江城、孟连、景谷等县的傣族村寨。章哈既是歌手称谓，也是作为曲艺表演形式的曲种名称。

章哈的演出形式有独唱和对唱两种，其中对唱有赛唱的性质。演出因伴奏乐器不同，也分为两种形式：一种以傣族拉弦乐器玎伴奏，称作“哈赛玎”，演唱内容多为山歌、情歌，多倾诉小伙子对姑娘的爱慕之情；另一种以单簧吹管乐器筚伴奏，称作“哈塞筚”。章哈的演唱既有即兴演唱，也有程式化的祝福歌、祈祷歌，还有固定本子的叙事长歌等。其曲调与唱词语调联系密切，朗诵性与歌唱性有机结合。章哈在傣族社会生活中有着不可替代的作用，傣族新年、关门节、开门节、祭寨神、赕佛及贺新房、婚嫁礼仪、孩子满月等喜庆场合都要请艺人演唱章哈。[①]章哈曲目众多，保存了诸多傣族最原始古老的歌谣、神话和传说，丰富了傣族群众的精神文化生活，起着儿童启蒙教育、倡导社会伦理道德、宣传生产知识等寓教于乐的重要作用。[②]

Item 1: Zhangha of the Dai Nationality

Item Serial Number: 280	Item ID Number: Ⅴ-44	Released Date: 2006 (Batch 1)	Category: Quyi (a general term for all Chinese talking-and-singing art forms)
Affiliated Province: Yunnan Province	Type: New Item	Application Province or Unit: Xishuangbanna Dai Autonomous Prefecture, Yunnan Province	

Zhangha of the Dai Nationality is a traditional performance form of Quyi (a general term for all Chinese talking-and-singing art forms) of the Dai nationality. It is primarily circulated in Xishuangbanna Dai Autonomous Prefecture, and the stockaded villages inhabited by the Dai people in counties of Jiangcheng, Menglian, Jinggu, etc. of Simao City, Yunnan Province. **Zhangha** is not only the name of the singer, but also the genre name of Quyi performance form.

The performance forms of **Zhangha** include solo singing and antiphonal singing, among which antiphonal singing has the nature of competition. Due to different accompaniment instruments, its performance is also divided into two forms. One is called “Hasaiding”, which is performed to the accompaniment of Ding, a stringed instrument of the Dai nationality. The content of its sing is mostly mountain songs and love songs, which mainly express young men’s adoration for girls. The other is called “Hasaibi”, performed to the accompaniment of Bi, a single-reed wind instrument. The performance of **Zhangha** includes impromptu singing,

① 《傣族章哈》，中国非物质文化遗产网，http://www.ihchina.cn/Article/Index/detail?id=13665，检索日期：2019 年 8 月 31 日。

② 《傣族章哈》，云南非物质文化遗产保护网，http://www.ynich.cn/view.php?id=1244&cat_id=11110，检索日期：2019 年 8 月 31 日。

stylized blessing songs and praying songs, as well as long narrative songs with fixed scripts. Its tunes and libretto intonations are closely related to each other, which has integrated its reciting nature and singing nature organically. **Zhangha** plays an irreplaceable role in the social life of the Dai people. On such festive occasions of the Dai nationality as the New Year, the Door-closing Festival, the Door-opening Festival, offering sacrifices to gods of stockaded villages, offering sacrifices to the Buddha, as well as celebrating the new house, wedding ceremonies and a baby's completion of its first month of life, they will invite artists to perform **Zhangha**. **Zhangha** has numerous pieces of repertoire, which have preserved many of the most primitive and ancient ballads, myths and legends of the Dai nationality, and have enriched the spiritual and cultural life of the Dai people, playing an important role in education through entertainment, such as enlightening and educating children, advocating social ethics and morals, and publicizing production knowledge.

第六章 传统体育、游艺与杂技

Chapter Six Traditional Sports, Recreations and Acrobatics

第 1 项：摔跤（彝族摔跤）

彝族摔跤

Wrestling of the Yi Nationality

项目序号：793	项目编号：Ⅵ-21	公布时间：2011（第三批）	类别：传统体育、游艺与杂技
所属地区：云南省	类型：扩展项目	申报地区或单位：云南省石林彝族自治县	

摔跤作为一项传统体育活动，在我国各民族中都比较常见，在云南省尤以彝族为甚。其中，石林县和元谋县彝族摔跤活动最受群众欢迎。

云南彝族摔跤与国际自由式摔跤相似，比赛一般采用三局两胜制。运动员双手从两侧抓住对方腰带，通过抱腰、抱单腿、过背、穿腿和夹臂翻等动作，将对方摔倒双肩着地为胜。败者退下，换另外运动员上场。胜者直至无人与其较量，被誉为“大力士”，并奖红布数丈。石林彝族自治县彝族（撒尼）同胞酷爱摔跤运动，每逢火把节和其他喜庆节日，各村寨常要开展摔跤比赛。摔跤赛的目的：一是为了祈求风调雨顺、五谷丰登；二是为了增强团结，增加节日喜庆气氛；三是为了锻炼身体，培养勇敢精神。元谋县小凉山乡彝族摔跤，彝语称为“格”，表示力量、技术的意思，是一项古老的为广大青少年男子喜爱的体育运动，能强健身体，鼓舞斗志，增进民族团结和社会和谐。摔跤表现了彝族人民的勇敢坚强和不屈不挠精神，与彝族自古尚武的观念和习俗密切相关。①

Item 1: Wrestling (Wrestling of the Yi Nationality)

Item Serial Number: 793	Item ID Number: Ⅵ-21	Released Date: 2011 (Batch 3)	Category: Traditional Sports, Recreations and Acrobatics
Affiliated Province: Yunnan Province	Type: Extended Item	Application Province or Unit: Shilin Yi Autonomous County, Yunnan Province	

As a traditional sport, wrestling is relatively common among all ethnic groups in China, especially the Yi nationality in Yunnan Province. Among them, **Wrestling of the Yi Nationality** in Shilin and Yuanmou counties are the most popular among the masses.

Wrestling of the Yi Nationality in Yunnan is similar to international freestyle wrestling, and the match generally adopts the best of three games. Athletes grasp the opponent's belt from both sides with both hands, and knock the opponent down with his shoulders touching the ground to win the game through actions of holding the waist, holding one leg, crossing the back, flinging the leg, clamping one arm to flip, etc. The loser withdraws from the match and another athlete participates in it. The winner is hailed as "Hercules" until no one can compete with him, and then he is rewarded with red cloth of several *zhang* (a Chinese unit of length, with one *zhang* roughly equal to 131 inches). The Yi people (the Sani branch) in Shilin Yi Autonomous County love wrestling. Whenever there comes the Torch Festival and other festive festivals, wrestling matches will often be held in all stockaded villages.

① 《摔跤（彝族摔跤）》，中国非物质文化遗产网，http://www.ihchina.cn/Article/Index/detail?id=13818，检索日期：2019 年 8 月 31 日。

There are three purposes: first, to pray for timely wind and rain as well as a bumper grain harvest; second, to enhance unity and increase the festive atmosphere; and third, to exercise the body and cultivate the spirit of bravery. **Wrestling of the Yi Nationality** in Xiaoliangshan Township of Yuanmou County is called "Ge" in the Yi language, which means strength and technique. It is an ancient sport loved by a large number of male teenagers, which can strengthen the body, inspire the fighting spirit, and promote national unity and social harmony. Wrestling shows the brave, strong and indomitable spirit of the Yi people, and is closely related to the concept and custom of the Yi nationality in advocating martial arts since ancient times.

第七章 传统美术

Chapter Seven
Traditional Fine Arts

第 1 项：纳西族东巴画

纳西族东巴画《神路图》
A Dongba Painting of the Naxi Nationality: The Road of God

项目序号：312	项目编号：Ⅶ-13	公布时间：2006（第一批）	类别：传统美术
所属地区：云南省	类型：新增项目	申报地区或单位：云南省丽江市	

东巴画是纳西族东巴文化艺术的一项重要内容，流传在云南省丽江市古城区和玉龙纳西族自治县。

东巴画以纳西族民间信奉的神灵、传说中的祖先及动物等为描绘内容。

主要有经卷图画、木牌画、纸牌画和卷轴画等形式。经卷图画包括东巴图画文字、封面装帧画、经书扉页和题图等。木牌画是在简易木牌面上绘制出的图像，主要用于纳西族的祭祀活动。纸牌画以自制的土纸为载体，主要分两类：一类是绘制的神像，或竖于神坛供人祭拜，或戴在祭司头顶；另一类是绘画谱典，或用作绘画者的规范，或用作绘画传承时的教本。卷轴画多绘于麻布或土布上，四周用蓝布装裱，上有天杆，下设地轴，绘画内容多为纳西族信奉的神祇。卷轴画的代表作《神路图》全长十几米，由一百多幅分格连环画组成，直幅长卷上共描绘了三百六十多个人物及动物形象，反映了纳西族灵魂不灭的生命意识和完善人生的伦理观念。东巴绘画主要以木片、东巴纸、麻布等为材料，用自制的竹笔蘸松烟墨勾画轮廓，然后敷以各种自然颜色，绚丽多彩，历经数百年而不褪色。其绘画形象具有强烈的原始意味，以线条表现为主，并不注重事物外部的形体比例，但朴实生动，野趣横生，色彩多用原色，鲜艳夺目。许多画面亦字亦画，保留了浓郁的象形文字书写特征。①

Item 1: Dongba Paintings of the Naxi Nationality

Item Serial Number: 312	Item ID Number: Ⅶ-13	Released Date: 2006 (Batch 1)	Category: Traditional Fine Arts
Affiliated Province: Yunnan Province	Type: New Item	Application Province or Unit: Lijiang City, Yunnan Province	

Dongba Paintings are an important part of the Dongba culture and art of the Naxi nationality. They are circulated in Ancient City District of Lijiang City and Yulong Naxi Autonomous County in Yunnan Province.

Dongba Paintings depict the god worshipped by the Naxi people, the legendary ancestors, animals, etc. Their forms mainly include sutra scroll paintings, wooden board paintings, paper board paintings and scroll paintings. Sutra scroll paintings include Dongba pictographic writing, cover binding paintings, sutra title pages and title paintings. Wooden board paintings are images painted on the simply-made wooden board, mainly used for the Naxi people's sacrificial activities. Paper board paintings use homemade paper as the carrier. They are mainly divided into two kinds:

① 《纳西族东巴画》，中国非物质文化遗产网，http://www.ihchina.cn/Article/Index/detail?id=13912，检索日期：2019 年 7 月 30 日。

one kind is the painted deity statues, which are either placed on the sacred altar for people to worship or worn on the heads of priests; the other kind is model paintings, which serve as standards of painters or teaching materials for the inheritance of paintings. Scroll paintings are mostly painted on linen or homespun cloth, mounted with blue cloth around, with a sky pole on the top and an earth axis on the bottom. The painting content is mostly deities worshiped by the Naxi people. The masterpiece of scroll paintings, The Road of God, is over ten meters in length and consists of more than one hundred divided serial pictures. On the long scroll for vertical hanging, more than 360 images of figures and animals are painted, reflecting the Naxi people's life consciousness of the immortality of the soul and their ethical concept of improving life. Wood chips, Dongba paper, linen, etc. are the main materials of **Dongba Paintings**. Painters use homemade bamboo pens dipped in pine smoke ink to outline the contours, and then apply various natural colors, which are brilliant and colorful, and will not fade for hundreds of years. The painting images have a strong primitive flavor, mainly expressed by using lines without the consideration of the external proportion of objects. They are simple and vivid, wild and interesting, with primary colors used, bright and eye-catching. Many picture planes are both written words and paintings, retaining a strong calligraphic feature of hieroglyphic writing.

傣族剪纸傣女
Paper Cutting of the Dai Nationality: A Woman of the Dai Nationality

第 2 项：傣族剪纸

项目序号：315	项目编号：Ⅶ-16	公布时间：2006（第一批）	类别：传统美术
所属地区：云南省	类型：新增项目	申报地区或单位：云南省潞西市	

傣族剪纸最早起源于傣族祭祀仪式所用的纸幡，后在佛教文化和中原文化影响下逐步发展，形成完善的剪纸并被广泛应用于祭祀、赕佛、丧葬、喜庆及居家装饰等方面。主要流行于云南省德宏傣族景颇族自治州潞西市。

潞西傣族剪纸以特制的剪刀、刻刀、凿子和锤子为工具。其剪刀和刻刀具有尖、利、仄、薄的特点，一般可剪八层纸；凿子和锤子有稳、钻、灵、活的特点，一次可凿五十余层纸。傣族剪纸分“剪”与“凿”两种方法，剪无需稿样，随手可剪；凿则需稿样，按样制作。傣族剪纸的主要制品为扎、董、佛幡、挂灯、吊幢等，多用以装饰佛殿的门窗、佛伞、佛幡及演出道具、节日彩棚、泼水龙亭等。傣族剪纸内容多与傣族所信仰的南部上座部佛教有关，涉及佛经故事、民间传说和边疆风物特产等，具有浓厚的生活气息和乡土风味。常见图形有龙凤、孔雀、大象、狮子、麒麟、马鹿、骏马、游鱼及各种奇兽异鸟，也有糯粘花、荷花、玫瑰花、菊花、茶花、杜鹃等花木，还有亭台楼阁、佛塔寺庙等建筑，形象生动。①

Item 2: Paper Cutting of the Dai Nationality

Item Serial Number: 315	Item ID Number: Ⅶ-16	Released Date: 2006 (Batch 1)	Category: Traditional Fine Arts

① 《剪纸（傣族剪纸）》，中国非物质文化遗产网，http://www.ihchina.cn/Article/Index/detail?id=13933，检索日期：2019 年 8 月 31 日。

Affiliated Province: Yunnan Province	Type: New Item	Application Province or Unit: Luxi City, Yunnan Province

Paper Cutting of the Dai Nationality originated from the Paper-made Soul-summoning Banners used in the sacrificial ceremonies of the Dai nationality. Later, under the influence of Buddhist culture and the culture of the Central Plains, it gradually developed and became a perfect art of **Paper Cutting**, widely applied to sacrificial offering, offering sacrifices to the Buddha, funerals, festive celebrations, home decoration, etc. It is mainly popular in Luxi City, Dehong Dai and Jingpo Autonomous Prefecture, Yunnan Province.

Paper Cutting of the Dai Nationality in Luxi City takes specially-made scissors, gravers, chisels and hammers as tools. Scissors and gravers have the characteristics of being pointed, sharp, narrow and thin. Generally, eight layers of papers can be clipped. Chisels and hammers have the characteristics of stability, drilling and flexibility, and over fifty layers of papers can be chiseled at a time. The methods of **Paper Cutting of the Dai Nationality** are divided into two kinds: clipping and chiseling. Clipping does not require a draft, and artisans can clip at will; but chiseling requires a draft, and artisans can chisel according to the draft. The main products of **Paper Cutting of the Dai Nationality** are Zha (small triangle-shaped colorful paper flags used to worship Buddha), Dong (colorful paper cuttings), banners used in Buddhist temples, hanging lamps, Diaochuang (hanging streamers), etc. They are mostly used to decorate the doors and windows of the Buddhist Palace, Buddha umbrellas, banners used in Buddhist temples as well as performance props, festival colored tents, the Water-splashing Dragon Pavilion, etc. The content of **Paper Cutting of the Dai Nationality** is mostly related to Theravada Buddhism believed by the Dai people, involving Buddhist stories, folk legends, frontier scenery and specialties, etc. It has a strong atmosphere of life and local flavor. Common patterns include dragons and phoenixes, peacocks, elephants, lions, kylin, red deer, horses, fish and various exotic animals and birds, as well as glutinous flowers, lotus flowers, roses, chrysanthemums, camellias, rhododendrons and other flowers and trees, together with towers, pavilions, pagodas, temples and other buildings, being lifelike and vivid.

第3项：彝族（撒尼）刺绣

彝族（撒尼）刺绣
(Sani) Embroidery of the Yi Nationality

项目序号：854	项目编号：Ⅶ-78	公布时间：2008（第二批）	类别：传统美术
所属地区：云南省	类型：新增项目	申报地区或单位：云南省石林彝族自治县	

彝族（撒尼）刺绣也叫“撒尼十字绣”，是流行于云南省石林彝族自治县彝族支系撒尼人聚居区的一种民间刺绣艺术。

撒尼妇女自幼习绣。撒尼刺绣按布纹的经纬运针走线，以斜十字针组成花纹，有单挑、双面挑、素色挑和彩色挑等多种手法，绣制品多系背包、桌布、窗帘、花包头、花围腰、服饰花边等生活日用品。其花样主要有三弦花、八角花、八舞花、太阳花、羊角花、蝴蝶花、四瓣花、八瓣花、狗齿纹、火焰纹、石榴纹、青蛙纹、树纹以及一些简单的菱角、三角形、条纹等图案。撒尼刺绣主要分为两类：一是平绣：以较为细腻柔和的写实性花卉图案为主，多取材于现实生活环境中的花草纹样，如山茶花、杜鹃花、石榴花和荷花等；二是镂空贴花，又叫“抠花”，其构图粗犷抽象，花样有云纹和波浪纹等。彝族撒尼刺绣凝结着撒尼人对民族文化、生活价值观念、宗教信仰和对世界的认识。其针脚细密，图案构思巧妙，花样搭配丰富，是彝族撒尼人对大自然审美价值的直观反映。①

① 《彝族（撒尼）刺绣》，中国非物质文化遗产网，http://www.ihchina.cn/Article/Index/detail?id=14189，检索日期：2019年8月31日。

Item 3: (Sani) Embroidery of the Yi Nationality

Item Serial Number: 854	Item ID Number: Ⅶ-78	Released Date: 2008 (Batch 2)	Category: Traditional Fine Arts
Affiliated Province: Yunnan Province	Type: New Item	Application Province or Unit: Shilin Yi Autonomous County, Yunnan Province	

(Sani) Embroidery of the Yi Nationality, also called "Sani Cross Stitch", is a kind of folk embroidery art popular in areas inhabited by the Sani branch of the Yi nationality in Shilin Yi Autonomous County, Yunnan Province.

Sani women learn embroidery since their childhood. The needling and threading of Sani Embroidery are done according to the warp and weft of the cloth, and its patterns are formed by using oblique cross stitches. There are various methods, such as single-sided cross stitch, double-sided cross stitch, plain-color cross stitch and multicolored cross stitch. The embroidery products are mostly daily necessities, such as backpacks, tablecloths, curtains, floral turbans, floral aprons and lace of costumes. The patterns are mainly Sanxian-shaped flowers, octagonal flowers, Eight-dance Flowers, sunflowers, Sheep-horn Flowers, pansies, four-petal flowers, eight-petal flowers, dogtooth patterns, flame patterns, pomegranate patterns, frog patterns, tree patterns as well as some simple patterns of water caltrops, triangles, stripes, etc. Sani Embroidery is mainly divided into two categories. The first one is Flat Embroidery. It focuses on delicate and soft realistic floral patterns, which are mostly based on flowers in real-life environments, such as camellias, rhododendrons, pomegranate flowers and lotus flowers. The other one is Hollowing and Decaling. It is also called "Hollowing Flowers", the composition of which is rough and abstract, having patterns of cloud and waves, etc. **Sani Embroidery of the Yi Nationality** embodies the Sani people's understanding of ethnic culture, life values, religious beliefs and the world. Its stitches are fine, its pattern designs are ingenious and its pattern combinations are rich, which directly reflect the aesthetic value of nature of the Sani people of the Yi nationality.

第 4 项：建筑彩绘（白族民居彩绘）

白族民居彩绘
Colored Paintings on the Residential Houses of the Bai Nationality

项目序号：872	项目编号：Ⅶ-96	公布时间：2008（第二批）	类别：传统美术
所属地区：云南省	类型：新增项目	申报地区或单位：云南省大理市	

白族民居彩绘流行于云南省大理市及周边白族地区，是大理白族文化的一朵奇葩，不仅用于神祠、庙宇和大型古建筑群的装饰，而且广泛应用于白族民居建筑。

大理境内的白族建筑多为土木结构，往往呈现青砖、白墙、灰瓦的外观。与此相协调，建筑彩绘的色彩也以黑、白、灰为主，着重突出素白这一白族民居建筑的主体色调。白族民居多在大门、照壁、山墙、腰线和龙马角等部位饰以精致的彩绘，其中香草纹、如意云纹和回纹三种图案出现最多，成为彩绘中最具民族特色的部分。彩绘工艺独具特色，最讲究彩绘的打底工序。木结构建筑一般多用猪血、桐油和石灰调和而成的猪血灰打底；泥砖墙上则用纯质熟石膏与白棉纸拌和，制成“纸筋灰”抹在需要彩绘的部位，待半干时再进行彩绘，这样可以保证彩绘不容易褪色。彩绘颜料多以矿物质颜料为主。[①]民居彩绘在以其独特的色彩和图案装饰房屋的同时，也被赋予了祛邪避灾，祈祥求福等丰富含义。白族民居彩绘是白族建筑艺术的精华，深受汉文化影响，将北方建筑的恢弘大气和南方建筑的精巧别致有机地融为一体，成为白族文化与汉族文化交流的印证。[②]

① 《白族民居彩绘》，云南非物质文化遗产保护网，http://www.ynich.cn/view.php?id=1144&cat_id=11111，检索日期：2019 年 8 月 31 日。

② 《建筑彩绘（白族民居彩绘）》，中国非物质文化遗产网，http://www.ihchina.cn/Article/Index/detail?id=14228，检索日期：2019 年 8 月 31 日。

Item 4: Architectural Colored Paintings (Colored Paintings on the Residential Houses of the Bai Nationality)

Item Serial Number: 872	Item ID Number: Ⅶ-96	Released Date: 2008 (Batch 2)	Category: Traditional Fine Arts
Affiliated Province: Yunnan Province	Type: New Item	Application Province or Unit: Dali City, Yunnan Province	

Colored Paintings on the Residential Houses of the Bai Nationality are popular in Dali City and the surrounding areas inhabited by the Bai nationality in Yunnan Province. They are an exotic flower of the Bai culture in Dali, not only used for the decoration of shrines, temples and large ancient buildings, but also widely applied to the residential houses of the Bai nationality.

The buildings of the Bai nationality in Dali are mostly constructed with earth and wood, often showing the appearance of blue bricks, white walls and gray tiles. In harmony with this, the colors of **Architectural Colored Paintings** are mainly black, white and gray, emphasizing plain white, the main hue of the residential buildings of the Bai nationality. The residential buildings of the Bai nationality are mostly decorated with exquisite paintings on gates, the Screen Wall, gables, waistlines, the Dragon-horse Horn, etc. Among them, vanilla patterns, propitious cloud patterns and Huiwen patterns are commonly used, becoming the part with the most typical ethnic feature in Colored Paintings. The craft of Colored Paintings has unique features, paying the most attention to their underpainting procedure. Wood-structure buildings are generally primed by using Zhuxuehui blended with pig blood, tung oil and lime. On the mud brick walls, the parts that need to be painted are plastered with "Zhijinhui" made by mixing pure plaster of paris and white cotton paper. When it is half dry, colored paintings are made, which can ensure that the corlored paintings will not fade easily. Pigments of Colored Paintings are mostly mineral pigments. While decorating houses with unique colors and patterns, **Colored Paintings on the Residential Houses** are also endowed with rich meanings, such as dispelling evil, avoiding disasters, and praying for auspiciousness and blessing. **Colored Paintings on the Residential Houses of the Bai Nationality** are the essence of the Bai architectural art, deeply influenced by the culture of the Han nationality. They organically integrate the magnificent atmosphere of northern architecture and the exquisite and uniqueness of southern architecture, becoming a testament of the exchange of Bai and Han cultures.

第 5 项：木雕（剑川木雕）

剑川木雕
Jianchuan Wood Carving

项目序号：834	项目编号：Ⅶ-58	公布时间：2011（第三批）	类别：传统美术
所属地区：云南省	类型：扩展项目	申报地区或单位：云南省剑川县	

剑川木雕已有一千多年的历史，主要流传于素有“木匠之乡”之称的云南省剑川县。

据史料记载，唐代时，剑川木匠就承担了南诏五华楼木雕构件的制作工作；宋代，曾有剑川木雕艺人进京献艺，轰动京华；清代时，剑川木雕木匠众多，流传普遍。中华人民共和国成立后，剑川木雕有了很大的发展。首都人民大会堂、民族文化宫等重要建筑都饰有剑川木雕。现今已发展成嵌石木雕家具、工艺挂屏和座屏系列、格子门系列、古建筑及室内装饰装修、旅游工艺品小件、现代家具六个门类两百六十多个花色品种，是集艺术价值、观赏价值、珍藏价值和实用价值于一身的传统文化产品。[①] 剑川木雕的产品多选用优质的红木、西南桦、缅甸红木以及天然植物漆和闻名于世的彩花大理石。其雕刻内容以花草、动植物图案为主，也有神仙传说故事的题材，常见的有“八仙过海”“八仙庆寿”等，木雕图案主要有香草、龙纹、凤纹、狮头、凤头、云纹等，变化多端，独具匠心。剑川木雕充分展示了白族人民高度的艺术水平和文化涵养，将原有的粗犷、豪放的风格和江南木雕的细腻、精巧糅为一体，成为全国木雕重要派别之一。剑川木雕造型美观大方，高雅别致，具有坚硬柔韧、抗腐蚀、不变形的特点。[②]

① 《木雕（剑川木雕）》，中国非物质文化遗产网，http://www.ihchina.cn/Article/Index/detail?id=14138，检索日期：2019 年 8 月 31 日。

② 《剑川白族传统木雕生产性保护税收政策初探》，云南非物质文化遗产保护网，http://www.ynich.cn/view.php?id=886&cat_id=12810，检索日期：2019 年 8 月 31 日。

Item 5: Wood Carving (Jianchuan Wood Carving)

Item Serial Number: 834	Item ID Number: Ⅶ-58	Released Date: 2011 (Batch 3)	Category: Traditional Fine Arts
Affiliated Province: Yunnan Province	Type: Extended Item	Application Province or Unit: Jianchuan County, Yunnan Province	

Jianchuan Wood Carving has had a history of more than a thousand years, mainly circulated in Jianchuan County, Yunnan Province, which is known as "the Hometown of Carpenters".

According to historical records, in the Tang Dynasty, Jianchuan carpenters undertook the production of the woodcarving components of Wuhua Building in Nanzhao; in the Song Dynasty, Jianchuan woodcarving artisans once went to the national capital to perform their talents, which caused a sensation in the capital city; and in the Qing Dynasty, there were numerous woodcarving carpenters in Jianchuan, who were distributed widely. Since the establishment of the People's Republic of China, **Jianchuan Wood Carving** has made great progress. Important buildings, such as the Great Hall of the People in the capital and the Cultural Palace of Nationalities, are decorated with **Jianchuan Wood Carving**. At present, it has developed into six categories with over 260 varieties of designs and colors, namely stone-inlaid wood-carved furniture, series of craft hanging screen and Zuoping (a screen with a base, which cannot be folded), lattice door series, ancient architecture and interior decoration, small tourist handicraft articles and modern furniture. They are traditional cultural products that integrate artistic value, ornamental value, collectible value and practical value. The products of **Jianchuan Wood Carving** mostly use high-quality mahogany, southwestern birches, Burmese mahogany, as well as natural plant lacquer and world-renowned colored marble. Its carving content is mainly the patterns of flowers, plants and animals. It also takes the legends of immortals as the theme. The common legends are "Eight Immortals Crossing the Sea", "Eight Immortals Celebrating the Birthday", etc. The wood carving patterns are mainly vanilla, dragon pattern, phoenix pattern, lion head, phoenix head, cloud pattern, etc., which are varied and unique. **Jianchuan Wood Carving** fully demonstrates the high artistic level and cultural cultivation of the Bai people. It combines the original rough and unrestrained style with the delicate and ingenious style of Jiangnan Wood Carving, becoming one of the important schools of Wood Carving in China. **Jianchuan Wood Carving** is beautiful, decent, elegant and unique, with the characteristics of hardness, flexibility, corrosion resistance and no deformation.

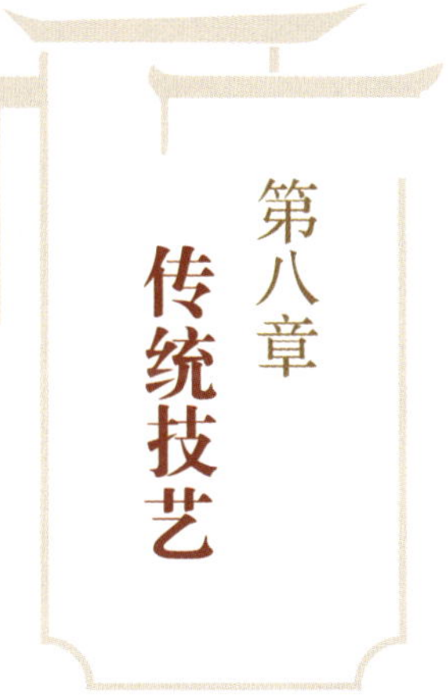

第八章 传统技艺

Chapter Eight

Traditional Craft

第 1 项：傣族慢轮制陶技艺

制陶工具慢轮

the Slow Wheel for Making Pottery

项目序号：355	项目编号：Ⅷ-5	公布时间：2006（第一批）	类别：传统技艺
所属地区：云南省	类型：新增项目	申报地区或单位：云南省西双版纳傣族自治州	

云南有长达四千余年的制陶史，西双版纳傣族自治州的景洪曼斗寨、勐罕曼峦站寨、勐海曼扎寨及勐龙寨等地均保留着较完整的傣族慢轮制陶技艺。

傣族自古喜爱用陶，制陶在傣语中称为“板磨”，俗称“土锅”。与其他民族不同的是，傣族制陶是由女性世代相承的。主要工具有转轮、木拍、竹刮和石球；主要技艺流程包括舂土、筛土、拌沙、渗水、安装转盘、制坯、打坯、干燥、准备烧陶和烧陶等环节；所生产的陶器按用途可分为生活用具、建材用具和赕佛用具。傣族制陶技艺最突出的特色为慢轮手工制作，器物表面均用有纹的木拍拍打出印纹。傣族陶器在用料上亦有讲究，主要以泥土加砂石料来改善成型性能。其焙烧方式也独具特色，有露天焙烧和封闭半焙烧等多种方法。成坯方法多样，有无转轮制坯、脚趾拨动慢轮和手拨动转轮等方式。这些远古时期的制陶技术，至今仍为傣族传承使用。傣族慢轮制陶技艺被国内外考古学家们视为我国原始陶艺的代表，是解开中国新石器时代烧陶之谜的钥匙。[①]

Item 1: the Craft of Making Pottery via Slow Wheels of the Dai Nationality

Item Serial Number: 355	Item ID Number: Ⅷ-5	Released Date: 2006 (Batch 1)	Category: Traditional Craft
Affiliated Province: Yunnan Province	Type: New Item	Application Province or Unit: Xishuangbanna Dai Autonomous Prefecture, Yunnan Province	

Yunnan Province boasts a history of more than 4,000 years of pottery making. The relatively complete **Craft of Making Pottery via Slow Wheels of the Dai Nationality** has been retained in such places as Mandou Stockaded Village of Jinghong City, Manluanzhan Stockaded Village of Menghan Township as well as Manzha Stockaded Village and Menglong Stockaded Village of Menghai County in Xishuangbanna Dai Autonomous Prefecture.

The Dai people have been fond of using pottery since ancient times. Pottery making is called "Banmo" in the Dai language, commonly known as "the Earth Pot". Unlike other ethnic groups, the craft of making pottery of the Dai nationality is inherited by women from generation to generation. The main tools are turning wheels, wooden bats, bamboo scrapers and stone balls. The main technical procedures include pounding clay, sieving clay, mixing sand, seeping water, installing turntables, making greenware, patting greenware, drying, getting prepared to fire pottery and firing pottery. According to its uses, the pottery produced can be divided into living utensils, utensils used as building materials and Buddha-worshiping utensils. The most prominent feature of the craft of making pottery of the Dai nationality is being

① 《傣族慢轮制陶技艺》，中国非物质文化遗产网，http://www.ihchina.cn/Article/Index/detail?id=14265，检索日期：2019 年 8 月 31 日。

made by hand via using slow wheels. The grains are patted on the utensil surfaces by using the wooden bats with grains. The pottery of the Dai nationality is particular about applying materials, mainly with sand added to clay to improve the formability. Its ways of firing are unique, which include many methods such as open-air firing and closed semi-firing. There are various methods of forming greenware, such as forming greenware without using the turning wheel, forming greenware by using toes to turn the slow wheel and forming greenware by using hands to move the turning wheel. These ancient techniques of pottery making are still used by the Dai people up to now. **The Craft of Making Pottery via Slow Wheels of the Dai Nationality** has been regarded as the representative of China's primitive pottery art by archaeologists at home and abroad, and is the key to exploring the mystery of pottery firing in the Neolithic Age of China.

白族扎染制品
the Product of Tie Dyeing of the Bai Nationality

第 2 项：白族扎染技艺

项目序号：376	项目编号：Ⅷ-26	公布时间：2006（第一批）	类别：传统技艺
所属地区：云南省	类型：新增项目	申报地区或单位：云南省大理市	

扎染是我国一种古老的纺织品染色技艺。白族扎染技艺流传于云南省大理白族自治州大理市喜州镇周城村和巍山彝族回族自治县的大仓、庙街等镇。其中，以周城村白族的扎染业最为著名，这里被文化部命名为“民族扎染之乡”。据史料记载，东汉时大理就有染织之法；明清时，洱海白族地区的染织技艺已达很高水平，明朝洱海卫红布、清代喜洲布和大理布均名噪一时。近代以来，大理染织业继续发展，周城成为远近闻名的手工织染村。

扎染一般以棉白布或棉、麻混纺白布为原料，染料主要是植物蓝靛（板兰根）。其主要步骤有画刷图案、绞扎、浸泡、染布、蒸煮、晒干、拆线和碾布等，技术关键是绞扎手法和染色技艺，主要工具有染缸、染棒、晒架和石碾。白族扎染品种多样，图案多为自然形的小纹样，分布均匀，题材寓意吉祥，具有重要的美学价值和实用功能，深受国内外消费者的好评。大理白族扎染显示出浓郁的民间艺术风格，一千多种纹样是千百年来白族历史文化的缩影，折射出白族的民情风俗，与各种工艺手段一起构成富有魅力的大理白族织染文化。[①]

① 《白族扎染技艺》，中国非物质文化遗产网，http://www.ihchina.cn/Article/Index/detail?id=14304，检索日期：2019 年 8 月 31 日。

Item 2: the Craft of Tie Dyeing of the Bai Nationality

Item Serial Number: 376	Item ID Number: Ⅷ-26	Released Date: 2006 (Batch 1)	Category: Traditional Craft
Affiliated Province: Yunnan Province	Type: New Item	Application Province or Unit: Dali City, Yunnan Province	

Tie Dyeing is an ancient textile dyeing technique in China. **The Craft of Tie Dyeing of the Bai Nationality** is spread in Zhoucheng Village of Xizhou Township, Dali City, Dali Bai Autonomous Prefecture, as well as Dacang and Miaojie townships, etc. in Weishan Yi and Hui Autonomous County of Yunnan Province. Among them, the tie-dyeing industry of the Bai nationality in Zhoucheng Village is the most famous. Here has been named as "the Hometown of Ethnic Tie Dyeing" by the Ministry of Culture. According to historical records, the skills of weaving and dyeing have emerged in Dali in the Eastern Han Dynasty. During the Ming and Qing dynasties, the crafts of weaving and dyeing in areas inhabited by the Bai nationality near the Erhai Lake have reached a high level. Weihong Cloth of the Erhai Lake in the Ming Dynasty and Xizhou Cloth and Dali Cloth in the Qing Dynasty have gained some fame for a time. Since modern times, the industry of weaving and dyeing in Dali has continued to develop, and Zhoucheng Village has become a well-known village of manual weaving and dyeing.

White cotton cloth or the white cloth blended cotton with hemp are the common raw materials for Tie Dyeing, and the colorant used for dying is mainly indigo plant (indigowoad root). The main steps include drawing and brushing patterns, tying and stitching, soaking, dyeing, steaming, drying, removing stitches and flattening the cloth. The key techniques are the tying-and-stitching technique and the dyeing technique. The main tools are dyeing vats, dyeing rods, drying racks and stone rollers. The products of Tie Dyeing of the Bai Nationality are diverse, and the patterns are mostly naturally-shaped small patterns, evenly distributed. Their subject matters imply auspiciousness, having important aesthetic value and practical functions, highly praised by consumers at home and abroad. The **Tie Dyeing of the Bai Nationality** in Dali shows a strong folk artistic style. More than one thousand patterns are the epitome of the history and culture of the Bai nationality for thousands of years, reflecting its customs. Together with various crafts, they constitute the charming weaving-and-dyeing culture of the Bai nationality in Dali.

第3项：苗族芦笙制作技艺

苗族芦笙制作技艺国家级传承人王杰锋制作芦笙照
a Photo of Making Lusheng Musical Instruments of Wang Jiefeng, the State-level Inheritor of the Craft of Making Lusheng Musical Instruments of the Miao Nationality

项目序号：383	项目编号：Ⅷ-33	公布时间：2006（第一批）	类别：传统技艺
所属地区：云南省	类型：新增项目	申报地区或单位：云南省大关县	

芦笙是苗族文化的一种象征，苗族芦笙在表演吹奏方面把词、曲、舞融为一体，保持了苗族历史文化艺术的原始性、古朴性。芦笙制作技艺历来都由师傅亲自教授，无文字资料留存，且技艺考究，传承比较困难。苗族传承芦笙制作技艺的师傅只用风箱、锤子、黄铜、斧子、凿子、锯子、钻子、苦竹、桐油和石灰（或乳胶）就能制作出精美实用的各式芦笙。

云南省昭通市大关苗族芦笙制作技艺主要存在于云南苗族聚居区的昭通市大关县天星镇。天星镇芦笙以苦竹、桦槁树皮、杉木和铜片为料，使用刀、锯、刨、凿、钻、锤、剪刀和炼炉等工具制作。芦笙通常由笙管、笙斗和簧片三部分组成，常见的芦笙发音管一般为六根，大关县芦笙制作传人王杰锋在继承祖传秘技的基础上进行了创新，将发音管改成八根或十根，又在高温冶炼黄铜笙簧片时加入一定比例的铅，增强了芦笙簧片的弹性及韧性，这样制成的芦笙发音更加响亮悦耳，传承百余年的天星“王芦笙”就此扬声滇黔交界的苗族村寨，为大关天星芦笙增添了光彩。①

① 《苗族芦笙制作技艺》，中国非物质文化遗产网，http://www.ihchina.cn/Article/Index/detail?id=14319，检索日期：2019年9月4日。

Item 3: the Craft of Making Lusheng Musical Instruments of the Miao Nationality

Item Serial Number: 383	Item ID Number: Ⅷ-33	Released Date: 2006 (Batch 1)	Category: Traditional Craft
Affiliated Province: Yunnan Province	Type: New Item	Application Province or Unit: Daguan County, Yunnan Province	

Lusheng Musical Instruments are a symbol of the culture of the Miao nationality. The performance of Lusheng Musical Instruments of the Miao nationality integrates lyrics, music and dances, maintaining the primitiveness and simplicity of the history, culture and art of the Miao nationality. Its making craft has always been taught by masters in person. There is no written material left, and this craftsmanship has particularity, so it's difficult to pass it on. The masters who inherit the craft of making Lusheng Musical Instruments of the Miao nationality can make all kinds of exquisite and practical Lusheng Musical Instruments only by using bellows, hammers, brass, axes, chisels, saws, drills, bitter bamboo, tung oil, and lime (or latex).

The Craft of Making Lusheng Musical Instruments of the Miao Nationality in Daguan County, Zhaotong City, Yunnan Province mainly exists in Tianxing Township where the Miao people inhabit. With bitter bamboo, birch bark, China fir and copper sheets as materials, Lusheng Musical Instruments in Tianxing Township are made by using the tools of knives, saws, planers, chisels, drills, hammers, scissors, furnaces, etc. Lusheng Musical Instruments are usually composed of three parts: vocal tubes, Shengdou (a container in Lusheng Musical Instruments where the air is retained and the reed is caused to vibrate) and the reeds. There are usually six vocal tubes in a commonly-seen Lusheng Musical Instrument. On the basis of inheriting the skills handed down from his ancestors, Wang Jiefeng, the inheritor of making Lusheng Musical Instruments in Daguan County, has made innovation and increased vocal tubes to eight or ten. In addition, when smelting the brass reed at high temperature, he has added a certain proportion of lead, which has enhanced the elasticity and toughness of the reeds of Lusheng Musical Instruments, making them louder and more pleasant in sound. The "King of Lusheng Musical Instruments" in Tianxing Township, which has been inherited for more than a hundred years, has become well known in villages of the Miao nationality on the border of Yunnan and Guizhou provinces, adding luster to Lusheng Musical Instruments in Tianxing Township of Daguan County.

第 4 项：阿昌族户撒刀锻制技艺

阿昌族户撒刀锻制图
a Picture of Forging Husa Knives of the Achang Nationality

项目序号：391	项目编号：Ⅷ-41	公布时间：2006（第一批）	类别：传统技艺
所属地区：云南省	类型：新增项目	申报地区或单位：云南省陇川县	

阿昌族户撒刀锻制技艺流传于云南省德宏傣族景颇族自治州陇川县户撒乡，主要集中在潘乐、户早、隆光、相姐、明社和曼炳六个村。

户撒刀是阿昌族人智慧的结晶，其先民在唐代就掌握了锻制和铸造铁器的要领，明代“三征麓川”（1441—1449）时，户撒成为“兵工厂”。阿昌族人吸收了汉族的兵器制造技术，形成独特的户撒刀锻制工艺，明末清初走向成熟，民国年间生产达到鼎盛。[①]户撒刀制作的工具主要有炉盘、锤、钳、铲、砧、风箱、锋钢刮刀和木质冷却槽等。其制作过程包括下料、制坯、打制刀样、修磨初加工、修饰刀叶、淬火、打磨抛光、制作刀柄刀鞘、制作背带和组装等十道工序，尤以淬火工艺最为关键，通过热处理使刀叶的硬度和韧性达到最佳状态，如史所称“柔可绕指，吹发即断，刚可削铁”。户撒刀锻制均为家庭作坊手工生产，工艺技术只在本家族中传承，决不外传。户撒刀品种繁多，主要有生产工具、生活用具及装饰性工艺品三大类一百二十多种。除服务周边民族和邻近地区及远销西藏、青海外，还出口东南亚地区。[②]

① 《阿昌族户撒刀锻制技艺》，中国非物质文化遗产网，http://www.ihchina.cn/Article/Index/detail?id=14339，检索日期：2019 年 8 月 31 日。

② 《阿昌族户撒刀锻制技艺》，云南非物质文化遗产保护网，http://www.ynich.cn/view.php?id=1249&cat_id=11110，检索日期：2019 年 8 月 31 日。

Item 4: the Craft of Forging Husa Knives of the Achang Nationality

Item Serial Number: 391	Item ID Number: Ⅷ-41	Released Date: 2006 (Batch 1)	Category: Traditional Craft
Affiliated Province: Yunnan Province	Type: New Item	Application Province or Unit: Longchuan County, Yunnan Province	

The Craft of Forging Husa Knives of the Achang Nationality has been passed down in Husa Township, Longchuan County, Dehong Dai and Jingpo Autonomous Prefecture, Yunnan Province, mainly concentrated in the six villages of Panle, Huzao, Longguang, Xiangjie, Mingshe and Manbing.

Husa Knive are the crystallization of the wisdom of the Achang people. Their ancestors have mastered the essentials of forging and casting ironware in the Tang Dynasty. During "the Three Time Conquest of Luchuan" (1441-1449) in the Ming Dynasty, Husa became a "munitions factory". Absorbing the weapon manufacturing technology of the Han nationality, the Achang people have developed a unique craft of forging Husa Knives. It matured in the late Ming and early Qing dynasties, with its production reaching its peak during the Republic of China. The tools for making Husa Knives mainly include a stove, a hammer, a pair of pincers, a shovel, an anvil, a bellow, a scraper made of high-speed steel and a wooden cooling tank. The production process includes ten procedures, such as preparing materials, making the basic form, making knife samples, grinding and preliminary processing, modifying the blade, quenching, grinding and polishing, making knife handles and scabbards, making straps and assembling. The quenching procedure is the most critical. Through heat treatment, the hardness and toughness of the blade can reach the best state. According to historical records, "the knife is so soft that it can be winded around fingers, so sharp that a hair can be cut when one blows a breath to it against the blade, and so tough that it can cut iron." Husa Knives are all handmade in the family workshop, and the craft is only passed down within the family and will never be passed down to outsiders. There are many varieties of Husa Knives, mainly including more than 120 kinds and classified into three categories, namely, the category of production tools, the category of daily goods and the category of decorative handcrafts. In addition to serving neighboring ethnic groups and areas, they are sold to distant places, such as Xizang Autonomous Region and Qinghai Province, and even exported to Southeast Asia.

傣族手工造纸
Papermaking by Hand of the Dai Nationality

纳西族手工造纸之舂料
Papermaking by Hand of the Naxi Nationality: Pounding Raw Materials

第 5 项：傣族、纳西族手工造纸技艺

项目序号：418	项目编号：Ⅷ-68	公布时间：2006（第一批）	类别：传统技艺
所属地区：云南省	类型：新增项目	申报地区或单位：云南省临沧市、香格里拉县	

傣族手工造纸技艺主要流传于云南省临沧市永德县永康镇芒石寨和耿马傣族佤族自治县孟定镇芒团村。其造纸原料为构树皮，技艺流程主要有采料、晒料、浸泡、拌灰、蒸煮、洗涤、捣浆、浇纸、晒纸、研光和揭纸等十一道工序。[①]首先，将2-3年生的构树皮采剥晒干后放凉水中浸泡发软；然后，用筛过的火灰将其涂抹均匀，以使其充分碱化。将碱化的构皮放入锅里加水中火蒸煮约十个小时。煮好后，冲洗净火灰及其他杂质，并将其置于石墩上，用木锤捶打至能在水中自然散开纤维。随后便可以浇纸，浇好的纸连同纸模一起晒（或烘）至七八成干时，用瓷碗轻轻打磨纸模表面，以使其更光滑、更有色泽，即研光。最后揭下整张纸，即完成制作。[②]临沧傣族手工造纸技艺保持一

① 《傣族手工造纸技艺》，云南非物质文化遗产保护网，http://www.ynich.cn/view.php?id=1247&cat_id=11110，检索日期：2019年8月31日。

② 黄琛、王海，《傣族手工造纸技艺：造纸活化石，本色千百年》，http://www.ynich.cn/view.php?id=3539&cat_id=11411，检索日期：2019年8月31日。

家一户的生产形式，传女不传子。

纳西族手工造纸技艺流传于迪庆藏族自治州香格里拉县三坝纳西族乡的白地村，其制品称白地纸，即纳西族东巴纸。造纸原料为当地独有的植物“阿当达”，即瑞香科丽江荛花，主要制作工具有纸帘、木框、晒纸木板和木臼等。其造纸流程主要由采集原料、晒干、浸泡、蒸煮、洗涤、舂料、再舂料、浇纸、贴纸和晒纸等工序组成，与傣族手工造纸技艺的流程基本相同，故不再详述。但其活动纸帘较为特殊，晒纸过程受到浇纸法的影响，又有抄纸法的痕迹，是中国造纸术与印巴次大陆造纸法兼容并蓄的结果。纳西族手工造纸技艺传子不传女，以家庭作坊生产且不外传。[①]

Item 5: the Craft of Making Paper by Hand of the Dai and Naxi Nationalities

Item Serial Number: 418	Item ID Number: Ⅷ-68	Released Date: 2006 (Batch 1)	Category: Traditional Craft
Affiliated Province: Yunnan Province	Type: New Item	Application Province or Unit: Lincang City and Shangri-La County of Yunnan Province	

The Craft of Making Paper by Hand of the Dai Nationality is mainly circulated in Mangshi Village of Yongkang Township in Yongde County, and Mangtuan Village of Mengding Township in Gengma Dai and Wa Autonomous County of Lincang City, Yunnan Province. Its raw material is the bark of paper mulberry. Its technical process mainly includes eleven procedures, namely, picking raw materials, drying raw materials in the sun, soaking, mixing with ash, boiling, washing, pulping, making paper by pouring pulp, drying paper in the sun, calendering and peeling paper. The bark of two to three-year-old paper mulberry is picked, peeled and get dried in the sun. Then, it is soaked in cold water to be softened. Next, the bark is evenly daubed with the sieved ash to get fully alkalized. The alkalized bark is put into a cauldron and boiled over a medium heat for about ten hours. After that, the ash and other impurities on it are washed off. Then, it is put on Shidun (a block of stone), and beaten by using a wooden hammer until its fibers can be dispersed naturally in the

① 《傣族、纳西族手工造纸技艺》，中国非物质文化遗产网，http://www.ihchina.cn/Article/Index/detail?id=14383，检索日期：2019 年 8 月 31 日。

water. At this time, paper can be made by pouring pulp onto the paper mold. When the poured paper and the paper mold are dried (or baked) to be 70-80% dry, workers should gently polish the surface of the paper mold with a porcelain bowl to make it smoother and have more luster, which is called calendering. Finally, the whole piece of paper is peeled off to complete the production. **The Craft of Making Paper by Hand of the Dai Nationality** in Lincang City remains a household production form, which is passed on to daughters instead of sons.

The Craft of Making Paper by Hand of the Naxi Nationality is spread in Baidi Village, Sanba Township of the Naxi nationality, Shangri-La County, Diqing Zang Autonomous Prefecture. Its products are called Baidi Paper, namely Dongba Paper of the Naxi Nationality. Its raw material is a unique local plant "Adangda", that is, *Wikstroemia lichiangensis* in Latin. The main production tools are curtains for making paper, wooden frames, boards for drying paper in the sun and wooden mortars, etc. Its papermaking process mainly consists of the procedures of collecting raw materials, drying in the sun, soaking, boiling, washing, pounding, pounding the second time, making paper by pouring pulp, sticking paper on boards, drying paper in the sun, etc. Since its making process is roughly the same as that of **the Craft of Making Paper by Hand of the Dai Nationality**, there is no need to describe in detail. However, its movable curtains are quite special. The procedure of drying paper in the sun is affected both by the method of making paper by pouring pulp and by the method of making paper by scooping pulp, which is the integration of Chinese papermaking technology and the papermaking method of Indian-Pakistani subcontinent. This craft is passed on to sons instead of daughters, and is produced within family workshops, without any external transmission.

第 6 项：陶器烧制技艺（藏族黑陶烧制技艺）

藏族黑陶：茶壶
the Black Pottery of the Zang Nationality: a Teapot

项目序号：881	项目编号：Ⅷ-98	公布时间：2008（第二批）	类别：传统技艺
所属地区：云南省	类型：新增项目	申报地区或单位：云南省迪庆藏族自治州	

云南省迪庆藏族自治州的藏族黑陶烧制技艺主要流传于香格里拉县尼西乡汤堆村。这里的藏族黑陶融实用性、观赏性和工艺性为一体，显示了藏族民间陶艺的创造力和表现力。

汤堆村的藏族黑陶烧制技艺采用黏性大、可塑性强的白色和红色陶土，加上风化沙石研磨而成的石粉，混合形成制坯原料。其制作工具极其原始、简单，以木拍、木刮、木垫和木榔头为主。与此相比，其烧制工艺却十分复杂，要经过选土、练土、制坯、镶瓷、磨光、装饰、阴干、烧制、渗炭和防裂等十二道工艺。制作陶坯采用泥条盘筑的方法，技术要求较高。先是取揉拌均匀的陶土，用木拍打成条状后置于基座上，而后再根据所需器物的形制，用手捏出轮廓，接着磨光内外器壁和沿口，然后镶嵌白瓷片，点缀以动物和几何纹图案，最后高温烧制约一小时后即成成品。汤堆村藏族黑陶手工艺产品主要有日常生活用品和宗教用具两大类，品种多样，用途广泛，藏族人民使用的各种餐具、炊具、茶具、酒具、饮具及香炉、酥油灯等均一应俱全。①

① 《陶器烧制技艺（藏族黑陶烧制技艺）》，中国非物质文化遗产网，http://www.ihchina.cn/Article/Index/detail?id=14459，检索日期：2019 年 9 月 5 日。

Item 6: the Craft of Firing Pottery (the Craft of Firing the Black Pottery of the Zang Nationality)

Item Serial Number: 881	Item ID Number: Ⅷ-98	Released Date: 2008 (Batch 2)	Category: Traditional Craft
Affiliated Province: Yunnan Province	Type: New Item	Application Province or Unit: Diqing Zang Autonomous Prefecture, Yunnan Province	

The Craft of Firing the Black Pottery of the Zang Nationality in Diqing Zang Autonomous Prefecture, Yunnan Province is mainly spread in Tangdui Village, Nixi Township, Shangri-La County. The Black Pottery of the Zang Nationality here integrates utility, appreciativeness and technological properties into one, demonstrating the creativity and expressiveness of the folk pottery art of the Zang nationality.

For **the Craft of Firing the Black Pottery of the Zang Nationality** in Tangdui Village, white and red clay with high viscosity and plasticity, as well as the stone powder made by grinding weathered sand are mixed as the raw materials for making greenware. The production tools are extremely primitive and simple, mainly including wooden bats, wooden scrapers, wooden mats and wooden hammers. On the contrary, the firing process is very complicated, which will go through twelve procedures, such as selecting clay, grinding and kneading clay, making greenware, inlaying porcelain pieces, polishing, decorating, drying in shade, firing, carburizing and crack prevention. Pottery greenware is made by using the method of coiling clay bars, which has high technical requirements. First, the evenly kneaded clay is prepared, patted into a bar by using wooden bats, and then placed on the base. After that, according to the shape of the required utensil, its outline is kneaded by hand. Then, the inner and outer walls and the edge of the utensil are polished, inlayed with white porcelain pieces, and decorated with animals and geometric patterns. Finally, the final pottery product is finished after being fired at high temperature for about one hour. The black pottery products of the Zang nationality in Tangdui Village mainly include articles for daily use and religious utensils. They have many varieties and a wide range of uses, including all kinds of tableware, cooking ware, tea sets, wine sets, drinking ware, incense burners and butter lamps used by the people of the Zang nationality.

建水紫陶：茶壶
Jianshui Purple Pottery: Teapot

第 7 项：

陶器烧制技艺
（建水紫陶烧制技艺）

项目序号：881	项目编号：Ⅷ-98	公布时间：2008（第二批）	类别：传统技艺
所属地区：云南省	类型：新增项目	申报地区或单位：云南省建水县	

建水紫陶被誉为“中国四大名陶”之一，产自云南省红河哈尼族彝族自治州建水县临安镇碗窑村，这里以烧制陶器闻名。

考古资料显示，建水县在新石器时代晚期就有泥条盘筑法烧制的陶器制品；清道光年间建水紫陶的技艺开始形成，并逐步发展为工艺美术陶，产品增加了文化内涵，品种更加丰富，有茶具、文具和酒具等。建水紫陶烧制技艺由镇浆制泥、手工拉坯、湿坯装饰、雕刻填泥、高温烧制和无釉磨光等六道工艺组成。[①] 首先将捣细的不同粘土原料按适当比例混合，放入池内加水制成浆状搅拌淘洗，待含砂浆泥沉落池底，勺取上面的浆泥倒入其他池内反复淘洗至泥浆自然凝干成膏状；然后在简易陶车上手工拉坯成需要的器型；之后便可以在湿坯上进行人工墨稿装饰，以保证填泥与坯体充分吻合；随后刻工艺人将湿坯上的墨迹雕刻成模，填敷各种色泥，填泥过程中要经过两到三次填压，以使填泥与刻模充分粘合。经修饰好的陶坯便可放入炉窑烧制，建水紫陶的烧制温度为 1150℃ -1200℃。出窑后，需要再进行人工打磨抛光，即制成成品。[②] 建水紫陶成品无铅、无毒、透气性能好，其品质明净如镜，叩之清脆如磬。建水紫陶多以传统中国书法、绘画作为装饰，风格古朴高雅。

---

① 《陶器烧制技艺（建水紫陶烧制技艺）》，中国非物质文化遗产网，http://www.ihchina.cn/Article/Index/detail?id=14458，检索日期：2019 年 9 月 3 日。

② 建水县文化和旅游局，《建水县非物质文化遗产保护名录》，昆明：云南人民出版社，2019 年，第 4-5 页。

Item 7: the Craft of Firing Pottery (the Craft of Firing Jianshui Purple Pottery)

Item Serial Number: 881	Item ID Number: Ⅷ-98	Released Date: 2008 (Batch 2)	Category: Traditional Craft
Affiliated Province: Yunnan Province	Type: New Item	Application Province or Unit: Jianshui County, Yunnan Province	

Jianshui Purple Pottery is acclaimed as one of "the Four Famous Pottery Products in China", produced in Wanyao Village, Lin'an Township, Jianshui County, Honghe Hani and Yi Autonomous Prefecture, Yunnan Province, which is famous for firing pottery.

According to archaeological data, there have been pottery products fired by using the method of coiling clay bars in Jianshui County in the late Neolithic period. During the reign of Emperor Daoguang of the Qing Dynasty, **the Craft of Firing Jianshui Purple Pottery** began to take shape and gradually developed into craft art pottery, with cultural connotations added to its products. Their varieties are more abundant, including tea sets, stationery and wine sets. This craft involves six procedures, namely depositing slurry and making clay, making greenware by hand, decorating the wet greenware, carving and mud-filling, firing at high temperature and unglazed polishing. First, different clay materials that have been finely mashed are mixed in proper proportion, then put into a tank, added with water to make slurry, stirred and elutriated. When the mortar settles at the bottom of the tank, the slurry above is scooped out, put into other tanks, and elutriated repeatedly until the slurry coagulates into paste naturally. Next, the naturally coagulated slurry is made into the required shape on a simple potter's wheel by hand. After that, artificial ink patterns can be decorated on the wet greenware to ensure that the filled clay fully matches the greenware body. Then, engravers carve the ink patterns on the wet greenware into molds and fill them with various colored clay. In the process of filling clay, 2-3 rounds of filling and pressing are needed to ensure that the filled clay is fully bonded to the carved molds. The decorated greenware can be put into the kiln for firing. The firing temperature of Jianshui Purple Pottery is 1150℃-1200℃. After leaving the kiln, the pottery needs to be polished manually and made into the finished products. Jianshui Purple Pottery products are lead-free and non-toxic, with good air permeability. They are as smooth as mirrors, and when they are knocked, the sounds are as crisp as those produced by the Chime Stone. Jianshui Purple Pottery is mostly decorated with traditional Chinese calligraphy and painting in simple and elegant style.

第 8 项：傣族织锦技艺

傣锦织机
the Loom for Weaving the Brocade of the Dai Nationality

项目序号：889	项目编号：Ⅷ-106	公布时间：2008（第二批）	类别：传统技艺
所属地区：云南省	类型：新增项目	申报地区或单位：云南省西双版纳傣族自治州	

傣族织锦技艺是傣族先民劳动的产物，是傣族传统手工艺最早期的重要品种，在傣族社会生活中占有相当重要的位置。

傣族织锦的原料是丝、棉、木棉、麻和毛等五类。从材料上看，傣锦以丝与棉使用较多，故傣锦主要有棉织锦和丝织锦两种。其工具有手摇纺车、织机、梭、综、镊、卷经轴、分经棍、卷布轴和幅撑等。工艺流程有备料、弹花、卷筵、纺线、整经、上机和染色等工序。织造时，傣族妇女首先将花纹组织用一根根细绳系在“纹板”（花本）上，用手提脚蹬的动作使经线形成上下两层后开始投纬，如此反复循环，织出漂亮的傣锦。傣锦图案，如荷花、槟榔、孔雀、大象、麒麟、龙凤和佛塔等图案表达了傣族人民对真善美的追求和向往。傣族织锦常以白底衬托单一独立的图案或多次重复的连续图案，还有些图案呈现为剪影式的侧面造型，形象生动、轮廓鲜明。此外，傣族织锦还强调图案的对称性、对比性和连续性，讲究疏密结合、具象和抽象结合，在我国织锦艺术中占有一席之地。①

Item 8: the Craft of Making Brocade of the Dai Nationality

Item Serial Number: 889	Item ID Number: Ⅷ-106	Released Date: 2008 (Batch 2)	Category: Traditional Craft

① 《傣族织锦技艺》，中国非物质文化遗产网，http://www.ihchina.cn/Article/Index/detail?id=14495，检索日期：2019 年 8 月 31 日。

Affiliated Province: Yunnan Province	Type: New Item	Application Province or Unit: Xishuangbanna Dai Autonomous Prefecture, Yunnan Province

The Craft of Making Brocade of the Dai Nationality is the result of the Dai ancestors' laboring. It is the earliest important variety of traditional handicrafts of the Dai nationality, occupying a very important position in the Dai people's social life.

The raw materials for making the Brocade of the Dai Nationality are silk, cotton, kapok, hemp and wool. In terms of materials, the Brocade of the Dai Nationality is made more by using silk and cotton, so it is mainly divided into two kinds: cotton brocade and silk brocade. The tools are hand-operated spinning wheels, looms, shuttles, Zeng (a device on a loom that separates the warp threads so that the shuttle can pass through), tweezers, warp beams, warp-splitting sticks, cloth rollers, Fucheng (a bamboo stick used to support the woven cloth so that it can maintain a relatively uniform width), etc. Its technological process involves the procedures of preparing raw materials, fluffing cotton, rolling cotton into threads, spinning, sorting out warp threads, weaving on the loom and dyeing. In the process of weaving, the Dai women first tie thin threads to "the Pattern Board" (Huaben) to form patterns. Next, through the lifting movements of their hands and the pedaling movements of their feet, they separate warp threads into the upper and lower layers, and then throw shuttles back and forth between these two layers to add weft threads. By repeating this process repeatedly, they can weave beautiful Dai Brocade. The patterns on it, such as lotus flowers, betel nuts, peacocks, elephants, kylin, dragons, phoenixes and pagodas, express the Dai people's pursuit of and yearning for truth, goodness and beauty. For the Brocade of the Dai Nationality, a single independent pattern or continuous patterns that are repeated many times are often set off on a white background, and some of its patterns are presented as silhouette-like side shapes, with vivid images and clear outlines. In addition, it also emphasizes the symmetry, contrast and continuity of patterns, and stresses the combination of sparsity and density and that of concreteness and abstractness, occupying an important place in Chinese brocade art.

第 9 项：斑铜制作技艺

双龙抱耳瓶
a Two-dragon-holding-ear Bottle

项目序号：901	项目编号：Ⅷ-118	公布时间：2008（第二批）	类别：传统技艺
所属地区：云南省	类型：新增项目	申报地区或单位：云南省曲靖市	

斑铜，因天然铜矿中含有各种金属，经冶炼熔铸后形成橘红色的斑纹而得名。斑铜制作技艺是云南独特的传统手工艺，主要流传于云南省曲靖市会泽县，已有三百余年的历史。

斑铜有“生斑”“熟斑”之分。生斑由高品位天然铜矿石加工而成，斑矿罕得，原料不易，产品甚少，极为珍贵；熟斑用工业熟铜通过独特的冶炼熔铸加工而成，工艺虽复杂，但原料丰富，产品较多。生斑制品的晶斑锃亮璀璨，富丽典雅，重量轻，色彩自然，光斑立体感和光泽度较好。斑铜制作工艺复杂，技术要求极高，需要经过选料、锻打、成型、烧斑、显斑和露斑等二三十道工序，历时两三个月才能完成。其中，选料是斑铜加工工艺的关键，要精选会泽、东川一带出产的天然铜（纯度达到 100%），用栗炭温火冶炼生斑，待纯铜原料烧红略显白色时取出，进行手工锻打成型，然后对初成品手工打磨、抛光，最后进行精加工。其制作工艺精湛，造型美观，色彩美仑美奂。主要品种有香炉、蜡台、火锅、鼎、盒、瓶以及各种工艺品。1914 年，会泽斑铜在巴拿马国际博览会上获得银奖。其产品远销日本、美国、澳大利亚和东南亚国家，在国际上享有一定声誉。[①]

① 《斑铜制作技艺》，云南非物质文化遗产保护网，http://www.ynich.cn/view.php?id=1159&cat_id=11111，检索日期：2019 年 8 月 31 日。

Item 9: the Craft of Making Variegated Copperware

Item Serial Number: 901	Item ID Number: Ⅷ-118	Released Date: 2008 (Batch 2)	Category: Traditional Craft
Affiliated Province: Yunnan Province	Type: New Item	Application Province or Unit: Qujing City, Yunnan Province	

Variegated Copperware is named after the orange variegation on the copperware that is formed after smelting and casting the natural copper ores which contain various kinds of metal. **The Craft of Making Variegated Copperware** is a unique traditional handicraft in Yunnan Province, mainly prevalent in Huize County of Qujing City, with a history of more than three hundred years.

Variegated Copperware is divided into "Shengban" and "Shuban". Shengban is made from high-grade natural copper ores. Due to the scarcity of raw materials, it is extremely rare and precious. Shuban is made from industrial wrought copper through unique procedures of smelting and casting. Although the making process is complex, due to the abundance of raw materials, it has more products. The variegation on the products made of raw copper are bright, shining, resplendent and elegant, light in weight, natural in color, and good in three-dimensional effect and glossiness. The process of making Variegated Copperware is complicated, with extremely high technical requirements. It needs to undergo 20-30 procedures, such as selecting materials, forging, shaping, burning and exposing variegation, which lasts 2-3 months. Among them, selecting materials is the key to the processing of Variegated Copperware. Natural copper ores (with a purity of up to 100%) mined from Huize County and Dongchuan District should be selected, and chestnut charcoal is used to smelt the ores with medium fire to make the variegation appear. When the pure copper raw materials are heated to be slightly white, they are taken out and forged into shape by hand. Then, the preliminary products are ground and polished by hand. Finally, they are processed finely. This craftsmanship is exquisite, the shapes of its products are beautiful, and their colors are gorgeous. The main products include incense burners, candlesticks, hotpots, Ding (an ancient cooking vessel with two loop handles and three or four legs), boxes, bottles and various other handicraft articles. In 1914, Huize Variegated Copperware won the silver medal at the Panama International Fair (EXPOCOMER). Its products are exported to Japan, the United States, Australia and Southeast Asian countries, enjoying a certain reputation internationally.

第10项：贝叶经制作技艺

僧人们在制作贝叶经
the Monks are Engraving Pattra-leaf Scriptures

项目序号：925	项目编号：Ⅷ-142	公布时间：2008（第二批）	类别：传统技艺
所属地区：云南省	类型：新增项目	申报地区或单位：云南省西双版纳傣族自治州	

贝叶经是用铁笔刻写在贝多罗树叶上的佛教经文。最早起源于古代印度，公元七世纪前后传入斯里兰卡，复经缅甸、泰国传入我国云南省西南边疆地区。云南省西双版纳傣族自治州、思茅区、临沧市和德宏傣族景颇族自治州一带是较完整地继承了贝叶经制作技艺的地区。

在西双版纳发现的贝叶经有巴利文本和傣文本两种，规格有每页四行式、五行式、六行式和八行式四种。贝叶经制作技艺包括砍贝叶、选贝叶、修整贝叶、煮贝叶、晾晒贝叶、压平贝叶、装模削平、刻写和装帧等程序。将贝叶砍下后削剪整齐，放入锅中，加淘米水烧火煮十多个小时后出锅，晾凉后用布刷洗干净，并晾晒。晾晒好后，将其反卷成团圈以压平（早上太阳未出来之前卷以免贝叶开裂），压平后将贝叶装模削平，用木板捆绑两面，以防再卷起。将已修平的贝叶两面弹上墨线，便可以进行刻写。刻写好后还需要涂墨，涂完后用锯末擦去油渍，以便字迹清楚地显示出来。此时再进行晾晒，晒好后用布擦锯末灰，再经过装模、修边、刨平、打磨、刷漆及金粉、分本册、穿线等程序后即制成成品。傣族人除利用加工后的贝叶刻写佛教经文外，还将傣族的天文历法、社会历史、法规、民俗、医药、生产、生活、伦理道德和文学艺术等内容记录在上面，因此傣人视傣文贝叶经为传世之宝，誉之为“运载傣族历史文化的神舟”，西双版纳的许多佛寺和普通百姓家都虔敬地加以珍藏。①

① 《贝叶经制作技艺》，中国非物质文化遗产网，http://www.ihchina.cn/Article/Index/detail?id=14582，检索日期：2019年8月31日。

Item 10: the Craft of Making Pattra-leaf Scriptures

Item Serial Number: 925	Item ID Number: Ⅷ-142	Released Date: 2008 (Batch 2)	Category: Traditional Craft
Affiliated Province: Yunnan Province	Type: New Item	Application Province or Unit: Xishuangbanna Dai Autonomous Prefecture, Yunnan Province	

Pattra-leaf Scriptures are the Buddhist scriptures engraved on the leaves of pattra trees by using a stencil pen. They originated from ancient India and were introduced to Sri Lanka around the 7th century, and then to the southwestern frontier region of Yunnan Province in China via Myanmar and Thailand. Xishuangbanna Dai Autonomous Prefecture, Simao District, Lincang City, and Dehong Dai and Jingpo Autonomous Prefecture in Yunnan Province are the areas where **the Craft of Making Pattra-leaf Scriptures** has been inherited relatively completely.

There are two kinds of Pattra-leaf Scriptures found in Xishuangbanna Dai Autonomous Prefecture: the Pali text and the Dai text. The specifications are four-line, five-line, six-line and eight-line per page. **The Craft of Making Pattra-leaf Scriptures** includes the procedures of cutting pattra leaves, selecting pattra leaves, trimming pattra leaves, boiling pattra leaves, drying pattra leaves in the sun, flattening pattra leaves, putting pattra leaves into the mold and trimming their edges, engraving and binding. First, pattra leaves are cut off, then trimmed neatly, and put in a pot with rice-washing water added to get boiled for more than ten hours. After that, they are taken out of the pot, get cooled, washed with a cloth and dry in the sun. After drying, they are rolled reversely into a circle to get flattened (before the sun comes out in the morning to prevent pattra leaves from cracking). After they get flattened, they are put in a mold, with their edges trimmed and both sides tied with two wooden boards in case of rolling up again. Next, the trimmed pattra leaves are marked with ink lines on both sides, and then can be engraved with scriptures. After engraving is finished, they need to be daubed with ink. After that, their oil stains are wiped off by using sawdust so that the handwriting on them can be seen clearly. At this time, they should dry in the air again. Then, the sawdust on them is wiped off with a cloth. Finally, after undergoing the procedures of putting them in the mold, trimming, planing, polishing, lacquering, coating them with gold powder, dividing them into volumes, threading, etc., the final products can be finished. The Dai people not only inscribe Buddhist scriptures on the processed pattra leaves, but also record the astronomical calendar, social history, laws and regulations, folk customs, medicine, production, life, ethics and morality, literature and art, etc. of the Dai nationality on them. Therefore, the Dai people regard Pattra-leaf Scriptures in the Dai language as a treasure handed down from generation to generation, praising them as “the divine boat carrying the history and culture of the Dai nationality”. They are treasured reverently in many Buddhist temples and common households in Xishuangbanna Prefecture.

第11项：普洱茶制作技艺（贡茶制作技艺）

贡茶制作技艺国家级传承人李兴昌制作贡茶照
the Picture of Making Tribute Tea of Li Xingchang, the State-level Inheritor of the Craft of Making Tribute Tea

项目序号：934	项目编号：Ⅷ-151	公布时间：2008（第二批）	类别：传统技艺
所属地区：云南省	类型：新增项目	申报地区或单位：云南省宁洱哈尼族彝族自治县	

云南普洱茶制作工艺历史悠久，最早可追溯到商周时期。至清代，普洱茶已被列为贡品，主要产于宁洱哈尼族彝族自治县和勐海县等地，在长期生产过程中形成了独特的制作技艺。

宁洱县普洱茶制作技艺又称“贡茶制作技艺”，是当地茶工在千百年的实践中积累经验而逐步形成的。这种技艺与地方民俗紧密结合在一起，茶叶采摘开始前必须先行祭礼，即向茶神行敬献仪式。仪式结束后，制作开始，制茶者按一定标准严格选择采摘地和采摘时节，遵照具体技术要求，以手摘方式采选原料。原料备齐后即进入杀青揉晒环节，以特定工艺将鲜叶加工成晒青茶。随后是蒸压成型，即通过蒸、揉、压、定型、干燥和包装等工序将晒青茶制成各种成品茶。普洱贡茶独特的传统制作技艺、深厚的历史文化内涵及与之相关的民俗文化是中华茶文化的重要组成部分，其合理的生产流程成为现代普洱茶工艺研发的基础。[①]

① 《普洱茶制作技艺（贡茶制作技艺）》，中国非物质文化遗产网，http://www.ihchina.cn/Article/Index/detail?id=14621，检索日期：2019年8月31日。

Item 11: the Craft of Making Pu'er Tea (the Craft of Making Tribute Tea)

Item Serial Number: 934	Item ID Number: Ⅷ-151	Released Date: 2008 (Batch 2)	Category: Traditional Craft
Affiliated Province: Yunnan Province	Type: New Item	Application Province or Unit: Ning'er Hani and Yi Autonomous County, Yunnan Province	

The Craft of Making Pu'er Tea has a long history, which can date back to the Shang and Zhou dynasties. By the Qing Dynasty, Pu'er Tea has been listed as a tribute, mainly produced in Ning'er Hani and Yi Autonomous County and Menghai County, etc. In the long-term production process, it has formed a unique making craft.

The Craft of Making Pu'er Tea in Ning'er County, also called "**the Craft of Making Tribute Tea**", has been formed by local tea workers who have accumulated experience through thousands of years of practice. This craft is closely related to local folk customs. Before picking tea leaves, tea workers must hold a sacrificial ritual, that is, an offering ceremony to the God of Tea. After the ceremony, the production begins. Tea workers select the place and time of picking tea leaves strictly according to certain standards, and pick the raw materials by hand in accordance with specific technical requirements. After the raw materials are prepared, they enter the procedures of heating green tea, kneading and drying, during which the fresh tea leaves are processed into dried green tea through specific crafts. Subsequently, the procedures of steaming, pressing and taking shape come, during which the dried green tea is made into various finished tea through the procedures of steaming, kneading, pressing, shaping, drying, packaging, etc. The unique traditional craft of making Pu'er Tribute Tea, its profound historical and cultural connotations, and related folk culture are important parts of Chinese tea culture. Its reasonable production process has become the basis for the research and development of modern Pu'er Tea.

大益茶
Dayi Tea

第12项：普洱茶制作技艺（大益茶制作技艺）

项目序号：934	项目编号：Ⅷ-151	公布时间：2008（第二批）	类别：传统技艺
所属地区：云南省	类型：新增项目	申报地区或单位：云南省勐海县	

“大益茶制作技艺”是唯一一个以生产企业品牌直接命名的非物质文化遗产项目。云南省勐海县旧称“佛海”，是世界茶树发源地之一。1939年，茶界名人范和钧创建勐海茶厂，生产“大益”牌普洱茶，经过六十多年的不懈努力，“大益”已成为国内外著名的茶叶品牌。2006年，“大益”普洱茶被农业部评为“中国名牌农产品”。

大益茶制作技艺的关键在于拼配和发酵。拼配是根据各个茶叶品种的特点进行有效、合理的组合，取长补短，以弥补单一品种之不足；发酵是指“人工后发”的特殊技艺。大益茶制作主要经过采茶菁、萎凋、杀青、揉捻和晒干等工序。普洱茶有生、熟之分。采收后的茶菁经萎凋后杀青、揉捻、晒干制成晒青毛茶，此时即是生的普洱茶原料，茶农会依客户需求，将生普洱茶分级后直接蒸压成型，慢慢越陈越香，以自然的方式陈放出普洱生茶品；熟普洱茶是将生普洱茶再经洒水、渥堆、晾干和筛分制成普洱散茶，即熟普洱之毛料，然后再蒸压成型至普洱熟茶品。①

① 《普洱茶制作技艺（大益茶制作技艺）》，中国非物质文化遗产网，http://www.ihchina.cn/Article/Index/detail?id=14622，检索日期：2019年8月31日。

Item 12: the Craft of Making Pu'er Tea (the Craft of Making Dayi Tea)

Item Serial Number: 934	Item ID Number: Ⅷ-151	Released Date: 2008 (Batch 2)	Category: Traditional Craft
Affiliated Province: Yunnan Province	Type: New Item	Application Province or Unit: Menghai County, Yunnan Province	

The Craft of Making Dayi Tea is the only intangible cultural heritage item directly named after the brand of the manufacturer. Menghai County of Yunnan Province, formerly known as "Fohai", is one of the birthplaces of tea trees in the world. In 1939, Fan Hejun, a celebrity in the tea industry, founded Menghai Tea Factory to produce Pu'er Tea with the brand name of "Dayi". After more than 60 years of unremitting efforts, "Dayi" has become a well-known tea brand at home and abroad. In 2006, Pu'er Tea of "Dayi" was rated as "Chinese Famous Agricultural Product" by the Ministry of Agriculture.

The key to **the Craft of Making Dayi Tea** lies in blending and fermentation. Blending is an effective and reasonable combination according to the characteristics of each tea variety, taking advantage of each other's strengths to make up for the shortcomings of a single variety. Fermentation refers to the special craft of "artificial post-fermentation". The production of Dayi Tea mainly involves the procedures of picking green tea leaves, withering, heating green tea leaves, kneading, drying, etc. Pu'er Tea is divided into two types: unfermented tea and fermented tea. The picked green tea leaves are withered, then heated, kneaded and dried to be made into dried green tea, which is the raw material of unfermented Pu'er Tea. According to customers' demands, the unfermented Pu'er Tea is graded, then directly steamed, pressed and shaped by tea growers. With time goes by, the tea becomes more and more fragrant. Then, the finished products of unfermented Pu'er Tea come into being in a natural way. The fermented Pu'er Tea is made by sprinkling water on, fermenting, drying and sifting the unfermented Pu'er Tea. After these procedures, the raw materials of fermented Pu'er Tea are made, and then they are steamed, pressed and shaped into the finished products of fermented Pu'er Tea.

第13项：乌铜走银制作技艺

乌铜走银制品——花瓶
a Product of Silver-plated Black Copperware: Vase

项目序号：1175	项目编号：Ⅷ-195	公布时间：2011（第三批）	类别：传统技艺
所属地区：云南省	类型：新增项目	申报地区或单位：云南省石屏县	

乌铜走银制作技艺由云南省石屏县岳家湾村抗金名将岳飞后裔岳永兄弟特创，为岳氏独家经营，曾与北京景泰蓝齐名，并称“天下铜艺双绝”。

乌铜走银制作技艺融汇了冶金、錾刻和绘画等传统技艺，“走银”即“镀银”，“乌铜走银”即在铜坯上镂刻出精美的纹饰图样，然后在阴刻的纹饰内镀银或金，再将铜坯表面处理成黑色，使其在黑底上衬托出银（金）光闪闪的灿烂饰纹。制作工具有风箱、熔炉、铁锤（大、小）、钳子和大小不一的錾子（錾刻花纹用）。[①] 制作过程是：将铜、金等贵金属按一定比例熔化后做成坯，在坯上雕刻各种花纹图案，然后将熔化的银（金）走入细密的花纹图案中，冷却后打磨光滑，再用祖传工艺使底铜变成乌黑色，透出银（金）纹图案，呈现出黑白（黄）分明的装饰效果。一般多以镶嵌白银为主，故称“乌铜走银”。制品多为墨盒、笔筒、酒壶、香炉和花瓶等日常用具，图案有麒麟吐书、八仙过海、花鸟虫鱼、飞禽走兽、梅兰竹菊和龙凤鹿鹤等，造型奇巧、制作精细。[②]

① 《乌铜走银制作技艺》，云南非物质文化遗产保护网，http://www.ynich.cn/view.php?id=1160&cat_id=11111，检索日期：2019 年 8 月 31 日。

② 《乌铜走银制作技艺》，中国非物质文化遗产网，http://www.ihchina.cn/Article/Index/detail?id=14714，检索日期：2019 年 8 月 31 日。

Item 13: the Craft of Making Silver-plated Black Copperware

Item Serial Number: 1175	Item ID Number: Ⅷ-195	Released Date: 2011 (Batch 3)	Category: Traditional Craft
Affiliated Province: Yunnan Province	Type: New Item	Application Province or Unit: Shiping County, Yunnan Province	

The Craft of Making Silver-plated Black Copperware was invented by the Yue Yong brothers, the descendants of the famous general Yue Fei who fought against the Jin Dynasty, in Yuejiawan Village, Shiping County, Yunnan Province. It is operated exclusively by the Yue family, once enjoying the same reputation as the craft of Beijing Cloisonne, both known as "the best two copper crafts in the world".

The Craft of Making Silver-plated Black Copperware incorporates the traditional techniques of metallurgy, chiseling and carving, painting, etc. "Silver-plated" means to be plated with silver. "Silver-plated Black Copperware" refers to the craft of engraving exquisite patterns on the copperware, plating silver or gold in the engraved patterns, and then making the copperware surface black, so that it can set off the brilliant silver (gold) patterns on the black background. Its production tools include bellows, furnaces, iron hammers (large and small ones), pliers, and chisels of different sizes (for chiseling patterns). The making process is as follows: First, precious metals, such as copper and gold, are melted in a certain proportion to make into a ware. Next, various patterns are engraved on the ware. Then, the molten silver (gold) is plated within the delicate patterns. After getting cooled, they are polished. After that, the base copper is changed into black by using the craft handed down from ancestors, with silver (gold) patterns becoming prominent, showing a sharp contrast between black and white (yellow) in decorative effect. Generally, silver is the main material for plating, so the products are named as "Silver-plated Black Copperware". They are mostly daily goods, such as ink cartridges, pen holders, liquor pots, incense burners and vases. The patterns are Kylin Bestowing Books, Eight Immortals Crossing the Sea, flowers, birds, insects and fish, birds and beasts, plum blossom, orchid, bamboo, chrysanthemum, dragons, phoenixes, deer, cranes, etc., which have ingenious designs and fine craftsmanship.

第 14 项：民族乐器制作技艺（傣族象脚鼓制作技艺）

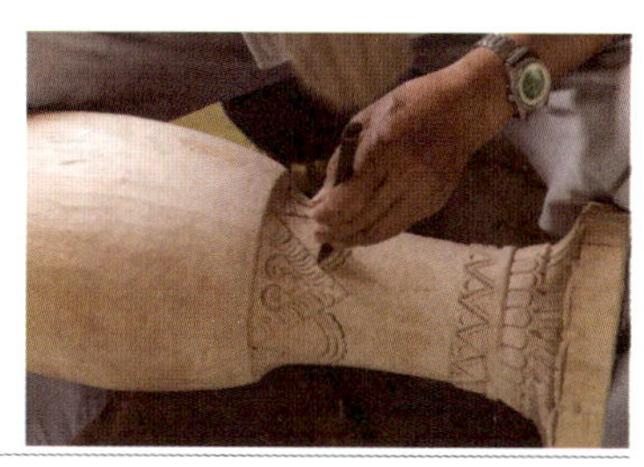

傣族象脚鼓制作图
the Picture of Making the Elephant-foot Drum of the Dai Nationality

项目序号：907	项目编号：Ⅷ-124	公布时间：2011（第三批）	类别：传统技艺
所属地区：云南省	类型：扩展项目	申报地区或单位：云南省临沧市临翔区	

傣族象脚鼓制作技艺流传于云南省临沧市临翔区，有五百多年的历史。临翔区傣族在泼水节、关门节（千灯节）、开门节和立幡杆节等民俗活动中都少不了象脚鼓。白象是傣族吉祥物，傣族人将传达吉祥声音的鼓制成白象腿形状的象脚鼓，体现了傣族的图腾崇拜。[①]

傣族象脚鼓制作技艺集木工雕刻、彩绘、制革和美术等技艺为一体，制作工具有锯、锤、斧、刀、刨、铲、凿、钻和锥等。工艺流程主要有：选料、开工仪式、下料、制作象脚鼓和竣工仪式。傣族象脚鼓的制作材料一般用椿树、杨柳树、云槐树和攀枝花树等，要在农历八月砍伐，此时树木质地好，不易虫蛀开裂。制作前，由村里德高望重的老人主持举行祭竜树、祭天官、祭水官、祭军事神、祭安全竜、祭寨心、祭叫魂神和祭佛祖等祭祀活动。祭祀完后，便可以下料制作，鼓长和鼓面直径比例 5:2，鼓的上中下比例是 4:2:4，鼓面直径小于鼓脚直径 2-6 厘米。象脚鼓初制完成后，要经过内部镂空打磨、外部凿刻打磨、雕刻吉祥物、蒙制鼓面和彩绘装饰等环节才算完工。制作完后还要举行竣工仪式，在佛塔前、古老的缅树下和佛寺里进行祭拜后才能将象脚鼓交给鼓手使用。[②]

---

① 《民族乐器制作技艺（傣族象脚鼓制作技艺）》，中国非物质文化遗产网，http://www.ihchina.cn/Article/Index/detail?id=14539，检索日期：2019 年 8 月 31 日。

② 黄琛、王海，《【喜迎十九大·文脉颂中华】傣族象脚鼓制作技艺：傣家真善美的追求》，http://www.ynich.cn/view.php?id=3535&cat_id=11411，检索日期：2019 年 8 月 31 日。

Item 14: the Craft of Making National Musical Instruments (the Craft of Making the Elephant-foot Drum of the Dai Nationality)

Item Serial Number: 907	Item ID Number: Ⅷ-124	Released Date: 2011 (Batch 3)	Category: Traditional Craft
Affiliated Province: Yunnan Province	Type: Extended Item	Application Province or Unit: Linxiang District, Lincang City, Yunnan Province	

The Craft of Making the Elephant-foot Drum of the Dai Nationality is circulated in Linxiang District, Lincang City, Yunnan Province, with a history of more than 500 years. The Dai people in Linxiang District play the Elephant-foot Drum in folk activities, such as the Water-splashing Festival, the Door-closing Festival (the Thousand-lantern Festival), the Door-opening Festival and the Flagpole-erecting Festival. The white elephant is the mascot of the Dai nationality. The Dai people made the drum that mimic the shape of the white elephant's leg to convey auspiciousness, which embodies the totem worship of the Dai nationality.

The Craft of Making the Elephant-foot Drum of the Dai Nationality integrates the techniques of wood carving, colored painting, leather making, fine arts, etc. The making tools include saws, hammers, axes, knives, planers, shovels, chisels, drills and awls. The main procedures include: selecting materials, the starting ceremony, cutting materials, making the Elephant-foot Drum and the completion ceremony. The common materials for making **the Elephant-foot Drum of the Dai Nationality** are Chinese toon, willow trees, locust trees, kapok trees, etc. They must be felled in the eighth lunar month. At this time, the wood of these trees boasts good texture and is not easy to be eaten and cracked by insects. Before making it, a respectable senior in the village presides over sacrificial activities, such as worshipping the dragon tree, worshipping the heavenly god, worshipping the water god, worshipping the military god, worshipping the dragon of safety, worshipping the village center, worshipping the soul-summoning god and worshipping the Buddha. After sacrificial activities are completed, the material can be cut and the making process begins. The ratio of the length of the drum to the diameter of the drumhead is 5:2. The ratio of the top, the middle and the bottom of the drum is 4:2:4, and the diameter of the drumhead is 2-6 cm shorter than that of the drum foot. When the preliminary production of the Elephant-foot Drum is completed, the drum can be finished only after going through the procedures of internal hollowing and grinding, external chiseling and polishing, carving mascots, covering the drumhead, painted decoration, etc. When its production is completed, a completion ceremony will be held. The Elephant-foot Drum can be handed to drummers for use only after it is worshipped in front of the pagoda, under the ancient banyan tree and in the Buddhist temple.

第15项：下关沱茶制作技艺

下关沱茶制作技艺之压制成型
the Craft of Making Xiaguan Bowl-shaped Compressed Tea: the Procedure of Being Compressed into Shape

项目序号：935	项目编号：Ⅷ-152	公布时间：2011（第三批）	类别：传统技艺
所属地区：云南省	类型：扩展项目	申报地区或单位：云南省大理白族自治州	

下关沱茶是白族人创造的十分典型的传统技艺，因创制于云南省大理市下关，故名“下关沱茶”。它由明代“团茶”演变而来，以云南大叶茶树良种加工的上等晒青毛茶为原料加工而成，多为手工操作。1902 年，大理喜洲白族商帮永昌祥在下关开设第一家茶叶精制加工厂，加工紧茶和饼茶，标志着沱茶工艺的诞生。①

下关沱茶生产工艺有原料配制、筛分、拣剔、称茶、蒸茶、揉捻、压制成型、定型、脱袋、干燥和包装等。加工中采取“细茶精制，粗茶细制，精提净取”的原则，形成了独特的加工工艺。其中，压制工艺是技术关键。1953 年以前，采用双手揉成，后改为木凳压制，凳上有凹凸槽模，运用杠杆原理进行压制，之后在布袋内冷却，等定型后解开布袋，置于木框上晾干，完成压制过程。下关沱茶制作技艺主要靠手口相传，凭长期实践经验才能掌握。下关沱茶分为生沱和普沱两种，未经发酵的为生沱，经过发酵的为普沱。特点是芽叶肥壮，滋味醇厚，茶叶内含成分丰富，色泽乌润显毫、香气清纯馥郁，汤色橙黄清亮。②

① 《黑茶制作技艺（下关沱茶制作技艺）》，中国非物质文化遗产网，http://www.ihchina.cn/Article/Index/detail?id=14626，检索日期：2019 年 7 月 29 日。

② 王晓云，《下关沱茶：百年茶香飘古道》，http://www.dlzfy.cn/dlml/ShowArticle.asp?ArticleID=247，检索日期：2019 年 8 月 31 日。

Item 15: the Craft of Making Xiaguan Bowl-shaped Compressed Tea

Item Serial Number: 935	Item ID Number: Ⅷ-152	Released Date: 2011 (Batch 3)	Category: Traditional Craft
Affiliated Province: Yunnan Province	Type: Extended Item	Application Province or Unit: Dali Bai Autonomous Prefecture, Yunnan Province	

Xiaguan Bowl-shaped Compressed Tea is a very typical traditional craft invented by the Bai people. Because it was created in Xiaguan Township, Dali City, Yunnan Province, it was named "**Xiaguan Bowl-shaped Compressed Tea**". Derived from "Tuancha Tea" of the Ming Dynasty, it is processed from the superior dried Yunnan large-leaf green tea, mostly by hand. In 1902, Yongchangxiang, a business group of the Bai nationality in Xizhou Township of Dali City, established the first tea refinery in Xiaguan to process compressed tea and tea bricks, marking the birth of Bowl-shaped Compressed Tea.

The production procedures of **Xiaguan Bowl-shaped Compressed Tea** include preparing raw materials, sifting, picking and choosing, weighing, steaming, kneading, compressing, shaping, removing bags, drying and packaging. During the making process, the principle of "excelsior" is adopted to form a unique processing technology. Among them, the compressing procedure is the key technology. Before 1953, **Xiaguan Bowl-shaped Compressed Tea** was kneaded with both hands. Later, it was compressed by using a wooden stool which has concave-convex grooves. First, by using the lever principle, the tea is compressed. Then, it is cooled in a cloth bag. After its shape is fixed, the cloth bag is unwrapped and the tea is placed on a wooden frame to get dried. By then, the compression procedure is finished. **The Craft of Making Xiaguan Bowl-shaped Compressed Tea** is mainly passed on from mouth to mouth, and can only be mastered through long-term practice. **Xiaguan Bowl-shaped Compressed Tea** is divided into two types: unfermented Bowl-shaped Compressed Tea and general Bowl-shaped Compressed Tea. The former is unfermented and the latter is fermented. The characteristics of Xiaguan Bowl-shaped Compressed Tea are: its bud leaves are plump and thick, its taste is mellow, it has a particularly abundant content of tea ingredients, it is dark and hairy, its aroma is pure and fragrant, and its soup color is orange yellow and clear.

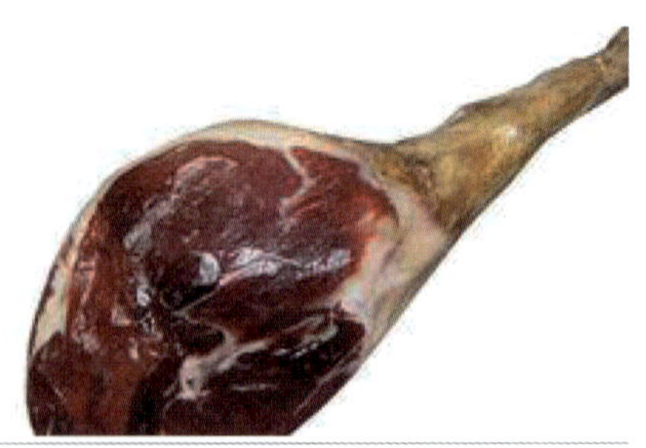

第16项：宣威火腿制作技艺

宣威火腿
Xuanwei Ham

项目序号：949	项目编号：Ⅷ-166	公布时间：2011（第三批）	类别：传统技艺
所属地区：云南省	类型：扩展项目	申报地区或单位：云南省宣威市	

宣威火腿，因产于宣威县而得名，素以风味独特而与浙江金华火腿齐名，蜚声中外。最迟明末产生，清雍正五年（1727）成名。1923 年参加广州名特食品会，获得优质奖章。20 世纪 80 年代再度获奖，90 年代实现专业化、规模化、系列化生产。

其传统加工工艺主要包括鲜腿修割定形、上盐腌制、堆码翻压、洗晒整形、上挂风干和发酵管理等六个环节。首先，将适当重量的鲜腿通风冷凉 10-12 小时后修割定形，刮去皮面残毛和污物，修去多余脂肪和结缔组织等，除净血渍。然后上盐腌制，腌制时将腿肉面朝下，皮面朝上，均匀撒盐，从蹄壳开始，逆毛孔向上用力揉搓皮层，使皮层湿润或盐与水呈糊状。腌制完成后，置于干燥、冷凉（7-10℃）的室内进行堆码翻压，翻压时底部的腿翻到上部，上部的翻到下部，以便排尽淤血。之后便可进行洗晒整形，整形后挂在室外阳光下继续晾晒 2-3 天后挂到仓库里风干，在此期间要做好发酵管理工作，根据气候变化，通过开关门窗、生火升湿来控制库房温、湿度，创造火腿发酵鲜化的最佳条件。宣威火腿的主要特点是：形似琵琶，只大骨小，皮薄肉厚，肥瘦适中；切开断面，香气浓郁，色泽鲜艳，瘦肉呈鲜红色或玫瑰色，肥肉呈乳白色，骨头略显桃红，似血气尚在滋润。其品质优良，是云南火腿的代表，故常称“云腿”。[①]

① 《火腿制作技艺（宣威火腿制作技艺）》，中国非物质文化遗产网，http://www.ihchina.cn/Article/Index/detail?id=14655，检索日期：2019 年 8 月 31 日。

Item 16: the Craft of Making Xuanwei Ham

Item Serial Number: 949	Item ID Number: Ⅷ-166	Released Date: 2011 (Batch 3)	Category: Traditional Craft
Affiliated Province: Yunnan Province	Type: Extended Item	Application Province or Unit: Xuanwei City, Yunnan Province	

Xuanwei Ham got its name because it was produced in Xuanwei County, which is as famous as Jinhua Ham of Zhejiang Province and well-known both at home and abroad for its unique flavor. Produced in the late Ming Dynasty at the latest, it became famous in the fifth year during the reign of Emperor Yongzheng of the Qing Dynasty (1727). In 1923, it participated in Guangzhou Fair of Famous and Special Foods, and won the Quality Medal. In the 1980s, it won this medal again. In the 1990s, its production became specialized, large-scale and serialized.

Its traditional processing technique mainly includes six steps: trimming and shaping fresh pork legs; salting; stacking, turning upside down and pressing; washing, drying and shaping; hanging and air drying; and fermentation management. First, fresh pork legs with a proper weight are ventilated and cooled for 10-12 hours, and then trimmed and shaped, with the residual hair and dirt on the skin scraped away, excessive fat and connective tissue trimmed off, and blood stains removed. Next, they are salted. In the process of salting, the leg meat side is placed downward and the skin side upward, evenly sprinkled with salt. Starting from the hoof shell, workers rub the skin upward in the opposite direction of the pores to make the skin moist or the salt change into the state of paste. After that, the salted legs are placed in a dry and cool (7-10°C) room for stacking, turning upside down and pressing. In this process, the salted legs at the bottom should be turned to the upper part, and those at the upper part should be turned to the lower one to drain the blood. Then, the salted legs can be washed, dried and shaped. After being shaped, they are hung outdoors in the sun to get dried for 2-3 days, and then hung in the warehouse for air drying. During this period, fermentation management should be done well. According to climate changes, workers should control the temperature and humidity of the warehouse by opening and closing doors and windows, lighting a fire and increasing the humidity, so as to create the best conditions for ham fermentation and freshness. The main characteristics of Xuanwei Ham are as follows: its shape is like Pipa (a plucked string instrument with a fretted fingerboard), with big size but small bones, thin skin but thick meat, and moderately fat and lean meat; when it is cut open, it will give off a rich aroma, showing a bright color, with its lean meat in bright red or rose colors, its fat meat in milky white color and its bones in slightly pink color, which appears to be still full of fresh blood. It has excellent quality and is a representative of the hams in Yunnan Province. Therefore, it is usually called “Yunnan Ham”.

第17项：蒙自过桥米线制作技艺

蒙自过桥米线
Mengzi Guoqiao Rice Noodles

项目序号：1349	项目编号：Ⅷ-235	公布时间：2014（第四批）	类别：传统技艺
所属地区：云南省	类型：新增项目	申报地区或单位：云南省蒙自市	

过桥米线是米线中的上品，是滇南地区特有的食品，起源于红河哈尼族彝族自治州蒙自市，已有百余年的历史。

蒙自过桥米线主要以米线、汤、肉片和佐料做成。其中，米线是主要食材，以细白、有韧性者为好，制作时先将大米用凉水浸泡半小时，控干水分后用石碾子或粉碎机碾（粉）碎成米面，然后加入适量的水糅合，最后将和好的米面团用专业压面机压成米线。蒙自过桥米线中的汤要用肥鸡和猪筒子骨等熬制而成，以清澈透亮为佳；肉片则是用鸡脯、猪里脊、肝、腰花、鲜鱼、火腿和鳅鱼等切成薄片制成，摆入碟内；佐料主要有豌豆尖、黄芽韭菜（韭菜苔或韭菜）、嫩菠菜、白菜心、葱花、豆芽、豆腐皮和玉兰片等，其中的蔬菜要用沸水略烫，切为约四厘米的长段。蒙自过桥米线集中原和边疆饮食文化之大成，多种味质不同的食物烹制在一起，形成营养丰富均衡、鲜美可口的独特佳肴，是云南食品中最具地方风味的小吃，云南省具有代表性的饮食文化品牌，荣获“中华名小吃”称号，为全国人民所熟知，在世界上也有一定的知名度。[①]

Item 17: the Craft of Making Mengzi Guoqiao Rice Noodles

Item Serial Number: 1349	Item ID Number: Ⅷ-235	Released Date: 2014 (Batch 4)	Category: Traditional Craft
Affiliated Province: Yunnan Province	Type: New Item	Application Province or Unit: Mengzi City, Yunnan Province	

① 《蒙自过桥米线》，蒙自市特产网，http://m.bytravel.cn/produce2/849981EA8FC768657C737EBF.html，检索日期：2019年7月23日。

Guoqiao Rice Noodles are the top grade among all rice noodles. As a unique food in the southern region of Yunnan Province, they originated from Mengzi City of Honghe Hani and Yi Autonomous Prefecture, with a history of more than one hundred years.

Mengzi Guoqiao Rice Noodles are mainly made with rice noodles, soup, sliced meat and condiments. Among them, rice noodles are the main ingredients and the fine, white and pliable ones are the best. In the process of making rice noodles, rice should be soaked in cold water for half an hour, then get drained, and ground into rice powder with a stone roller or a grinder. With an appropriate amount of water added, the rice powder is made into the rice dough. Then, the rice dough is made into rice noodles by using a professional noodle machine. The soup for Mengzi Guoqiao Rice Noodles should be made by stewing fat chicken and pork leg bones, and it is better to be clear and translucent. The sliced meat is made of chicken breast, pork tenderloin, liver, kidney, fresh fish, hams, loach, etc. that are sliced into thin pieces and put in a dish. The condiments mainly include the tips of pea sprouts, yellow-sprouts chives (Chinese chives), baby spinach, cabbage hearts, chopped green onions, bean sprouts, thin sheets of bean curd and dried slices of tender bamboo shoots. The vegetables should be boiled slightly in hot water and cut into 4-cm sections. Mengzi Guoqiao Rice Noodles integrate the food cultures of the Central Plains and the frontier regions. A variety of foods with different flavors are cooked together, forming a unique cuisine that has rich and balanced nutrition and delicious taste. They are the snack that has the most local flavor among all Yunnan foods, and are a representative food culture brand in Yunnan Province, winning the title of "Famous Chinese Snack". They are well-known to the whole Chinese people, and also have a certain popularity in the world.

鹤庆银器锻制品——茶壶
Heqing Silverware Product: a Tea Pot

第 18 项：银饰锻制技艺（鹤庆银器锻制技艺）

项目序号：390	项目编号：Ⅷ-40	公布时间：2014（第四批）	类别：传统技艺
所属地区：云南省	类型：扩展项目	申报地区或单位：云南省鹤庆县	

鹤庆银器锻制技艺主要流传于云南省大理白族自治州鹤庆县新华村，有五百多年的历史。

鹤庆银器锻制的工具主要有熔银炉、风匣、手锤、手钳、凿子和多功能成套錾切工具等。主要工艺有捶揲、焊接、抛光、錾刻、花丝和剔空等，其中錾刻和花丝工艺最具特色。鹤庆银器锻制的錾刻工艺主要有阳錾、阴錾、平錾和镂空等方法，錾刻工具主要有一把锤子和一套钢制錾子，其錾头被磨制成尖、圆、方、平、凹槽、月牙、花瓣等形状，以錾刻出需要的图案。錾刻时，银器锻制艺人左手执錾，右手握锤，选用适形的錾子，将纹饰錾刻在银片器形的表面。花丝工艺指艺人用极细的金银丝进行编制、堆垒、掐花和焊接，做成各种平面或立体的图形纹饰。鹤庆县新华村的银器造型丰富、种类繁多、工艺精湛、质量上乘。主要产品分为汉式银器、藏式银器和其他一些民族的银佩饰等三种，工艺造型主要有壶、九龙杯、鹤阳八景酒具、手镯、戒指、项链、耳环、银包木碗、青稞酒壶、净水壶、大中小法号、唢呐、百家锁、胸佩、胸链、帽链、门环、藏刀和佛盒等。鹤庆白族银饰的纹样以植物、花鸟和鱼虫为主。鹤庆银器工艺品远近闻名，远销各省市及美国、日本、印度、马来西亚、尼泊尔、泰国、巴基斯坦等国家，深受世人称赞。①

① 王青，《鹤庆白族银器加工工艺》，载《今日民族》，2012 年第 10 期，第 38 页。

Item 18: the Craft of Making Silver Ornaments (the Craft of Making Heqing Silverware)

Item Serial Number: 390	Item ID Number: Ⅷ-40	Released Date: 2014 (Batch 4)	Category: Traditional Craft
Affiliated Province: Yunnan Province	Type: Extended Item	Application Province or Unit: Heqing County, Yunnan Province	

The Craft of Making Heqing Silverware is mainly spread in Xinhua Village, Heqing County, Dali Bai Autonomous Prefecture, Yunnan Province, with a history of more than five hundred years.

The tools for making Heqing Silverware mainly include a silver-melting furnace, a wind box, a hammer, a plier, a chisel and a set of multi-functional chiseling and cutting tools. The main procedures include hammering, welding, polishing, chiseling and carving, making filigree and hollowing out, among which chiseling and carving as well as making filigree are the most distinctive. The procedure of chiseling and carving mainly involves the methods of Yang chiseling, Yin chiseling, flat chiseling and hollowing out. The tools for chiseling and carving mainly include a hammer and a set of steel chisels. The chisel heads are ground into the pointed shape, round shape, square shape, flat shape, groove shape, crescent shape, petal shape, etc. to carve the required patterns. When carving it, the artisan who makes silverware holds a chisel in the left hand and a hammer in the right one, choosing an appropriate chisel to carve decorative patterns on the surface of silverware. The filigree procedure refers to artisans' weaving, stacking, making flowers via pinching, and welding by using extremely fine gold and silver wires to make various flat or three-dimensional decorative patterns. The silverware in Xinhua Village of Heqing County is rich in shape and variety, with exquisite craftsmanship and high quality. Its main products are divided into three types: the Han-style silverware, the Zang-style silverware and the silver ornaments of some other nationalities. They are mainly pots, Nine Dragon Cups, wine sets engraved with eight scenic spots of Heyang, bracelets, rings, necklaces, earrings, silver-wrapped wooden bowls, highland barley liquor pots, water pots, large-, medium- and small-sized Fahao (a kind of bass wind instruments), Suona Horn (a woodwind instrument), Baijia locks, chest accessories, chest chains, hat chains, door knockers, knives of the Zang nationality, Buddha boxes, etc. The patterns on the silver ornaments of the Bai nationality in Heqing County are mainly plants, flowers, birds, fish and insects. Heqing silverware handicrafts are well-known far and near, and are exported to various provinces and cities, as well as the United States, Japan, India, Malaysia, Nepal, Thailand, Pakistan and other countries, highly praised by customers.

滇红茶制作的揉捻工艺
the Procedure of Rubbing and Kneading in the Making of Yunnan Black Tea

第19项：

红茶制作技艺

（滇红茶制作技艺）

项目序号：932	项目编号：Ⅷ-149	公布时间：2014（第四批）	类别：传统技艺
所属地区：云南省	类型：扩展项目	申报地区或单位：云南省凤庆县	

滇红茶属发酵茶，以云南大叶种茶树鲜叶为原料，手工操作而成。因加工精细，费时较多，被称为“工夫红茶”；又因其成条形，亦称“红条茶”。主要流传于云南省凤庆县。

滇红茶制作工艺从采摘到成品茶需经过初制和精制两个步骤。初制：初制工序包括萎凋、揉捻、发酵和干燥。滇红茶的鲜叶经过这四道工序处理后，称毛茶。在此过程中，茶叶发生了物理和化学变化，才得以成为汤色鲜红、滋味甘醇的红茶。精制：精制工序包括整理茶条形状、剔除劣质异形、调剂品质、控制水份和增进香气。为达到精制加工的目的，需要将初制的滇红茶划分本身茶、原身茶和轻身茶三路产品区分加工：本身茶，条索紧直、苗锋秀丽、芽毫显露、色泽油润、嫩度较高，为条型茶中最好的产品；原身茶，条索短秃、芽毫少、围度大、嫩度低，与本身茶相比，品质次之；轻身茶，叶质轻而芽毫显，条索欠紧结，色泽杂而显干枯，外形低于本身茶而优于原身茶，内质欠于原身茶。优质滇红茶主要有外形条索紧结、汤色鲜红、香气鲜浓、滋味醇厚和耐冲泡的特点。

Item 19: the Craft of Making Black Tea (the Craft of Making Yunnan Black Tea)

Item Serial Number: 932	Item ID Number: Ⅷ-149	Released Date: 2014 (Batch 4)	Category: Traditional Craft
Affiliated Province: Yunnan Province	Type: Extended Item	Application Province or Unit: Fengqing County, Yunnan Province	

Yunnan Black Tea belongs to fermented tea, which is made of the fresh leaves of Yunnan large-leaf tea as raw materials by hand. Because it is processed finely, consuming a lot of time, it is called "Kongfu Black Tea"; and due to its strip shape, it is also called "Strip Black Tea". It is mainly spread in Fengqing County, Yunnan Province.

From picking tea leaves to making final products, the production process of Yunnan Black Tea needs to undergo two steps: primary processing and refined processing. Primary processing: Its procedures include withering, rubbing and kneading, fermenting and drying. After undergoing these four procedures, the fresh leaves of Yunnan Black Tea are made into raw tea. In this process, tea leaves undergone physical and chemical changes, becoming black tea with a bright red color and a sweet taste. Refined processing: Its procedures include improving the shape of tea strips, removing inferior and deformed ones, adjusting the quality, controlling the moisture and enhancing the aroma. In order to achieve the goal of refined processing, it is necessary to divide the primarily-processed Yunnan Black Tea into three grades: Benshen tea, Yuanshen tea and Qingshen tea, and process them differently. Benshen tea is the best product in strip-shaped tea, with tight and straight shape, beautiful seedlings, visible tea hairs, oily color and high degree of tenderness. Yuanshen tea, with short and bald tea strips, few tea hairs, large girth and low degree of tenderness, is inferior to Benshen tea in quality. Qingshen tea has light leaves and visible tea hairs, less tight tea strips and mixed and dry colors, so it is inferior to Benshen tea and superior to Yuanshen tea in appearance, while inferior to Yuanshen tea in quality. High-quality Yunnan Black Tea mainly has the characteristics of tightly-shaped tea strips, bright red color, strong aroma, mellow taste and lasting long time.

第九章 传统医药

Chapter Nine

Traditional Medicine

第 1 项：彝医药（彝医水膏药疗法）

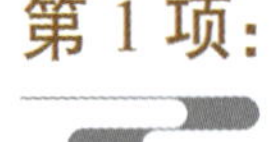

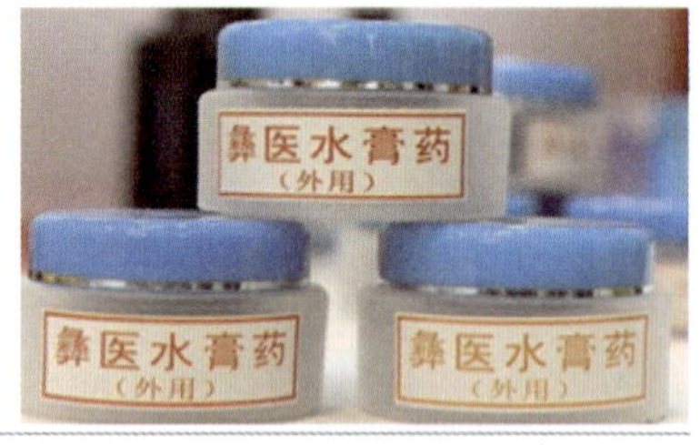

彝医水膏药制品

the Products of the Ointments Mixed with Water of the Yi Nationality

项目序号：1194	项目编号：Ⅸ-19	公布时间：2011（第三批）	类别：传统医药
所属地区：云南省	类型：新增项目	申报地区或单位：云南省楚雄彝族自治州	

彝医药是彝族人民的传统医药，分布于云南省楚雄彝族自治州和四川凉山彝族自治州等地。彝医学将天地元气分为清、浊二气，蕴生金、木、水、火、土五行作为基本物质。人体以清气络胸、腹、五脏，以浊气循肌表、腹、背，上下六气贯通，制衡内外邪毒。这是彝族人民对生命和健康的认知，成为彝医学的基础理论。

彝医水膏药疗法是一种清热解毒的外治法。彝族地区气候湿热，虫虺蚊蚋为害，瘴疠疫气为毒，疖肿痈疽时有发生。当疖肿疮毒尚未破溃时，将一种或多种草药切碎捣烂，加水调成糊状，敷于红肿热痛部位，外用纱布包住，1-2天更换一次。所用水指井水、冰水或雪水（在冬天或从高山收集后贮于瓦罐内备用）；所用草药主要是青叶胆、地胆、迎春花和野菊花等。这些草药结合水的凉性，具有清热、解毒、消肿和镇痛的作用。现在彝医水膏药已经制成了成品，使用十分方便。①

Item 1: the Medicine of the Yi Nationality (the Therapy of Ointments Mixed with Water of the Yi Nationality)

Item Serial Number: 1194	Item ID Number: Ⅸ-19	Released Date: 2011 (Batch 3)	Category: Traditional Medicine
Affiliated Province: Yunnan Province	Type: New Item	Application Province or Unit: Chuxiong Yi Autonomous Prefecture, Yunnan Province	

The Medicine of the Yi Nationality is the traditional medicine of the Yi people, distributed in Chuxiong Yi Autonomous Prefecture of Yunnan Province, Liangshan Yi Autonomous Prefecture of Sichuan Province, etc. **The Medicine of the Yi Nationality** divides the vitality of the heaven and the earth into Qingqi and Zhuoqi, which has generated five elements of gold, wood, water, fire and earth as basic substances. In the human body, Qingqi serves to connect the chest, the abdomen and five internal organs, and Zhuoqi flows through the skin, the abdomen and the back. The six kinds of Qi (vital energy) are interconnected, balancing the internal and external evil toxins. This is the Yi people's understanding of life and health, which has become the basic theory of **the Medicine of the Yi Nationality**.

The Therapy of Ointments Mixed with Water of the Yi Nationality is an external therapy for clearing away heat and deintoxication. The climate in areas where the Yi people live is hot and humid. Here insects, mosquitoes, gnats and miasma can cause serious diseases, and furuncle and gangrene occur from time to time. When furuncle and gangrene have not ruptured, the doctors chop up one or more medicinal herbs, mash them up, add water to make a paste, apply it to the red, swollen, hot and

① 《彝医药（彝医水膏药疗法）》，中国非物质文化遗产网，http://www.ihchina.cn/Article/Index/detail?id=14893，检索日期：2019 年 8 月 31 日。

painful area, and wrap it with gauze for external use, once every 1-2 days. The water used is well water, ice water or snow water (stored in crocks in winter or after being collected from high mountains for later use). The medicinal herbs used are mainly Qingyedan Herb (*Swertia mileensis* in Latin), Didan Herb (*Elephantopus scaber* in Latin), winter jasmine, wild chrysanthemum flower, etc. Combined with the coolness of water, these herbs have the effects of clearing heat, deintoxication, subsiding the swelling and easing pains. Now, **the Therapy of Ointments Mixed with Water of the Yi Nationality** has been made into end products, which is very convenient for users.

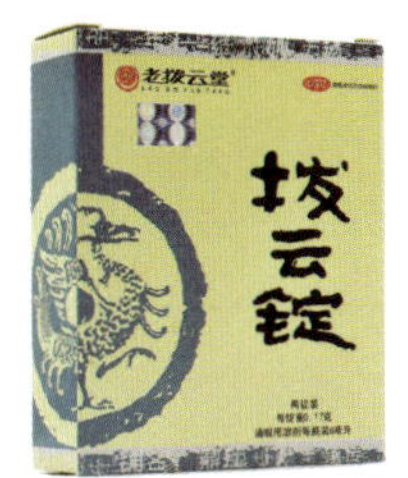

拨云锭制品
the Products of Boyun Pastille

第 2 项：彝医药（拨云锭制作技艺）

项目序号：1194	项目编号：Ⅸ-19	公布时间：2014（第四批）	类别：传统医药
所属地区：云南省	类型：扩展项目	申报地区或单位：云南省楚雄市	

彝医药——拨云锭传统配方及制作工艺是我国目前唯一的中药眼科锭剂制品，是中国民族医药学会评定的首个彝族药品种。据《云南省志·医药志》记载："清雍正六年（1728 年），通海秀山沈育柏创建老拨云堂，生产拨云锭眼药，首开云南制药先河"[①]，距今已有 280 多年的历史。

"拨云锭"由彝族传统配方通过传统工艺制成，药物配方主要有麝香、龙胆草等十味中药，有解毒散结、消炎止痛、明目退翳等显著疗效，用于暴发火眼，目赤肿痛，沙眼刺痛，目痒流泪，翼状胬肉，牙龈肿痛，咽喉红肿等病症。外用，取本品两锭，加入滴眼用溶剂中，振摇至完全溶解，摇匀后滴入眼睑内，一日 2 至 4 次；牙龈肿痛、喉舌炎症可含服，一次一锭，一日三次。光绪末年，"拨云锭"声名远扬，销售至中原、青海、新疆和甘肃等地，并经由茶马古道远销至越南、缅甸、泰国、老挝和马来西亚等东南亚国家，曾一度作为货币在市场上流通。"拨云锭"获得清朝皇室和民国云南政府的嘉奖并荣载史册，至新中国成立前，其年产销量高达 300 万锭。新中国成立以后，老拨云堂生产的"拨云锭"获得诸多荣誉。"拨云锭"是民族传统文化和现代科学相结合的见证。[②]

① 云南省地方志编纂委员会，《云南省志·医药志》，昆明：云南人民出版社，1995 年，第 2 页。

② 《彝医药——拨云锭传统配方及制作工艺》，楚雄州非遗网，http://www.cxfy.org.cn/file_read.aspx?id=565，检索日期：2019 年 8 月 31 日。

Item 2: the Medicine of the Yi Nationality (the Craft of Making Boyun Pastille)

Item Serial Number: 1194	Item ID Number: Ⅸ-19	Released Date: 2014 (Batch 4)	Category: Traditional Medicine
Affiliated Province: Yunnan Province	Type: Extended Item	Application Province or Unit: Chuxiong City, Yunnan Province	

The traditional formula and craft of making Boyun Pastille, **the Medicine of the Yi Nationality**, is the only ophthalmic pastille product of traditional Chinese medicine. It is the first Yi medical product appraised by China Medical Association of Minorities. According to *Annuals of Yunnan Province·Annuals of Medicine*: "In the 6th year during the reign of Emperor Yongzheng of the Qing Dynasty (1728), Shen Yubai in Xiushan (Township) of Tonghai (County) founded the ancient Boyun Hall, producing the eye medicine of Boyun Pastille, the first pharmaceutical pioneer in Yunnan Province." It has had a history of more than 280 years up to now.

Boyun Pastille is made by adopting the traditional Yi medical formula and the traditional craft. The formula mainly includes ten Chinese medicinal herbs, such as musk and gentian. It has the miraculous effects of deintoxication, diminishing stagnation, relieving pain and inflammation, improving eyesight, reducing leukoma, etc. It is used for epidemic conjunctivitis, swollen and painful eyes, trachoma with stabbing pains, itchy eyes, tearing, pterygium, swollen and painful gums, red and swollen throats, etc. For external use, patients should take out two pastilles, add them to the solvent for eye drops, shake the solvent to dissolve the pastilles, and drip them into the eyelids after shaking well, 2-4 times a day. For the swellings and pains of gums, as well as the inflammations of tongues and throats, patients can take the pastilles sublingually, one pastille per time, three times a day. In the last year during the reign of Emperor Guangxu, Boyun Pastille became famous and was sold to the Central Plains, Qinghai, Xinjiang, Gansu, etc. It was also exported to the Southeast Asian countries, such as Vietnam, Myanmar, Thailand, Laos and Malaysia through the Tea-horse Ancient Road. It had once been used as a currency to circulate in the market. Boyun Pastille had been awarded by the royal family of the Qing Dynasty and Yunnan government of the Republic of China, going down in history. Before the founding of the People's Republic China, its annual sales volume had reached three million pastilles. After the founding of the People's Republic of China, Boyun Pastille produced by the ancient Boyun Hall has received many honors. It is a testimony to the integration of traditional ethnic culture and modern science.

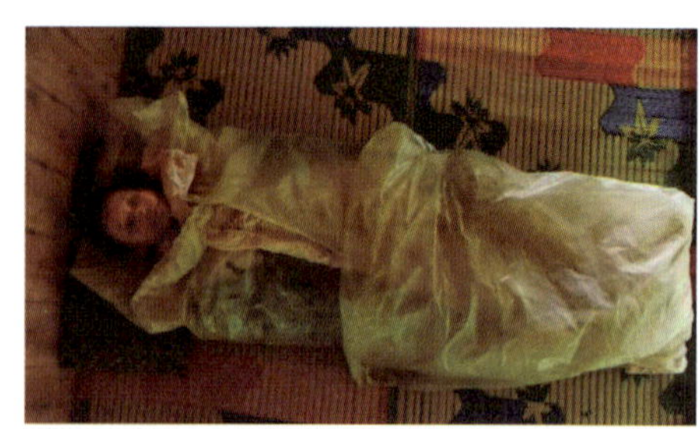

第 3 项：傣医药（睡药疗法）

睡药疗法
the Therapy of Sleeping in Herbs

项目序号：1195	项目编号：Ⅸ-20	公布时间：2011（第三批）	类别：传统医药
所属地区：云南省	类型：新增项目	申报地区或单位：云南省西双版纳傣族自治州、德宏傣族景颇族自治州	

傣医药是傣族人民在总结本民族传统医药经验的基础上，吸取和借鉴印度古典医学和中医学知识，形成以“四塔、五蕴”[①]和“解药理论”为核心的传统医学体系。

睡药疗法是傣医药传统外治法之一，用于治疗中风、风湿病及高热昏厥等病症。分冷睡和热睡两种。冷睡疗法治热病，热睡疗法治寒病。冷睡疗法即根据病情所需，选择相应的处方，采集傣药鲜品（或干品）切碎捣烂，加入适量的药酒、旱莲草汁拌匀后，把药平摊在睡药床上，让患者睡在药上，然后将余药均匀地包敷周身（除面部外），再用布包裹。一次治疗时间视病情而定，具有清火解毒、退热镇惊、祛风止痛、保护脏器之功，用于治疗发热性疾病出现高热不退、惊厥抽搐、神昏谵语、类风湿病、痛风、周身关节肌肉红肿热痛等病症。热睡疗法针对寒病，按病情所需，配备相应的傣药鲜品或干品，置于锅内，加适量水和酒，炒热后平摊在睡药床上，待温度适中，让患者平睡在药上，再取余药包裹周身（除面部外），用布包住，覆盖被褥，一次约 30 分钟左右，令其发汗，以达到开汗孔、通气血、除风毒、止疼痛的目的，用来治疗风湿病、中风偏瘫后遗症、月子病和老年性腰腿痛等。睡药疗法符合傣医理论和群众习俗，药物就地取材，资源丰富，使用方便。[②]

① “四塔”：即土、水、火、风；“五蕴”：即色、识、受、想、行。

② 《傣医药（睡药疗法）》，中国非物质文化遗产网，http://www.ihchina.cn/Article/Index/detail?id=14895，检索日期：2019 年 8 月 31 日。

Item 3: the Medicine of the Dai Nationality (the Therapy of Sleeping in Herbs)

Item Serial Number: 1195	Item ID Number: Ⅸ-20	Released Date: 2011 (Batch 3)	Category: Traditional Medicine
Affiliated Province: Yunnan Province	Type: New Item	Application Province or Unit: Xishuangbanna Dai Autonomous Prefecture and Dehong Dai and Jingpo Autonomous Prefecture of Yunnan Province	

The Medicine of the Dai Nationality is a traditional medical system with "the Four Pagodas and the Five Aggregates"① and "the Antidote Theory" as the core, which is formed by the Dai people on the basis of summarizing their traditional medical experience, absorbing and drawing on the knowledge of Indian classical medicine and traditional Chinese medicine.

The Therapy of Sleeping in Herbs is one of the traditional external therapies of **the Medicine of the Dai Nationality**. It is used to treat diseases, such as strokes, rheumatism, and faint due to a high fever. There are two types: cold therapy and hot therapy. The cold therapy cures the hot disease, and the hot therapy cures the cold disease. According to the condition of the disease, appropriate prescriptions of the cold therapy are applied. The process is as follows: collect fresh Dai medicinal herbs (or dried herbs), chop them up, and then pound them to a pulp; add an appropriate amount of medicinal liquor and eclipta juice, mix them thoroughly, and then spread the mixed medicine evenly on the bed; let the patient lie on the medicine, and evenly cover his/ her body (except the face) with the remaining herbs, and then wrap him/her with a cloth. The duration of one treatment depends on the condition of the patient. It has the functions of clearing heat, detoxification, relieving fever and convulsions, removing wind and relieving pains, as well as protecting visceral organs. It is used to cure the symptoms resulting from febrile diseases, such as recurrent fever, convulsions, delirium, rheumatoid diseases, gout, and the swellings and pains of the joints and muscles all over the body. The hot therapy is to cure the cold disease. The process is as follows: according to the conditions of the disease, prepare

① "The Four Pagodas" refers to earth, water, fire and winds; "the Five Aggregates" refers to colors, knowledge, reception, thought and action.

corresponding fresh or dried Dai medicinal herbs; put them in a pot, add appropriate amount of water and liquor, heat the herbs and then spread them evenly on the bed; when the temperature is moderate, let the patient lie on the medicine; cover his/ her body (except the face) with the remaining herbs, wrap him/her with a cloth, and then cover him/her with a quilt for about 30 minutes at a time to make him/her sweat, with the purpose of opening sweat pores, promoting the circulation of Qi (vital energy) and blood, eliminating wind and poison, as well as relieving pains. The hot therapy can treat rheumatism, stroke hemiplegia sequelae, puerperal fever and senile waist-and-leg pains. **The Therapy of Sleeping in Herbs** is in line with the theory of the Dai medicine and the custom of the Dai people. Its medicine is made from local materials, with rich resources and great convenience.

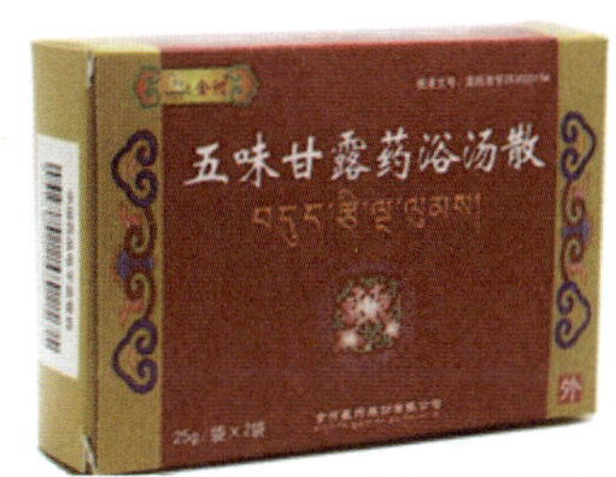

第 4 项：
藏医药（藏医骨伤疗法）

藏医骨伤疗法的骨折后期所用药物——《五味甘露药浴汤散》
the Medicine Used at the Later Stage of Bone Fracture of the Therapies for Bone Injuries of the Zang Medicine: Five-flavor Ganlu Medicine (powder) for Medicated Bath

项目序号：448	项目编号：Ⅸ-9	公布时间：2011（第三批）	类别：传统医药
所属地区：云南省	类型：扩展项目	申报地区或单位：云南省迪庆藏族自治州	

迪庆藏医骨伤疗法是以传统藏医创伤学理论为基础，运用具有接骨功效的天然鲜草药捣成糊状外敷和内服传统藏药相结合，结合当地资源条件，形成的独具特色的疗法。

迪庆藏医骨伤疗法由整复、外敷药加夹板或牵引固定、功能锻炼三个步骤构成。其中，外敷药加夹板或牵引固定最具特色。这个步骤包含骨折初期、中期、后期。初期应用具有清热、消肿、止痛、活血化瘀功效的外敷药伤科一号（由铁箍散、冰片、红花、雪山一枝蒿等组成），并根据不同情况用夹板固定或持续牵引固定，内服传统藏药桑琼丸、十味乳香丸、十八味杜鹃花丸，其药理作用是舒通筋骨脉络和活血化瘀。中期应用具有接骨、舒筋功效的外敷药伤科二号（由铁箍散、红花、骨碎补、当归、秦皮等组成），并根据病情用夹板外固定或持续牵引，内服藏药接骨消炎丸、八味秦皮丸和达尔强散，主要药理作用是促进骨细胞生成、骨化、骨连接和消炎。后期用五味甘露药浴和内服具有补肾壮骨、益气养血强筋骨功效的石榴日轮丸、巴桑母酥油丸等，并适当进行功能锻炼。五味甘露药浴具有消炎止痛、活血化瘀、强筋壮骨、防止肌肉萎缩、防止关节僵硬等作用。迪庆藏医骨伤疗法外敷药材均就地取材，按藏医理论处方，受到周边群众及国内外患者的信任。①

---

① 《藏医药（藏医骨伤疗法）》，中国非物质文化遗产网，http://www.ihchina.cn/Article/Index/detail?id=14865，检索日期：2019 年 7 月 28 日。

Item 4: the Zang Medicine (the Therapies for Bone Injuries of the Zang Medicine)

Item Serial Number: 448	Item ID Number: Ⅸ-9	Released Date: 2011 (Batch 3)	Category: Traditional Medicine
Affiliated Province: Yunnan Province	Type: Extended Item	Application Province or Unit: Diqing Zang Autonomous Prefecture, Yunnan Province	

Based on the theory of traumatology of traditional Zang medicine, **the Therapies for Bone Injuries of the Zang Medicine** in Diqing are a unique way of treatment formed by the combination of the external application of the mashed natural fresh herbs that have the effect of setting broken bones and the oral administration of traditional Zang medicine, which takes the advantage of local resources.

The Therapies for Bone Injuries of the Zang Medicine in Diqing involve three steps: resetting, external application of medicine and splint or traction and fixation, and functional exercise. Among them, the external application of medicine and splint or traction and fixation is the most distinctive. This step includes the initial, middle and later stages of bone fracture. At the initial stage, patients should use the medicine for external application, Trauma No. 1 (consisting of *Schisandra propinqua*, borneol, safflower, *Aconitum racemulosum* Franch., etc.) which has the efficacy of clearing heat, reducing swellings, relieving pains, promoting blood circulation and removing stasis. Besides, fixed splints or continuous traction and fixation should be applied according to different conditions, with the traditional Zang medicines of Sangqiong Pills, Ten-flavor Ruxiang Pills and Eighteen-flavor Azalea Pills taken, the effects of which are to unblock the arteries and veins in muscles and bones, promote blood circulation and remove stasis. At the middle stage, patients should use the medicine for external application, Trauma No. 2 (consisting of S*chisandra propinqua*, safflower, the rhizome of *davallia*, Chinese Angelica, ash bark, etc.) which has the efficacy of bonesetting and unblocking the blood vessels in muscles. Besides, fixed splints or continuous traction should be applied according to different conditions, together with the oral administration of the Zang medicines of Pills for Bonesetting and Diminishing Inflammation, Eight-flavor Ash Bark Pills and Da'er Strengthening Powder, the effects of which are mainly to promote the formation of bone cells, ossification and bone connection and to diminish inflammation. At the later stage, patients should have a medicated bath of Five-flavor Ganlu Medicine, take Pomegranate Rilun Pills and Basangmu Butter Pills that have the efficacy of nourishing kidneys and strengthening bones, nourishing Qi (vital energy) and blood and strengthening muscles and bones, and do functional exercises appropriately. The medicated bath of Five-flavor Ganlu Medicine has the functions of relieving inflammations and pains, promoting blood circulation and removing stasis, strengthening muscles and bones, and preventing muscle atrophy and joint stiffness. The medicinal herbs used in the external application of **the Therapies for Bone Injuries of the Zang Medicine** in Diqing are all from local resources. The prescriptions are made according to the theory of the Zang medicine, which have been trusted by the masses in surrounding areas and the patients at home and abroad.

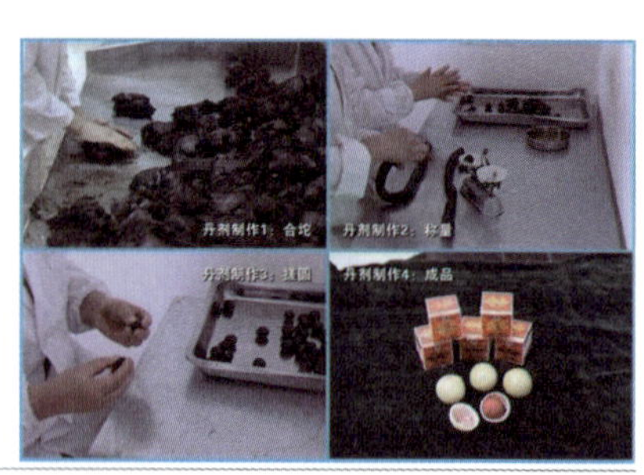

昆中药丹剂的制作工序
the Procedures of Making Pellets of Kun Traditional Chinese Medicine

第 5 项：

中医传统制剂方法

（昆中药传统中药制剂）

项目序号：443	项目编号：Ⅸ-4	公布时间：2014（第四批）	类别：传统医药
所属地区：云南省	类型：扩展项目	申报地区或单位：云南省昆明市	

昆中药是在明朝初年随皇帝朱元璋派遣的入滇大军传入云南才逐渐在滇发展起来的，已有 600 多年历史，目前已成为中国中药五大老号之一。

昆中药一直秉持中医药应回归到“阴阳平衡”“整体调养”和“治未病”上来的原则，逐步形成了舒肝、清肺和养心等养生理念和方法。昆中药药工制药“选材优良，灰碎之杂质不敷；做工细腻，配方之斤两弗疏”。各老药铺先后创制众多精品国药，自成一体。清肺化痰丸是昆中药独家品种；双美号的朱氏善用水酒和小儿化风丹；其他驰名的昆中药制剂有：体德堂的“郑氏女金丹”、万松草堂的“小儿救急丹”、长春坊的“阮氏上清丸”、福元堂的“保产达生丸”、姚济药号的“姚济资生丸”、福林堂的“再造丸”和“感冒疏风丸”、玉六堂的“止咳丸”、姚荫轩的“桑菊银翘散”、成春堂的“疥疮药膏”、萧光汉的生三七丸和熟三七丸等。这些产品配方独到，疗效确切，在明、清、民国时期就已驰名。昆中药的制作技艺丰富多样，“炮炒煅炙，丸散膏丹”，这些炮炙技法由药工口口相传。①

① 《昆中药传统中药制剂》，昆中药网，http://www.kunmingzhongyao.com/view/zycPC/1/52/view/47.html，检索日期：2019 年 8 月 31 日。

Item 5: the Preparation Methods of Traditional Chinese Medicine (the Preparations of Kun Traditional Chinese Medicine)

Item Serial Number: 443	Item ID Number: Ⅸ-4	Released Date: 2014 (Batch 4)	Category: Traditional Medicine
Affiliated Province: Yunnan Province	Type: Extended Item	Application Province or Unit: Kunming City, Yunnan Province	

Kun Traditional Chinese Medicine was introduced to Yunnan with the army dispatched by Emperor Zhu Yuanzhang in the early Ming Dynasty and gradually developed in Yunnan, having a history of more than 600 years. At present, it has become one of the five old brands of traditional Chinese medicine in China.

Kun Traditional Chinese Medicine has always been adhering to the principles of traditional Chinese medicine, such as "the balance of Yin and Yang", "holistic recuperation" and "preventive treatment of diseases", and has gradually formed the concepts and methods of health preservation, such as soothing the liver, clearing away the lung-heat and nourishing the heart. When making medicines, the pharmaceutical workers of **Kun Traditional Chinese Medicine** adhere to the principle of "the selection of excellent materials, no impurities, exquisite workmanship and enough amount of the formula". Each old pharmacy has successively created many fine Chinese medicines, having a style of its own. Pills for Clearing Away the Lung-heat and Eliminating Phlegm are the exclusive variety of **Kun traditional Chinese Medicine**; Shuangmei Shop, run by the Zhu family, is well-known for its medicinal liquor and Pills for Dispelling Infants' Wind. Other well-known preparations of **Kun Traditional Chinese Medicine** include: the Zheng Family's Nüjin Pellets of Tide Hall, Infant Emergency Pellets of Wansong Thatched Cottage, the Ruan Family's Shangqing Pills of Changchun Workshop, Childbirth-ensuring Pills of Fuyuan Hall, Yaoji Life-activating Pills of Yaoji Pharmacy, Revival Pills and Pills for Curing Influenza and Dispelling Wind of Fulin Hall, Cough-relieving Pills of Yuliu Hall, Powder of Mulberry Leaf, Daisy, Lonicera and Forsythia of Yaoyinxuan, Scabies Ointment of Chengchun Hall, Raw Pseudo-ginseng Pills and Cooked Pseudo-ginseng Pills made by Xiao Guanghan. These products have unique formulas and good effects, well-known in the Ming and Qing dynasties and the Republic of China. The crafts of making **Kun Traditional Chinese Medicine** are rich and diverse, including "drying by heat, frying, calcining, roasting, making pills, making powder, making ointments and making pellets". These crafts are passed down from mouth to mouth by pharmaceutical workers.

第十章 民俗

Chapter Ten Folk Custom

第 1 项：傣族泼水节

浴佛活动

the Activity of Bathing the Buddha

项目序号：456	项目编号：X-8	公布时间：2006（第一批）	类别：民俗
所属地区：云南省	类型：新增项目	申报地区或单位：云南省西双版纳傣族自治州	

傣族泼水节又名“浴佛节”，傣语称为“比迈”（意为新年），是西双版纳最隆重的传统节日之一，是全面展现傣族水文化、音乐舞蹈文化、饮食文化、服饰文化和民间崇尚等传统文化的综合舞台，在傣历六月中旬（农历清明前后十天左右）举行。

泼水节为傣族的新年，起源于印度，曾是婆罗门教的一种宗教仪式，其后为佛教所吸收，约在 13 世纪末到 14 世纪初经缅甸传入中国云南傣族地区。随着“南传上座部”佛教在傣族地区影响的增大，泼水节的习俗也日益流行起来。这一节日现已成为傣族最主要的民俗节日。西双版纳傣族泼水节内容包括民俗活动、艺术表演和经贸交流等，具体节日活动有泼水、赶摆、赛龙舟、浴佛、诵经、章哈演唱和孔雀舞、白象舞表演等。节日期间，傣族男女老少都穿上节日盛装，挑着清水，先到佛寺浴佛，然后开始互相泼水，泼出的清水象征着吉祥、幸福、健康，年轻人还将手里明亮晶莹的水珠视作甜蜜爱情的象征。①

Item 1: the Water-splashing Festival of the Dai Nationality

Item Serial Number: 456	Item ID Number: X-8	Released Date: 2006 (Batch 1)	Category: Folk Custom
Affiliated Province: Yunnan Province	Type: New Item	Application Province or Unit: Xishuangbanna Dai Autonomous Prefecture, Yunnan Province	

The Water-splashing Festival of the Dai Nationality, also known as “the Festival of Bathing the Buddha”, is called “Bimai” (New Year) in the Dai language. It is one of the grandest traditional festivals in Xishuangbanna Dai Autonomous Prefecture, and a comprehensive platform where the traditional cultures of the Dai nationality, such as water culture, music and dance culture, food culture, costume culture and folk worship, are displayed. It is held in the middle of the 6th month of the Dai calendar (about ten days before or after the Tomb Sweeping Festival of the lunar calendar).

The Water-splashing Festival is the New Year of the Dai nationality. It originated from India and was once a religious ritual of Brahmanism. Later, it was absorbed by Buddhism and introduced to regions inhabited by the Dai nationality in Yunnan Province of China via Myanmar around the late 13th century to the early 14th century. With the increasing influence of Theravada Buddhism in regions inhabited by the Dai nationality, the custom of the Water-splashing Festival has become more and more popular. This festival has become the most important folk

① 《傣族泼水节》，中国非物质文化遗产网，http://www.ihchina.cn/Article/Index/detail?id=14943，检索日期：2019 年 8 月 31 日。

festival of the Dai nationality by now. The content of **the Water-splashing Festival of the Dai Nationality** in Xishuangbanna Dai Autonomous Prefecture includes folk activities, artistic performances, as well as economic and trade exchanges. Specific activities include splashing water, Ganbai (going to a fair), racing the Dragon Boat, bathing the Buddha, reciting scriptures, singing Zhangha, as well as performing the Peacock Dance and the White Elephant Dance. During the festival, the Dai people, regardles of age and gender, all wear festive costumes, carry clean water, first go to the Buddhist temple to bathe the Buddha, and then start splashing water at each other. The splashed clean water symbolizes auspiciousness, happiness and health. The young people also view the bright water drops in their hands as symbols of sweet love.

第 2 项：傣族泼水节

德宏傣族泼水节活动
the Activities of the Water-splashing Festival of the Dai Nationality in Dehong

项目序号：456	项目编号：X-8	公布时间：2008（第二批）	类别：民俗
所属地区：云南省	类型：扩展项目	申报地区或单位：云南省德宏傣族景颇族自治州	

德宏傣族泼水节是世居云南省德宏傣族景颇族自治州的傣族、德昂族和阿昌族盛大的传统节日，节期在清明节后第 7-10 天。德宏地区的傣族又称此节日为“尚罕”和“尚键”，源于梵语，意为周转、变更和转移，指太阳已经在黄道十二宫运转一周开始向新的一年过渡。

泼水节已有近千年的历史，是在傣族稻作文明基础上融合 11 至 13 世纪南传的上座部佛教而逐渐形成的，是南传佛教宗教仪式与德宏傣族传统礼仪相结合的产物，呈现了傣族传统文化的显著特点。德宏傣族泼水节的活动形式多姿多彩，具有丰富的人文内涵，主要活动有民众采花、信众赕佛、祭祀龙亭、浴佛仪式、洒水祝福、歌舞活动、武术表演、男女丢包（抛绣球）及燃放孔明灯、飘水灯和放高升等。德宏傣族泼水节较完整地体现了傣族稻作文明和水文化的精髓，具有广泛的文化及社会功能，是傣族物质和精神文明传承的重要载体。①

Item 2: the Water-splashing Festival of the Dai Nationality

Item Serial Number: 456	Item ID Number: X-8	Released Date: 2008 (Batch 2)	Category: Folk Custom

① 《傣族泼水节》，中国非物质文化遗产网，http://www.ihchina.cn/Article/Index/detail?id=14944，检索日期：2019 年 8 月 30 日。

Affiliated Province: Yunnan Province	Type: Extended Item	Application Province or Unit: Dehong Dai and Jingpo Autonomous Prefecture, Yunnan Province

The Water-splashing Festival of the Dai Nationality in Dehong is a grand traditional festival of the Dai, De'ang and Achang nationalities living in Dehong Dai and Jingpo Autonomous Prefecture, Yunnan Province for generations. This festival is 7-10 days after the Tomb Sweeping Festival. The Dai people in Dehong also call it "Shanghan" and "Shangjian", which derive from Sanskrit, with the meanings of turnover, alteration and transference. It means that the sun has already moved a circle around the Twelve Signs of the Ecliptic, starting to transition to a new year.

The Water-splashing Festival has had a history of nearly a thousand years. It has been gradually formed on the basis of the rice-farming civilization of the Dai nationality by integrating Theravada Buddhism that spread from the 11th to the 13th centuries. It is a product of the combination of the religious ritual of Theravada Buddhism and the traditional etiquette of the Dai nationality in Dehong, showing the salient characteristics of the traditional culture of the Dai nationality. The activities of **the Water-splashing Festival of the Dai Nationality** in Dehong are diverse in form, boasting rich humanistic connotations. The main activities include people picking flowers, worshipping the Buddha, offering sacrifices to the Dragon Pavilion, the ceremony of bathing the Buddha, splashing water to pray for blessings, singing and dancing activities, performing martial arts, young men and women's Diubao (throwing the Embroidered Ball), igniting and letting off the Kongming Lantern, floating the Water Lamp, and setting off firecrackers made of explosive, bamboo tubes and bamboo poles by the Dai people. **The Water-splashing Festival of the Dai Nationality** in Dehong completely demonstrates the essence of the rice-farming civilization and the water culture of the Dai people, with a wide range of cultural and social functions, acting as an important carrier of the material and spiritual civilization of the Dai nationality.

第 3 项：

火把节（彝族火把节）

楚雄彝族火把节
the Torch Festival of the Yi Nationality in Chuxiong Yi Autonomous Prefecture

项目序号：458	项目编号：X-10	公布时间：2006（第一批）	类别：民俗
所属地区：云南省	类型：新增项目	申报地区或单位：云南省楚雄彝族自治州	

彝族火把节又称“过大年”，是楚雄彝族自治州最盛大的传统节日，于每年农历六月二十四至二十七日举行，流传于云南省楚雄州各县市的彝族村寨。

节日期间，彝族各村寨都要举行隆重的祭祀活动，祭天地、祭火、祭祖先、驱邪除恶，祈求六畜兴旺、五谷丰登、家宅平安，体现了彝族人民尊重自然规律、追求幸福生活的美好愿望。除了祭祀、祈福活动外，彝族人民还要探亲访友，听老人唱古歌，开展赛装、对歌、跳脚、摔跤、斗牛和磨担秋等文艺体育活动。楚雄州十个县、市彝族聚居地区过火把节的方式各有不同特点，但主要内容相似。楚雄市比较注重祭火神、祭庄稼神及除家秽的仪式；树苴乡要跳民间祭祀舞蹈十二兽舞，由 12 名青壮年男女模仿十二兽的习性动作，同时有农耕、栽种、收割和十二兽相生相克等内容，祈求来年风调雨顺、五谷丰登；双柏县罗武支系的彝族，火把节节期为五天；双柏县法脿小麦地冲一带的彝族地区要跳“老虎笙”舞；禄丰县高峰地区彝族从六月二十日就开始“迎火把”，此后一连几天都是分户过节。彝族火把节是宗教、祭祀、文艺、体育、社交和农产品交流的集中活动场所，凡具代表性的彝族歌舞在火把节期间都能得到最好展现。[①]

① 《彝族火把节》，云南非物质文化遗产保护网，http://www.ynich.cn/view.php?id=1407&cat_id=11110，检索日期：2019 年 8 月 30 日。

Item 3: the Torch Festival (the Torch Festival of the Yi Nationality)

Item Serial Number: 458	Item ID Number: X-10	Released Date: 2006 (Batch 1)	Category: Folk Custom
Affiliated Province: Yunnan Province	Type: New Item	Application Province or Unit: Chuxiong Yi Autonomous Prefecture, Yunnan Province	

The Torch Festival of the Yi Nationality, also known as "Celebrating the New Year", is the grandest traditional festival in Chuxiong Yi Autonomous Prefecture. It is held from the 24th to the 27th days of the 6th lunar month every year, and spread in the villages of the Yi nationality in all counties and cities of Chuxiong Prefecture, Yunnan Province.

During the festival, grand sacrificial activities will be held in every Yi village, such as offering sacrifices to the heaven, the earth, fire and ancestors, as well as expelling and eliminating evil, to pray for the prosperity of livestock and five cereals and the safety of households. They reflect the Yi people's respect for the laws of nature and their good wish to pursue a happy life. In addition to offering sacrifices and praying for blessings, the Yi people will also visit relatives and friends, listen to the elderly singing ancient songs, and carry out cultural and sports activities, such as costume competitions, antiphonal singing, Foot-jumping Dance, wrestling, bullfighting and Modanqiu Sport. The ways of celebrating the Torch Festival in the ten counties and cities in Chuxiong Prefecture inhabited by the Yi nationality are different in characteristics, but the main content is similar. In Chuxiong City, the rituals of offering sacrifices to the god of fire, offering sacrifices to the god of crops and removing domestic filth are paid more attention. In Shuju Township, a folk sacrificial dance, known as the Twelve-beast Dance is performed. Twelve young men and women imitate the behaviors of twelve beasts and other content, such as farming, planting, harvesting and the mutual generation and restriction of the twelve beasts, with the purpose of praying for timely wind and rain and a bumper grain harvest in the coming year. For the Luowu branch of the Yi nationality in Shuangbai County, the Torch Festival lasts for five days. In areas inhabited by the Yi nationality in Xiaomaidichong Village, Fabiao Township of Shuangbai County, the Tiger Sheng Dance is performed. The Yi people in Gaofeng Township of Lufeng County begin to “welcome the torch” on the 20th day of the 6th lunar month, and for several days thereafter, they celebrate the festival in each household. **The Torch Festival of the Yi Nationality** is a gala for religious activity, sacrificial activity, literature and art, sports, social intercourse and exchanges of agricultural products. All the representative songs and dances of the Yi nationality can be best displayed during **the Torch Festival**.

第 4 项：景颇族目瑙纵歌

景颇族目瑙纵歌节盛况
the Grand Occasion for the Munao Zongge Festival of the Jingpo Nationality

项目序号：459	项目编号：X-11	公布时间：2006（第一批）	类别：民俗
所属地区：云南省	类型：新增项目	申报地区或单位：云南省陇川县	

目瑙纵歌又称“总戈”，意为“欢聚歌舞”，是景颇族最隆重的传统节日，于每年农历正月十五、十六日举行，流传于云南省德宏傣族景颇族自治州的景颇族聚居区。

目瑙纵歌的最主要活动是跳目瑙纵歌舞。正式活动前，人们在舞场中心立起四根木柱，用来祭祀太阳和指示舞蹈路线。柱侧置刀、矛，象征人民强悍刚毅的性格。根据目瑙舞起源于鸟类舞的传说，在柱档两端设木雕犀鸟、孔雀各一只。柱前立活竹高竿，象征生命常青。上方挂有横匾，画有景颇传说中的起源地喜马拉雅山。目前，目瑙纵歌节已成为景颇人民欢庆丰收的歌舞娱乐的民俗节日。其最具代表性的表现形式是目瑙纵歌，包括苏目瑙（招财庆丰收）、巴当目瑙（庆祝胜利）、定栓目瑙（庆贺新居落成）和结如目瑙（出征誓师）等。与目瑙纵歌配合的舞蹈动作不多，顿步摆肩的韵律鲜明独特，是景颇族舞蹈的代表性动作。[①]举行目瑙纵歌活动时，方圆百十里有上万人参加，数万人踩着同一个鼓点起舞，规模宏大、震撼力很强，气氛十分隆重，极富民族感召力和凝聚力。目瑙纵歌节也因此被视为中国西部地区的民族狂欢节，有“天堂之舞”“万人狂欢舞”的美称。

① 《景颇族目瑙纵歌》，中国非物质文化遗产网，http://www.ihchina.cn/Article/Index/detail?id=14949，检索日期：2019 年 8 月 30 日。

Item 4: the Munao Zongge Festival of the Jingpo Nationality

Item Serial Number: 459	Item ID Number: X-11	Released Date: 2006 (Batch 1)	Category: Folk Custom
Affiliated Province: Yunnan Province	Type: New Item	Application Province or Unit: Longchuan County, Yunnan Province	

Munao Zongge, also known as “Zongge”, means “a happy gathering of singing and dancing”. It is the grandest traditional festival of the Jingpo nationality, held on the 15th and the 16th days of the first lunar month every year, and spread in areas inhabited by the Jingpo nationality in Dehong Dai and Jingpo Autonomous Prefecture, Yunnan Province.

The most primary activity of the Munao Zongge Festival is to perform Munao Zongge Dance. Before the formal event, people erect four wooden pillars in the center of the Dance Square to offer sacrifices to the sun and to indicate the dance route. Knives and spears are placed by the side of the pillars, symbolizing the tough and resolute character of the people. According to the legend that Munao Dance originated from birds' dances, wood carvings of one hornbill and one peacock are set at both ends of the crosspiece between pillars respectively. Tall living bamboo poles are erected in front of the pillars, symbolizing eternal life. There is a horizontal plaque hanging above, with the place of origin, the Himalayas, in the legend of the Jingpo nationality painted. At present, **the Munao Zongge Festival** has become a folk festival of singing, dancing and entertainment for the Jingpo people to celebrate a bumper harvest. Its most representative form of expression is Munao Zongge Dance, which includes Sumunao (to pray for wealth and celebrate a bumper harvest), Badang Munao (to celebrate a victory), Dingshuan Munao (to celebrate the completion of a new house) and Jieru Munao (to take a mass pledge before going out to battle). There are not many dance movements for the performance of Munao Zongge Dance. With distinctive rhythms, step stamping and shoulder swinging are the representative dance movements of the Jingpo nationality. When the activity of Munao Zongge is held, tens of thousands of people, within about a-hundred-li radius, participate in it, dancing to the same rhythm of the drum. It is large in scale, and grand with breath-taking atmosphere, full of national appeal and cohesion. **The Munao Zongge Festival** is therefore regarded as an ethnic carnival in western China, and has the laudatory names of “the Dance of Heaven” and “the Carnival Dance of Ten Thousand People”.

第 5 项：独龙族卡雀哇节

剽牛祭天活动

the Activity of Offering Sacrifices to the Heaven by Slaughtering Cattle

项目序号：471	项目编号：X-23	公布时间：2006（第一批）	类别：民俗
所属地区：云南省	类型：新增项目	申报地区或单位：云南省贡山独龙族怒族自治县	

独龙族卡雀哇节流传于云南省怒江傈僳族自治州贡山独龙族怒族自治县西部独龙江流域的所有独龙族村寨，在每年农历腊月，即公历的 12 月至次年的 1 月之间举行。1991 年，公历 1 月 10 日被定为独龙族的卡雀哇节。

节庆内容包括木刻传信、跳锅庄、射击猎物模型、火塘烧松叶求吉祥、喝木罗酒和剽牛等。各家族之间用木刻传信的方式相互邀请好友前来过节，木刻上刻有几道缺口就表示再过几天举行庆祝仪式，受邀者按时间带上各种食物前往，互致祝贺。第一天，宾主共饮水酒，相互对歌，晚上全村人聚在一起，围着篝火品尝食物，青年男女跳锅庄，共庆年节。第二天，有些村寨还要举行射猎庆典，铓锣齐鸣，人们围成圈边唱边舞。第三天，各家在火塘中烧松叶，祈祷来年家人平安吉祥。第四天，全村人聚在一起喝木罗酒，唱歌跳舞直至深夜。第五天，大家一起吃喝到太阳落山，卡雀哇节结束。整个节日活动中，最隆重的是剽牛祭天活动。剽牛时，全村男女围成大圆圈将牛围在中间，随铓锣声有节奏地跳翻手舞。居住于独龙江上游的村落最先揭开序幕，由上游经中游至下游各村寨，依序进入节期，整个独龙江流域的卡雀哇庆典前后相续一个月。① 卡雀哇节保留着木刻传信的信息传播方式，是研究无文字族群的社会组织机制的珍贵样本。②

① 《独龙族卡雀哇节》，云南非物质文化遗产保护网，http://www.ynich.cn/view.php?id=1405&cat_id=11110，检索日期：2019 年 8 月 30 日。

② 《独龙族卡雀哇节》，中国非物质文化遗产网，http://www.ihchina.cn/Article/Index/detail?id=14965，检索日期：2019 年 8 月 30 日。

Item 5: the Kaquewa Festival of the Dulong Nationality

Item Serial Number: 471	Item ID Number: X-23	Released Date: 2006 (Batch 1)	Category: Folk Custom
Affiliated Province: Yunnan Province	Type: New Item	Application Province or Unit: Gongshan Dulong and Nu Autonomous County, Yunnan Province	

The Kaquewa Festival of the Dulong Nationality is spread in all Dulong villages in the Dulong River Basin in the western part of Gongshan Dulong and Nu Autonomous County, Nujiang Lisu Autonomous Prefecture, Yunnan Province. It is held in the 12th month of the lunar calendar, that is between December and January of the next year of the solar calendar. In 1991, January 10th of the solar calendar was designated as **the Kaquewa Festival of the Dulong Nationality**.

The activities of the festival include: delivering messages via woodcuts, performing Guozhuang Dance, shooting prey models, burning pine leaves in the Fire Pit to pray for auspiciousness, drinking Muluo Liquor, and slaughtering cattle. All families use woodcuts to send messages to each other to invite friends to come to celebrate the festival. The number of notches on the woodcut indicates the number of the days after which the celebration ceremony will be held. The invitees bring a variety of food on the day and express good wishes to each other. On the first day, the host and the guest drink liquor and sing songs in antiphonal style. In the evening, all villagers gather around the bonfire to taste food, and young men and women perform Guozhuang Dance to celebrate the festival together. On the second day, in some villages, shooting and hunting celebrations will also be held. With Mangluo (a copper percussion instrument used by the ethnic minorities in Yunnan Province) ringing, people form a circle while singing and dancing. On the third day, pine leaves are burned in the Fire Pit of each family to pray for the safety and auspiciousness of the family members in the coming year. On the fourth day, all villagers gather together to drink Muluo Liquor, singing and dancing until late at night. On the fifth day, they eat and drink together until the sun sets, and the Kaquewa Festival ends. During the whole festival, the most solemn event is the activity of slaughtering cattle to offer sacrifices to the heaven. When slaughtering cattle, all men and women in the village form a big circle to surround the cattle, and perform the Flip-hand Dance to the rhythm of Mangluo (a copper percussion instrument used by the ethnic minorities in Yunnan Province). Villages in the upper reaches of the Dulong River unveil the prologue to celebrating this festival firstly. Villages, from the upper reaches through the middle reaches to the lower reaches of the Dulong River, enter the festival period in sequence. The celebration of **the Kaquewa Festival** in the entire Dulong River Basin lasts one month. The Kaquewa Festival preserves the way of disseminating information, that is, delivering messages via woodcuts, and is a precious sample for studying the social organization mechanism of the ethnic group with no written words.

接圣水
Collecting Holy Water

第 6 项：怒族仙女节

项目序号：472	项目编号：X-24	公布时间：2006（第一批）	类别：民俗
所属地区：云南省	类型：新增项目	申报地区或单位：云南省贡山独龙族怒族自治县	

怒族仙女节又称“鲜花节”，是怒族最盛大的传统节日，于每年农历三月十五日举行，延续三天，流传于云南省怒江傈僳族自治州贡山独龙族怒族自治县丙中洛乡的怒族聚居区。

节庆活动包括祭祀仙女洞并迎接圣水、歌舞求福、体育竞技三项。怒族信奉仙女，以祈求安泰。为了纪念传说中的仙女阿茸姑娘，在她死后的第二年农历三月十五，人们举行祭拜活动，逐渐形成仙女节习俗。[①]仙女节每年的参与者达数千人，人人穿上节日盛装，带着祭祀品、牲礼和酒，从周围村寨聚到仙女洞前，由普化寺的喇嘛击鼓诵经，众人叩头献礼，奉献鲜花、种子和酒。传说洞内由阿茸化作的钟乳石会流出仙乳，即“圣水”，由青年女子进洞接圣水，然后众人共饮，载歌载舞，通宵达旦，祈求仙女、山神保佑安康幸福、五谷丰登、六畜兴旺。同时，还开展射弩、赛跑和扳腕等民族体育活动。怒族仙女节蕴涵着丰富的怒族文化，体现了怒族的自然信仰和生殖信仰，带有藏传佛教的特征。[②]

① 《怒族仙女节》，中国非物质文化遗产网，http://www.ihchina.cn/Article/Index/detail?id=14966，检索日期：2019 年 8 月 30 日。

② 《怒族仙女节》，云南非物质文化遗产保护网，http://www.ynich.cn/view.php?id=1404&cat_id=11110，检索日期：2019 年 8 月 30 日。

Item 6: the Fairy Maiden Festival of the Nu Nationality

Item Serial Number: 472	Item ID Number: X-24	Released Date: 2006 (Batch 1)	Category: Folk Custom
Affiliated Province: Yunnan Province	Type: New Item	Application Province or Unit: Gongshan Dulong and Nu Autonomous County, Yunnan Province	

The Fairy Maiden Festival of the Nu Nationality, also known as "the Flower Festival", is the grandest traditional festival of the Nu nationality. It is held on the 15th day of the 3rd lunar month every year and lasts three days. It is spread in regions inhabited by the Nu nationality in Bingzhongluo Township, Gongshan Dulong and Nu Autonomous County, Nujiang Lisu Autonomous Prefecture, Yunnan Province.

The activities during the festival include three kinds, namely offering sacrifices to the Fairy Maiden Cave and collecting holy water, singing and dancing to pray for blessings, and Sports Contests. The Nu people believe in the fairy maiden to pray for peace and prosperity. In order to commemorate the legendary fairy maiden, Arong, on the 15th day of the 3rd lunar month of the second year after her death, people held worship activities and gradually formed the custom of **the Fairy Maiden Festival**. Thousands of people attend this festival every year. Everyone wears festive costumes, brings sacrifices and liquor, and gathers together in front of the Fairy Maiden Cave from surrounding villages. Lamas in Puhua Temple beat the drum and recite the sutra, and everyone kowtows to offer sacrifices, such as flowers, seeds and liquor. Legend has it that the stalactites transformed from Arong in the cave will flow out fairy milk, that is, "holy water". Young women enter the cave to collect holy water, and then drink it with everyone. They sing and dance all night long, praying for the fairy maiden's and the mountain god's protection of a secure, healthy and happy life, a bumper grain harvest and the thriving of the domestic animals. At the same time, ethnic sports activities, such as crossbow shooting, race running and arm wrestling, are also carried out. **The Fairy Maiden Festival of the Nu Nationality** contains rich culture of the Nu nationality, and embodies the natural belief and reproductive belief of the Nu people, with the feature of Tibetan Buddhism.

第 7 项：傈僳族刀杆节

“上刀山”表演
the Performance of “Climbing the Mountain of Knives”

项目序号：475	项目编号：X-27	公布时间：2006（第一批）	类别：民俗
所属地区：云南省	类型：新增项目	申报地区或单位：云南省泸水县	

傈僳族刀杆节是居住在云南省怒江傈僳族自治州泸水县境内的傈僳族和彝族的传统节日，每年正月十五日举行。相传明代兵部尚书王骥受朝廷派遣，率兵到云南边陲傈僳族居住地平叛。在收复失地，赶走入侵者后，他带领傈僳青年习武练勇，以保边境民富兵强。后来皇帝听信谗言，毒死王骥。傈僳族人即以过“刀杆节”的方式纪念这位爱国将领。

“上刀山，下火海”是刀杆节中主要的习俗表演活动，是最惊心动魄的环节，包括点花、点刀、耍刀、迎花、设坛、祭刀杆、竖杆、祭龙、上刀、拆刀和下火海等步骤，有一套严格的仪式，再现了山地民族翻山越岭的生活经历及攀藤附葛、艰苦卓绝的精神。“上刀山”是将 36 把利刀捆扎于 4-5 丈高的栗树杆上，每把刀相距尺许，刀刃朝上，表演者赤脚踏着锋利的钢刀，爬至刀杆顶端，依次进行开天门、挂红和撒谷等表演。“下火海”是表演者下刀杆后又踏入通红炽热的炭火中，表演绝技。现在节日中，原始信仰的内容已被展现健康新颖的唱词和手上舞蹈动作丰富的“跳嘎”所取代，体现了爱国主义精神和不畏艰险的民族精神。①

① 《傈僳族刀杆节》，中国非物质文化遗产网，http://www.ihchina.cn/Article/Index/detail?id=14970，检索日期：2019 年 8 月 30 日。

Item 7: the Daogan (knife ladder) Festival of the Lisu Nationality

Item Serial Number: 475	Item ID Number: X-27	Released Date: 2006 (Batch 1)	Category: Folk Custom
Affiliated Province: Yunnan Province	Type: New Item	Application Province or Unit: Lushui County, Yunnan Province	

The Daogan (knife ladder) Festival of the Lisu Nationality is a traditional festival of the Lisu and Yi nationalities living in Lushui County, Nujiang Lisu Autonomous Prefecture, Yunnan Province. It is held on the 15th day of the first lunar month every year. According to legend, Wang Ji, the Minister of War of the Ming Dynasty, was dispatched by the imperial court to lead his troops to the border area of Yunnan inhabited by the Lisu nationality to suppress a rebellion. After recapturing the lost territory and driving away invaders, he led the young men of the Lisu nationality to practice martial arts so as to make the people in the border area prosperous and soldiers there strong and powerful. Later, the emperor heard and believed slanders and poisoned Wang Ji. The Lisu people commemorate this patriotic general by celebrating **the Daogan (knife ladder) Festival**.

"Climbing the mountain of knives and crossing the sea of fire" are the major folk custom activities and the most thrilling performance sessions in this festival, including the procedures of Dianhua (offering sacrifices to colored paper flowers by using blood from a cockscomb), Diandao (offering sacrifices to knives by using blood from a cockscomb), playing with knives, welcoming the colored paper flowers, setting up an altar, offering sacrifices to Daogan (knife ladder), erecting Daogan (knife ladder), offering sacrifices to the dragon, climbing the knives, unfixing the knives, and crossing the sea of fire. They have a set of strict ritual. The performance reproduces the life experience of the ethnic groups in mountainous regions who have crossed mountains and climbed up by pulling the creepers, as well as their spirit of overcoming great hardship. "Climbing the mountain of knives" is an activity, in which 36 sharp knives are tied to two chestnut tree trunks with the height of 4-5 *zhang* (a Chinese unit of length, with one *zhang* roughly equals to 131 inches), and with the interval between two knives about one *chi* (a Chinese unit of length, with one *chi* roughly equals to 13 inches) apart and each knife blade facing upward, and then performers climb to the top of Daogan (knife ladder) with their bare feet stepping on the sharp steel knives, making performances such as opening the Heavenly Gate, hanging red decorations and sprinkling millet in sequence. “Crossing the sea of fire” means that performers step into the fiery red and hot charcoal fire to perform unique skills after descending Daogan (knife ladder). Now at the festival, the content concerning the primitive belief has been replaced with “Tiaoga Dance” that has healthy novel lyrics and rich dance movements of hands, which embodies the patriotic spirit and the national spirit of being fearless of danger and difficulty.

第 8 项：白族绕三灵

白族绕三灵的队伍

a Procession of "Raosanling (worshipping three gods in parades)"

项目序号：489	项目编号：X-41	公布时间：2006（第一批）	类别：民俗
所属地区：云南省	类型：新增项目	申报地区或单位：云南省大理白族自治州	

白族绕三灵，流传于云南省大理白族自治州，迄今有一千多年历史，每年农历四月二十三日至二十五日举行。节日期间，白族群众成群结队，携带祭祀用具、行李、食品和炊具等从四面八方赴会。人们希望通过虔诚的祭拜，祈求神灵保佑风调雨顺、五谷丰登、阖家平安。

“绕三灵”队伍分为三部分：前导为一男一女两位手执柳树枝和牛尾的老人（称花柳树老人）；中部除吹笛子的一人外，还有手执“霸王鞭”“金钱鼓”的男女舞者数十人；队尾由吹树叶的一人和数十位手执扇子或草帽的妇女组成，排成“一字长蛇阵”，在花柳树老人带领下，于农历四月二十三日早晨，聚集到大理古城城隍庙，点燃香烛，准备行装。当日，聚集的群众从城隍庙出发，一路载歌载舞，沿点苍山麓向北，先到崇圣寺燃香祭拜；继而又北行至苍山五台峰下的朝阳村本主庙祭拜“抚民皇帝”本主，称为“南朝（拜）”；再往北到庆洞村，祭拜“神都”的庆洞“本主”庙，称为“北朝（拜）”。然后，在寺院内外场地，打“霸王鞭”和“金钱鼓”，跳扇子舞、唱白族调子，傍晚在神都周围埋锅造饭，当晚夜宿庆洞庙宇和四周野地树林中。这里是“绕三灵”活动的中心场所，人们尽情歌舞，通宵达旦。四月二十四日，祭拜象征洱海之神的斩蟒英雄段赤诚本主。四月二十五日，到大理城北洱海边的马久邑村，祭拜“本主”保安景帝。这三天里，“绕三灵”群众要行走 40 多公里路程，吹吹打打，载歌载舞，对歌应答。绕三灵传承历史久远，活动规模庞大，体现出白族在文化上的包容吸纳能力和高度的创新精神。[①]

① 《白族绕三灵》，中国非物质文化遗产网，http://www.ihchina.cn/Article/Index/detail?id=14999，检索日期：2019 年 8 月 30 日。

Item 8: Raosanling (worshipping three gods in parades) of the Bai Nationality

Item Serial Number: 489	Item ID Number: X-41	Released Date: 2006 (Batch 1)	Category: Folk Custom
Affiliated Province: Yunnan Province	Type: New Item	Application Province or Unit: Dali Bai Autonomous Prefecture, Yunnan Province	

Raosanling (worshipping three gods in parades) of the Bai Nationality is circulated in Dali Bai Autonomous Prefecture, Yunnan Province, with a history of more than 1,000 years so far. It is held from the 23rd to the 25th days of the fourth lunar month every year. During the festival, the Bai people flock together to attend it from all directions, carrying sacrificial utensils, luggage, food, cooking utensils, etc. They hope to pray to the gods for timely wind and rain, a bumper grain harvest, and the safety and soundness of all family members through devout worship.

The procession of "**Raosanling (worshipping three gods in parades)**" is divided into three parts. In the front part, there is a male and a female old people holding willow branches and oxtails (known as the Flower and Willow Tree Elderly). In the middle part, in addition to a flute player, there are dozens of male and female dancers holding "Bawang Whip" and "Jinqian Drum" in hands. The end of the procession consists of one person who blows leaves and dozens of women who hold fans or straw hats, forming a long line of "snake formation". Led by the Flower and Willow Tree Elderly, they gather at Chenghuang Temple in the Ancient City of Dali, lighting incense and candles and preparing for packages in the morning of the 23rd day of the 4th lunar month. On the same day, the assembled people set off from Chenghuang Temple, singing and dancing all the way. Heading north along the foot of the Diancang Mountain (also called the Cangshan Mountain), they first go to Chongsheng Temple to burn incense and worship. Then, they go north to the local temple in Chaoyang Village under the Wutai Peak of the Cangshan Mountain to worship the local god of "Fumin Emperor", which is called "the Southern Worship". Next, they go further north to Qingdong Village, worshipping Shendu Temple, the local temple in Qingdong, which is called "the Northern Worship". After that, on the grounds inside and outside the temple, they play "Bawang Whip" and "Jinqian Drum", perform the Fan Dance, and sing local tunes of the Bai nationality. In the evening, they cook and have dinner in the surrounding area of Shendu Temple, and spend the night in the temples in Qingdong Village as well as the surrounding wild fields and woods. Here is the center for the activity of "**Raosanling (worshipping three gods in parades)**", where people sing and dance to their heart's content all night till dawn. On the 24th day of the 4th lunar month, they worship the local god Duan Chicheng, a hero who have slayed a python for people, symbolizing the god of the Erhai Lake. On the 25th day of the 4th lunar month, they arrive at Majiuyi Village by the Erhai Lake in the north of Dali City to worship the local god, Bao'anjing Emperor. In these three days, the paraders have to travel more than 40 kilometers, blowing and beating, singing in antiphonal style and dancing. **Raosanling (worshipping three gods in parades)**, a large-scale activity, has a long history of inheritance, reflecting the inclusiveness and high degree of innovation of the culture of the Bai nationality.

第 9 项：苗族服饰（昌宁苗族服饰）

昌宁苗族服饰展示
Display of the Costumes of the Miao Nationality in Changning County

项目序号：513	项目编号：X-65	公布时间：2006（第一批）	类别：民俗
所属地区：云南省	类型：新增项目	申报地区或单位：云南省保山市	

昌宁苗族服饰流传于云南省保山市昌宁县耈街彝族苗族乡的苗族村寨，从中可以追溯苗族历史的发展进程和文化沉积。

昌宁苗族服饰的原料主要为当地生产的火麻土布。当地苗人将火麻剥出的麻丝用手摇机纺成线，再用土布机织成火麻土布，再根据自己的爱好在麻布缝制成的衣裙上缝出各种图案。男子服装或短衣长裤，或大襟长衫；女装一般为上衣下裙（统一采用百褶裙），或上衣下裤，服饰配件多，图案精美，色彩艳丽。昌宁苗族妇女的服装分为盛装、二等盛装和便装三类。不同场合，穿不同服装。盛装相当于“礼仪服”“婚礼服”“宗教服”“寿衣”，不仅在盛大的节日、宗教活动或出嫁时穿，死后还要作寿衣。二等盛装在走亲戚、回娘家、陪客和赶集等活动时穿。便装为日常生活、劳动穿的衣服，花纹较简单。其中，盛装集中体现了苗族服饰文化的全部精髓。[①] 一套完整的苗族妇女盛装有包头、上衣、披肩、围腰、腰带和短褶裙等 18 件套，被称作“十八一朵花”。用色大胆是昌宁苗族服饰的显著特点，其色调以红、黄、橙和白为主，并以刺绣取胜。[②]

① 《昌宁苗族服饰》，保山日报网，http://www.baoshandaily.com/html/20110610/content_130767539416090.html，检索日期：2019 年 9 月 10 日。

② 《苗族服饰（昌宁苗族服饰）》，中国非物质文化遗产网，http://www.ihchina.cn/Article/Index/detail?id=15044，检索日期：2019 年 8 月 30 日。

Item 9: the Costumes of the Miao Nationality (the Costumes of the Miao Nationality in Changning County)

Item Serial Number: 513	Item ID Number: X-65	Released Date: 2006 (Batch 1)	Category: Folk Custom
Affiliated Province: Yunnan Province	Type: New Item	Application Province or Unit: Baoshan City, Yunnan Province	

The Costumes of the Miao Nationality in Changning County is circulated in the Miao villages in Goujie Yi and Miao Township, Changning County, Baoshan City, Yunnan Province, from which the development process and cultural deposits of the Miao nationality can be traced back.

Its raw material is mainly locally-handwoven hemp cloth. The local Miao people spin the hemp silk peeled from the hemp stalk into thread by using a hand-cranked spinning wheel, and weave it into hemp cloth by using a wooden loom. Then, they embroider various patterns on the costumes made of hemp cloth according to their preference. Men's clothing includes short tops and long trousers, or long gowns with big Jin (two fronts of an upper garment). Women's clothing generally consists of tops and skirts (uniform pleated skirts), or tops and trousers, with many accessories, exquisite patterns and gorgeous colors. Women's Costumes of the Miao Nationality in Changning County are divided into three categories: splendid attire, second-class splendid attire and casual clothes, with different clothes for different occasions. Splendid attire is equal to "ceremonial clothing", "wedding clothes", "religious clothing" and "Shouyi (clothes for the dead)". It not only is worn on the occasions of grand festivals, religious activities or weddings, but also serves as Shouyi (clothes for the dead). Second-class splendid attire is worn on the occasions of visiting relatives, visiting parents' homes, entertaining guests, going to the market, etc. Casual clothes are clothes for daily life and labor, with simple patterns. Among them, splendid attire embodies all the essence of the costume culture of the Miao nationality. A complete set of the Miao women's splendid attire contains 18 pieces, such as headscarves, tops, shawls, aprons, belts and short pleated skirts, known as "Eighteen Petals of a Flower". A bold use of colors is a prominent feature of **the Costumes of the Miao Nationality in Changning County**. Their color tones are mainly red, yellow, orange and white, and the embroidery on them makes these costumes the best.

第10项：德昂族浇花节

德昂族浇花节歌舞表演
the Singing and Dancing Performance at the Flower-watering Festival of the De'ang Nationality

项目序号：985	项目编号：X-78	公布时间：2008（第二批）	类别：民俗
所属地区：云南省	类型：新增项目	申报地区或单位：云南省德宏傣族景颇族自治州	

浇花节是德昂族一年一度的传统佳节，从清明节后第七天开始，前后历时三天，涉及德昂族的宗教礼仪、民间歌舞、民间工艺、婚姻习俗和传统饮食等多方面内容，主要流传于云南省德宏傣族景颇族自治州。

浇花节主要活动有浇佛、供品品尝比赛、祭拜天地、念经祈求风调雨顺、打水给老人洗手、对歌和传烟、浇水、歌舞表演以及送花篮等。节日第一天，德昂族群众穿起节日盛装，背上从井里打来的清水，带着准备好的食物，手捧鲜花，汇集到本寨的奘房中。节日仪式由寨内的长老主持，仪式过程中，男青年敲响象脚鼓，女青年和着鼓点跳起“堆沙舞”，其他群众则身背精致的小花篮，手捧竹水筒举过头顶，依次往水龙槽里倒水，为佛像冲浴，以祈来年风调雨顺。仪式后，人们将带来的食物摆到佛像前的供盘中，齐声朗诵祭词，然后尽情品尝各种食物。食毕排成长队，以象脚鼓队为前导，翻山越岭来到井旁或泉边取水。每次取水都很讲究，要举行取水供物仪式，男女青年还要进行传烟、对歌和赛舞等表演。[①] 送花篮是德昂族小伙子向姑娘表达爱慕之情的方式。浇花节前，小伙子们便忙着用竹篾编制漂亮花篮，送给和自己相处好的姑娘。跳浇花舞时，以鼓、铓和镲伴奏，女子身背花篮，男子手持竹筒做浇花状，表示男女双方相互泼水祝福。[②]

① 《德昂族浇花节》，中国非物质文化遗产网，http://www.ihchina.cn/Article/Index/detail?id=15100，检索日期：2019年8月30日。

② 《德昂族浇花节》，云南非物质文化遗产保护网，http://www.ynich.cn/view.php?id=1172&cat_id=11111，检索日期：2019年8月30日。

Item 10: the Flower-watering Festival of the De'ang Nationality

Item Serial Number: 985	Item ID Number: X-78	Released Date: 2008 (Batch 2)	Category: Folk Custom
Affiliated Province: Yunnan Province	Type: New Item	Application Province or Unit: Dehong Dai and Jingpo Autonomous Prefecture, Yunnan Province	

The Flower-watering Festival is an annual traditional festival of the De'ang nationality, held from the 7th day after the Tomb Sweeping Festival and lasting three days. It involves many aspects of the De'ang nationality, such as religious ceremonies, folk songs and dances, folk crafts, marriage customs and traditional diet, mainly spread in Dehong Dai and Jingpo Autonomous Prefecture, Yunnan Province.

The main activities of **the Flower-watering Festival** include bathing the Buddha, the competition of tasting sacrifices, offering sacrifices to the heaven and the earth, chanting sutras to pray for timely wind and rain, fetching water to wash hands for the elderly, antiphonal singing, passing tobacco, watering, singing and dancing performances, as well as sending flower baskets. On the first day of the festival, the De'ang people put on festive costumes, carry the clean water fetched from the well on their backs, bring the prepared food, hold flowers in their hands and gather in the temple of the village. The festival ceremony is presided over by the elders in the village. During the ceremony, young men play the Elephant-foot Drum, and young women perform Duisha Dance to the rhythm of the drumbeats. Other people carry delicate flower baskets on their backs, hold bamboo tubes with water above their heads, and pour water into the Water Dragon Trough one by one to bathe the Buddha statue and to pray for timely wind and rain in the coming year. After the ceremony, people put the food they have brought on the plates for holding sacrifices in front of the Buddha statue, recite sacrificial words in unison, and then taste all kinds of food to their heart's content. After eating, they stand in a long queue. Led by the Elephant-foot Drum team, they traverse mountains and ridges to the well or spring to fetch water. Fetching water should be given particular attention, with a water-supply ceremony held before each fetching. Besides, young men and women will also give performances, such as passing tobacco, antiphonal singing and dance competition.

Sending flower baskets is a way for young men of the De'ang nationality to express their love to young women. Before the Flower-watering Festival, young men are busy making beautiful flower baskets with thin bamboo slices, and then give the baskets to the girls who get along well with them. The Flower-watering Dance is performed to the accompaniment of drums, Mang (a folk copper percussion instrument) and small cymbals. Women carry flower baskets on their backs, and men hold bamboo tubes in their hands to imitate the action of watering flowers, indicating that men and women express their mutual blessings through splashing water.

第11项：石宝山歌会

石宝山歌会民俗活动
the Folk Acticity of the Singing Festival of the Shibao Mountain

项目序号：1012	项目编号：X-105	公布时间：2008（第二批）	类别：民俗
所属地区：云南省	类型：新增项目	申报地区或单位：云南省剑川县	

石宝山歌会是白族地区盛大的民族传统节日，以对歌、赛歌为特色，于每年农历七月二十七至八月初一在云南大理州剑川县石宝山举行，已有上千年的历史。

石宝山歌会主要活动有万人弹弦对歌、演唱白曲、民间艺人演奏“阿吒力”佛教音乐及表演乐舞等，龙头三弦、三弦曲、霸王鞭舞、白族调和大白曲（本子曲）等都是歌会上表演的独具风格的民间艺术。歌会上对唱的调子，俗称“白族调”，即白族民间歌谣，有劳动歌、时政歌、仪式歌、情歌、生活歌、反意歌、一字歌和叙事长歌“本子曲”等。歌会上演唱的剑川白族调属山歌类，曲调优美动听。弹弦对歌是白族青年谈情说爱的巧妙方式，石宝山歌会正是他们择偶的好机会。对歌不但唱情，也比智慧，要求即兴创作演唱，一问一答间不能停顿。每年歌会都有来自剑川县、洱源县、丽江市、大理市和兰坪县等地的群众参加。除了唱歌对歌外，还有石龙霸王鞭舞等白族舞蹈和白族“阿吒力”佛教法事活动、朝拜白族地区的中央本主及“阿央白”（石刻女阴）等民俗活动。[①] 石宝山歌会是白族歌谣诞生的摇篮和发展传播的基地。[②]

① 《石宝山歌会》，云南非物质文化遗产保护网，http://www.ynich.cn/view.php?id=1166&cat_id=11111，检索日期：2019 年 8 月 30 日。

② 《石宝山歌会》，中国非物质文化遗产网，http://www.ihchina.cn/Article/Index/detail?id=15245，检索日期：2019 年 8 月 30 日。

Item 11: the Singing Festival of the Shibao Mountain

Item Serial Number: 1012	Item ID Number: X-105	Released Date: 2008 (Batch 2)	Category: Folk Custom
Affiliated Province: Yunnan Province	Type: New Item	Application Province or Unit: Jianchuan County, Yunnan Province	

The Singing Festival of the Shibao Mountain is a grand traditional ethnic festival in areas inhabited by the Bai nationality, characterized by antiphonal singing and singing contests. It is held in the Shibao Mountain of Jianchuan County, Dali Prefecture, Yunnan Province from the 27th day of the 7th lunar month to the 1st day of the 8th lunar month every year, with a history of over one thousand years.

The main activities of **the Singing Festival of the Shibao Mountain** include ten thousand people's performances of stringed instruments and antiphonal singing, singing the tunes of the Bai nationality, folk artists' playing of "Azhali" Buddhist music, and their performance of music and dance. Dragon-head Sanxian (a three-stringed plucked musical instrument), Sanxian Tunes, Bawang Whip Dance, the tunes of the Bai nationality and Dabai Tune (Benzi Tune), etc., are all unique folk arts performed at **the Singing Festival**. The tunes for antiphonal singing performed at **the Singing Festival** are commonly known as "the tunes of the Bai nationality", that is, the folk songs of the Bai nationality, including labor songs, songs concerning current affairs, ritual songs, love songs, life songs, ironic songs, Yizi songs (with one character repeated in each line of lyrics), and the long narrative song of "Benzi Tune". The tunes of the Bai nationality in Jianchuan County sung at **the Singing Festival** belong to the category of the folk song, with melodies sweet and pleasant to the ear. Performing stringed instruments and antiphonal singing is an ingenious way of courting for young people of the Bai nationality, and **the Singing Festival of the Shibao Mountain** is a good opportunity for them to choose their spouses. Antiphonal singing is not only about the singing of love, but also about the competition between two singers' intelligence, requiring extemporaneous creation and singing, during which there can't be any pauses between questioning and answering. Every year, people from Jianchuan County, Eryuan County, Lijiang City, Dali City, Lanping County and other places participate in the festival. In addition to antiphonal singing, there are also folk activities, such as Bawang Whip Dance of Shilong Village, the dance of the Bai nationality; "Azhali" Buddhist ritual activities of the Bai nationality; worshipping the highest local god in areas inhabited by the Bai nationality; worshiping "Ayangbai" (the carved stone pudendum), etc. **The Singing Festival of the Shibao Mountain** is the birth place of the folk songs of the Bai nationality and the home base for their development and dissemination.

第12项：大理三月街

大理三月街开幕式
the Opening Ceremony of Dali March Street

项目序号：1013	项目编号：X-106	公布时间：2008（第二批）	类别：民俗
所属地区：云南省	类型：新增项目	申报地区或单位：云南省大理市	

大理三月街是白族盛大的传统节日，流传于云南省大理白族自治州大理市大理古城。它集白族民俗、宗教和经济文化交流于一体，由庙会演变而来，其产生与佛教在大理的传播有密切关系，从农历三月十五日开始，为期七天。每年赶赴三月街的人数以百万计，全国各地及海外都有人参加。

大理三月街期间有丰富多彩的民族文体活动，同时进行物资交易和文化交流。除保留有传统的药材、大牲畜和日用百货交易外，大理三月街还新增了“洋人街”和地方民族食品一条街，又增设了珠宝玉器和电脑产品等交易市场，扩大了地方名特优新产品的销售规模。节日期间，大理古城张灯结彩，街市上搭出“花山”，各家各户也在门前放置花木，将集风花雪月自然风光和人文景象为一体的大理装饰成娱乐的世界、商贸的海洋。人们既可以赶街购货，又可以在街旁的山坡、广场和集市里参与山歌对唱、民族器乐演奏、灯展、花展、民族服饰表演及射弩、秋千、摔跤、赛马、龙舟和民族歌舞比赛等文体活动。①

① 《大理三月街》，中国非物质文化遗产网，http://www.ihchina.cn/Article/Index/detail?id=15246，检索日期：2019年8月30日。

Item 12: Dali March Street

Item Serial Number: 1013	Item ID Number: X-106	Released Date: 2008 (Batch 2)	Category: Folk Custom
Affiliated Province: Yunnan Province	Type: New Item	Application Province or Unit: Dali City, Yunnan Province	

Dali March Street is a grand traditional festival of the Bai nationality, which is circulated in the Ancient City of Dali, Dali City, Dali Bai Autonomous Prefecture, Yunnan Province. It integrates the folk customs, religions, as well as economic and cultural exchanges of the Bai nationality into one, evolving from the Temple Fair. Its emergence is closely related to the spread of Buddhism in Dali, held from the 15th day of the 3rd lunar month and lasting seven days. Every year, millions of people from all over China and overseas arrive at March Street to participate in this festival.

During the festival of **Dali March Street**, a variety of ethnic cultural and sports activities will be held, and the trade of goods and cultural exchanges will be carried out at the same time. In addition to the trade of traditional medicinal materials, large livestock and articles of daily use, a "Foreigner Street" and a local ethnic food street have been opened up, and the trading markets of jewelry, jade and computer products, etc. have also been added during the festival of **Dali March Street**, which have expanded the sales scale of the famous, special and high-quality new products. During the festival, the Ancient City of Dali is decorated with lanterns and festoons, and "flower hills" are erected at the street market. Flowers are also placed in front of the doors of all households, making Dali, which integrates the natural scenery of wind, flowers, snow and the moon with humanistic scenery, into a world of entertainment and an ocean of commerce. People can not only go to the street market to buy goods, but also participate in cultural and sports activities on the street-side hillside, on the square and at the market, such as antiphonal singing of folk songs, ethnic instrumental performances, lantern shows, flower shows, ethnic costume performance, as well as the competitions of crossbow shooting, playing on swings, wrestling, horse racing, dragon boats and ethnic songs and dances, etc.

第13项：祭寨神林

祭寨神林
Offering Sacrifices to Gods of Stockaded Villages

项目序号：1208	项目编号：X-133	公布时间：2011（第三批）	类别：民俗
所属地区：云南省	类型：新增项目	申报地区或单位：云南省元阳县	

祭寨神林，汉语意为“春耕节”，是哈尼族每年春耕开始前（一般在一月中旬）举行的一种祭祀活动，祈求来年风调雨顺、五谷丰登、人畜平安，主要流传于云南省哈尼族村落。元阳县各乡镇的祭寨神林是所有哈尼族村落最隆重的节庆大典。

祭寨神林各地的节期略有不同。元阳县哈播村一带的祭寨神林，从农历腊月第一个辰龙日开始，持续到午马日，节期为三天。节日第一天清扫寨子，杀鸡，舂糯米粑粑，染三色鸭蛋。由德高望重的寨老带领数名家道兴旺、品行端正的男子，杀牲祭祀寨神林。祭祀牺牲按全村家庭平均分配，家庭成员和禽畜都必须尝一口，还必须拌进五谷种子里。第二和第三天，摆长街宴，通宵达旦吟唱古老的哈吧（古歌），老人向子孙后代讲述祖先迁徙的历史、传授安身立命的伦理道德、梯田耕作的技术，对每个村民一年来的德行做出评价。祭寨神林也是春耕备耕的序曲，全面彰显了哈尼族山区梯田耕作的礼仪、技术和禁忌等知识系统。祭寨神林展现了哈尼族传统文化，特别是其太阳历法和物候历法、创世迁徙史诗和叙事长诗、音乐舞蹈等文化要素，充分体现了哈尼族体察天意、顺应自然以及追求天人和谐的世界观。①

① 《祭寨神林》，中国非物质文化遗产网，http://www.ihchina.cn/Article/Index/detail?id=15291，检索日期：2019年8月31日。

Item 13: Offering Sacrifices to Gods of Stockaded Villages

Item Serial Number: 1208	Item ID Number: X-133	Released Date: 2011 (Batch 3)	Category: Folk Custom
Affiliated Province: Yunnan Province	Type: New Item	Application Province or Unit: Yuanyang County, Yunnan Province	

Offering Sacrifices to Gods of Stockaded Villages, which means "the Spring Plowing Festival" in Chinese, is a sacrificial activity held by the Hani people every year before the start of spring plowing (usually in the middle of the 1st lunar month) to pray for timely wind and rain, a bumper grain harvest and the safety of people and livestock in the coming year. It is mainly spread in the Hani villages in Yunnan Province. **Offering Sacrifices to Gods of Stockaded Villages** held in all townships of Yuanyang County is the grandest festival ceremony of all Hani villages.

The dates of **Offering Sacrifices to Gods of Stockaded Villages** vary slightly in different regions. In Habo Village of Yuanyang County, it starts from the first Dragon Day of the 12th month of the lunar calendar and continues to the Horse Day, lasting three days. On the first day of the festival, stockaded villages are cleaned, chickens are killed, the cooked glutinous rice is pounded into sticky cakes, and duck eggs are dyed three colors. Several men with prosperous family and good conduct led by the venerable Zhailao (a head of a stockaded village) kill animals to offer sacrifices to gods of stockaded villages. Sacrifices offered are divided equally among all families in the village. Family members and livestock must have a taste of the sacrifices, which must be mixed with the seeds of the five cereals. On the second and third days, people will have a Long Street Banquet, singing the ancient Haba (ancient songs) all night till dawn. The elderly men tell the history of ancestral migration to their descendants, teach them the ethics and morality to settle down and get on with life as well as the techniques of terrace cultivation, and evaluate the moral conduct of each villager over the past year. **Offering Sacrifices to Gods of Stockaded Villages** is also the prelude to preparing for spring plowing, fully demonstrating the knowledge concerning the etiquette, techniques and taboos of terrace cultivation in the mountain areas inhabited by the Hani nationality. It shows the traditional culture of the Hani nationality, especially the cultural elements, such as the solar calendar, the phenological calendar, the epic of creation and migration, the long narrative poem, music and dance, which fully reflects the Hani people's world views of perceiving the will of heaven, conforming to nature, and pursuing harmony between heaven and man.

第14项：

抬阁（通海高台）

通海高台："许仙借伞"
Tonghai High Stage: "Xu Xian Borrows an Umbrella"

项目序号：994	项目编号：X-87	公布时间：2011（第三批）	类别：民俗
所属地区：云南省	类型：扩展项目	申报地区或单位：云南省通海县	

通海高台是在云南省通海县传统节庆民俗活动中保留的一种抬阁表演形式。明清时军屯移民将粤、闽等省的"抬阁"和"飘色"传到云南。清嘉庆、道光年间，七街、通海县城、河西县城、四街、杨广（今通海县辖镇）相继成立了"高台会"，传承至今。

高台巡游多在每年农历正月十六日举行，俗称"迎"高台。平年有12台，闰年有13台。制作高台手艺的难点是做到不露"筋骨"。所谓"筋骨"，指的是支撑整个舞台的铁杆。做到顺乎自然、天衣无缝，是高台艺人的绝活。高台是一个流动舞台，一台高台就是一出戏。经过挑选并训练过的4-5岁孩子装扮各种角色，表现的内容多为戏曲故事。[①]传统节目有历史故事"文王访贤""孙渊哭洞""孟母教子""岳飞出世"等，还有民间传说"三打白骨精""花果山""三借芭蕉扇""许仙借伞""水漫金山""鹊桥会""木兰从军"等。高台巡游，有吹打乐伴随，还有毛驴灯和龙灯等民俗表演。通海高台融戏剧、小说、历史传奇、民间故事、雕塑、绘画、美工和装饰于一体，成为富有戏剧性、故事性、可移动的立体舞台艺术。[②]

① 《抬阁（通海高台）》，中国非物质文化遗产网，http://www.ihchina.cn/Article/Index/detail?id=15212，检索日期：2019年8月31日。

② 李琼，《通海县举办通海高台装裱制作技艺培训班》，http://www.ynich.cn/view.php?id=2353&cat_id=11411，检索日期：2019年8月31日。

Item 14: Pavilion Lifting (Tonghai High Stage)

Item Serial Number: 994	Item ID Number: X-87	Released Date: 2011 (Batch 3)	Category: Folk Custom
Affiliated Province: Yunnan Province	Type: Extended Item	Application Province or Unit: Tonghai County, Yunnan Province	

Tonghai High Stage is a form of pavilion-lifting performance retained in the traditional festivals and folk activities in Tonghai County, Yunnan Province. In the Ming and Qing dynasties, the military immigrants brought the folk activities of "Pavilion Lifting" and "Floating Colors" from Guangdong and Fujian provinces to Yunnan Province. During the reigns of Emperor Jiaqing and Emperor Daoguang of the Qing Dynasty, "the Union of the High Stage" has been established successively in Qijie Village, the city proper of Tonghai County, the city proper of Hexi County, Sijie Township and Yangguang Township (today under the jurisdiction of Tonghai County), which has been passed down up to now.

The high-stage parade is usually held on the 16th day of the first lunar month every year, known as "welcoming" the High Stage. There are 12 High Stages in a common year and 13 ones in a leap year. The difficulty in making the High Stage is to keep its "tendons and bones" invisible. The so-called "tendons and bones" refer to the iron poles that support the entire stage. To make the High Stage in the course of nature without any trace is the unique skill of the artists who make it. A High Stage is a mobile stage, each telling a story. The selected and trained 4- to 5-year-old children are dressed up as various roles, mostly performing opera stories. Traditional programs include historical stories, such as "King Wen of Zhou Visits the Virtuous", "Sun Yuan Cries over the Cave", "Mencius's Mother Teaches Her Son" and "The Birth of Yue Fei", as well as folk legends, such as "Beating the White Bone Demon Three Times", "The Huaguo Mountain", "Borrowing the Palm-leaf Fan Three Times", "Xu Xian Borrows an Umbrella", "The Flooding of Jinshan Temple", "Meeting on the Magpie Bridge" and "Mulan Joins the Army". The high-stage parade is accompanied by wind music, percussion music, as well as the folk performances of the Donkey Lantern and the Dragon Lantern, etc. **Tonghai High Stage** integrates dramas, novels, historical romance, folk tales, sculpture, painting, art designing and decoration into one, becoming a dramatic, storytelling and movable three-dimensional stage art.

第15项：

苗族花山节

苗族花山节活动展示
the Activity Show of the Flower Hill Festival of the Miao Nationality

项目序号：1359	项目编号：X-146	公布时间：2014（第四批）	类别：民俗
所属地区：云南省	类型：新增项目	申报地区或单位：云南省屏边苗族自治县	

苗族花山节也称“踩花山”或“踩山”，于每年农历正月初二至初五举行，主要流传于云南省红河哈尼族彝族自治州屏边苗族自治县，是该县各乡镇苗族一年一度的传统节日，也是展示苗族服饰和歌舞艺术的平台。节日期间，会举行多种文体表演与竞赛活动，内容丰富、积极健康。

苗族花山节通常由无子嗣而为祈求子嗣者主办。主办人负责择定吉日，抱着公鸡，在选定的平缓坝坡上竖立一棵高约 2 ～ 3 丈的五彩花杆（多用大龙树），陈设好酒于花山场内。届时，远近各村寨男女穿着节日盛装涌向花山场，吹起芦笙，爬花杆、耍武术、打陀螺、踢鸡毛毽、蹬脚架、斗牛、斗鸡、斗画眉鸟、赛马、跳芦笙舞和对唱山歌。其中，爬花杆是主要的比赛项目，有顺爬、倒爬、顺倒旋环爬和口吹芦笙爬等四种形式。男女青年对唱山歌选择伴侣也是花山节的主要内容。花山节一般要持续 4 ～ 6 天，结束时，组织者要抱着公鸡祭献花杆，进行倒花杆仪式。花杆倒下后，人们将悬挂的布条剪下，拴在孩子手腕上，以祈求孩子健康，花杆则拿来做床，有容易生子之意。①

① 《苗族花山节》，云南非物质文化遗产保护网，http://www.ynich.cn/view.php?id=1171&cat_id=11111，检索日期：2019 年 9 月 4 日。

Item 15: the Flower Hill Festival of the Miao Nationality

Item Serial Number: 1359	Item ID Number: X-146	Released Date: 2014 (Batch 4)	Category: Folk Custom
Affiliated Province: Yunnan Province	Type: New Item	Application Province or Unit: Pingbian Miao Autonomous County, Yunnan Province	

The Flower Hill Festival of the Miao Nationality, also known as "Stepping on the Flower Hill" or "Stepping on the Hill", is held from the 2nd to the 5th days of the first lunar month. It is mainly spread in Pingbian Miao Autonomous County, Honghe Hani and Yi Autonomous Prefecture, Yunnan Province. It is an annual traditional festival of the Miao nationality in various townships of this county, and also a platform to display the costumes and the art of singing and dancing of the Miao nationality. During the festival, a variety of cultural and sports performances and competitions will be held, with rich, positive and healthy content.

The Flower Hill Festival of the Miao Nationality is usually organized by those who have no children and pray for offspring. The organizer is responsible for choosing an auspicious day, holding a rooster, erecting a colorful flower pole (mostly made of a big dragon tree) with a height of about 2-3 *zhang* (a Chinese unit of length, with one *zhang* roughly equal to 131 inches) on the selected gentle slope, and setting out good liquor on the spot of the Flower Hill. At that time, men and women from villages far and near flock to the spot of the Flower Hill in festive costumes, playing Lusheng Musical Instruments, climbing the flower pole, performing martial arts, whipping tops, kicking the shuttlecock, Dengjiaojia (kicking competition), bullfighting, cockfighting, thrush fighting, horse racing, performing Lusheng Dance and singing Mountain Songs in antiphonal style. Among them, climbing the flower pole is the main competition event, which includes four types of climbing, namely upward climbing, downward climbing, upward-and-downward circular climbing, and climbing while playing Lusheng Musical Instruments. Young men and women's performing antiphonal singing of Mountain Songs to choose their spouses is also the main content of **the Flower Hill Festival**. The festival usually lasts 4-6 days. When it comes to the end, the organizer will hold the rooster in hands to offer sacrifices to the flower pole, and carry out the ceremony of toppling the flower pole. After it falls to the ground, people will cut off the hanging cloth strips and tie them around children's wrists to pray for children's health. The flower pole is used to make beds, which has the meaning of giving birth to kids easily.

楚雄彝族武定纳苏支系青年女子服饰
Young Women's Costumes of the Nasu Branch of the Yi Nationality in Wuding County of Chuxiong

第16项：彝族服饰

楚雄彝族男子服饰
Men's Costumes of the Yi Nationality in Chuxiong

项目序号：1369	项目编号：X-156	公布时间：2014（第四批）	类别：民俗
所属地区：云南省	类型：新增项目	申报地区或单位：云南省楚雄彝族自治州	

由于彝族支系众多，居住分散，各地的彝族服饰样式各异，带有浓厚的地域色彩。楚雄彝族服饰主要流行于云南楚雄彝族自治州各县及邻近地区。这里是古代各部彝族辗转迁徙之地，属东、南、西、北、中彝语六大方言的交汇地带，因此其服饰尤显纷繁多彩。

楚雄彝族服饰有370多种款式，色彩绚丽、富有创意，或精致时尚，或传统古典，常以大量银制品和刺绣装饰，全部由彝人手工完成。楚雄彝族服饰一方面兼具传统古典和现代时尚的特点，因此一些流传了几千年的传统古典服饰和刺绣被完整地保存下来；另一方面又与时俱进、兼容并包，因此一些与时代同步、与汉族服饰交融的彝族服饰也广为流传。[①] 总体上看，上穿右衽大襟短上衣，下着长裤，是现代女装的基本款式。女上装花饰繁多，色彩艳丽，图案以云纹和马樱花一类的花卉为主，多装饰在上衣的胸前、盘肩等特定部位，工艺以镶补、平绣为普遍。妇女头饰大体可分为包帕、缠头、绣花帽三类。楚雄彝族男子服饰与凉山地区的不同，多用黑布包头，不留"天菩萨"，不扎"英雄髻"，耳朵不戴耳珠子。楚雄彝族男子平日身穿蓝色或黑色的对襟窄袖上衣，衣衔及腹，衣襟以两排布钮扣装饰，有的在右袋边镶以花卉。裤子又肥又短，以便利上山和下田干活。然而，节日盛装则呈现出丰富多彩的特色。[②]

Item 16: the Costumes of the Yi Nationality

Item Serial Number: 1369	Item ID Number: X-156	Released Date: 2014 (Batch 4)	Category: Folk Custom
Affiliated Province: Yunnan Province	Type: New Item	Application Province or Unit: Chuxiong Yi Autonomous Prefecture, Yunnan Province	

Due to the numerous branches of the Yi nationality and scattered residences, **the Costumes of the Yi Nationality** vary greatly in styles from place to place, having strong regional features. Chuxiong Costumes of the Yi Nationality are mainly popular in all counties in Chuxiong Yi Autonomous Prefecture of Yunnan Province, and its adjacent areas. This is the place to which various branches of the Yi nationality traveled and migrated in ancient times, belonging to the convergence zone of the six major dialects of the Yi language in the eastern, southern, western, northern and central parts. Therefore, the costumes here are particularly diverse, complicated and colorful.

There are more than 370 styles of Chuxiong Costumes of the Yi Nationality, with gorgeous colors and full of creativity, either exquisite and fashionable, or traditional and classical. They are often decorated with a large number of silver products and embroidery patterns, all handmade by the Yi people. On the one hand, Chuxiong

① 楚《彝族服饰》，雄州非遗网，http://www.cxfy.org.cn/file_read.aspx?id=566，检索日期：2019 年 8 月 31 日。

② 《楚雄彝族男子服饰》，中国网，http://www.china.com.cn/aboutchina/zhuanti/yz/2009-07/20/content_18170369.htm，检索日期：2020 年 8 月 8 日。

Costumes of the Yi Nationality have the characteristics of both classical tradition and modern fashion. Therefore, some traditional classical costumes and embroidery that have been passed down for thousands of years have been completely preserved. On the other hand, they also keep pace with the times and absorb anything and everything, so some costumes of the Yi nationality that synchronize with the times and blend with the costumes of the Han nationality are also widely spread. Generally speaking, Youren big-Jin short tops with the left fronts of the tops covering the right ones and long trousers are the basic style of modern women's clothing. There are a variety of floral decorations on women's upper clothing, which has gorgeous colors. The patterns are mainly clouds and Maying Flowers (*Rhododendron delavayi Franch* in Latin), mostly decorated on the specific parts of the upper clothing, such as chests and shoulders. Patchwork embroidery and plain embroidery are common techniques. Women's headwear can be roughly divided into three categories: headscarves, head wrappings and embroidered hats. Chuxiong Yi men's costumes are different from those in Liangshan Yi Autonomous Prefecture. They usually use black cloth to wrap their heads, with no "Tianpusa (a strand of hair on top of the head of a Yi man)" or "Hero's Coiled Hair", and there are no earrings on their ears. Men of the Yi nationality in Chuxiong usually wear blue or black narrow-sleeved Duijin tops with two fronts of the tops opposite each other. The hems of the tops reach their abdomens, with two fronts of the tops decorated with two rows of cloth buttons in the middle. Some are adorned with flowers beside the right pockets. The trousers are loose and short, convenient for laboring in the mountains and fields. However, the festive costumes of the Yi nationality present the characteristics of being rich and colorful.

第17项：民间信俗（梅里神山祭祀）

藏胞祭祀梅里神山
a Zang Compatriot's Offering Sacrifices to the Meili Sacred Mountain

项目序号：992	项目编号：X-85	公布时间：2014（第四批）	类别：民俗
所属地区：云南省	类型：扩展项目	申报地区或单位：云南省德钦县	

梅里神山祭祀流传于云南省迪庆藏族自治州德钦县境内。梅里雪山是康巴地区最大的神山，藏传佛教的朝觐圣地，每年秋末冬初，藏族人民都会牵羊扶拐，口念佛经，绕山焚香朝拜（转经）。

祭山是我国藏地流行的一种民间习俗，核心是神山信仰。就藏族的神山崇拜观念而言，人们并非仅仅崇拜作为自然物体的山，而是崇拜隐居于山背后的被认为具有超自然的神灵。为了表示虔诚及得到神灵的护佑，藏族人民通过祭祀神山，找到了人与神灵沟通的途径。梅里雪山转山线路有三条：大转、中转和小转，大转围绕整座山脉，中转围绕主峰群，小转在主峰正面腹地进行叩拜。德钦县祭山活动十分流行，形式有煨桑、悬挂经幡和风马旗。煨桑是祭山活动最隆重的形式，既有以村落为单位的集体祭山仪式，也有以家户为形式的祭山仪式。祭山地点分别有山头、村间公房、家户房顶。祭山仪式上有招福仪式、刀赞、喀夏（说笑话）和迎宾祝酒等习俗。德钦县的祭山仪式程式完整、内容丰富，包含传统知识、民间文学、服饰、雕塑、舞蹈和说唱等方面，是德钦县集合度高、内容包罗万象的民俗活动。[①]

① 《国家级非遗｜梅里神山祭祀：康巴藏民一生至少一次的朝圣》，迪庆非物质文化遗产保护网，http://www.dqich.cn/baohuminglu/detail/21/155，检索日期：2019年8月31日。

Item 17: the Folk-belief Custom (Offering Sacrifices to the Meili Sacred Mountain)

Item Serial Number: 992	Item ID Number: X-85	Released Date: 2014 (Batch 4)	Category: Folk Custom
Affiliated Province: Yunnan Province	Type: Extended Item	Application Province or Unit: Deqin County, Yunnan Province	

Offering Sacrifices to the Meili Sacred Mountain is prevalent in Deqin County, Diqing Zang Autonomous Prefecture, Yunnan Province. The Meili Snow Mountain is the largest sacred mountain in Kham area and a sacred place of pilgrimage of Tibetan Buddhism. In late autumn and early winter every year, the Zang people lead sheep on crutches, reciting Buddhist scriptures and making a pilgrimage to the mountain by circling around it while burning incense.

Offering sacrifices to mountains is a folk custom popular in Zang areas in China, and its core is the belief in sacred mountains. As far as the concept of worshipping the sacred mountains of the Zang nationality is concerned, people don't only worship the mountains as natural objects, but worship the gods who hide behind mountains and are believed to possess supernatural abilities. In order to show piety and get blessings from gods, the Zang people find a way to communicate with gods by offering sacrifices to sacred mountains. There are three routes to circle around the Meili Snow Mountain: large circling, medium circling and small circling. The large circling involves the circling around of the entire mountain ranges, the medium circling involves the circling around of the main peak group, and the small circling is to worship in the front hinterland of the main peak. The activity of offering sacrifices to mountains in Deqin County is very popular, the forms of which include Weisang (burning pine and cypress branches), and hanging Jingfan (prayer flags) and Fengma Flags. Weisang (burning pine and cypress branches) is the most solemn form of offering sacrifices to mountains. There are both collective ceremonies of worshipping mountains with one village as a unit and the rituals of worshipping mountains performed by individual households. The places for offering sacrifices to mountains include the tops of mountains, public houses in villages and the roofs of households. In the ceremony of offering sacrifices to mountains, there are customs such as praying for blessings, Daozan (a Zang sacrificial talking-and-singing ceremony), Kaxia (telling jokes), welcoming guests and drinking a toast. The ceremony of offering sacrifices to mountains in Deqin County is complete in procedure and rich in content, including traditional knowledge, folk literature, costumes, sculpture, dancing as well as talking-and-singing. It is a highly integrated and all-encompassing folk activity in Deqin County.

第18项：民间信俗

（女子太阳山祭祀）

请太阳仪式
the Ceremony of Welcoming the Sun

项目序号：992	项目编号：X-85	公布时间：2014（第四批）	类别：民俗
所属地区：云南省	类型：扩展项目	申报地区或单位：云南省西畴县	

女子太阳山祭祀流传于云南省文山壮族苗族自治州西畴县的上果村。上果村被称为“太阳村”，保留着世上唯一的活态传承母系社会原始部落祭祀太阳的习惯——“女子太阳节”，又称“女人节”，起源于母系氏族社会先民对太阳的崇拜。每年农历二月初一，所有年满16岁的壮族女子沐浴净身祭祀太阳。

女子太阳山祭祀程序与仪式主要有制作黄米饭、净身更衣、请太阳和送太阳等。祭祀前一天需要制作黄米饭，黄米饭代表了太阳金色的光芒。祭祀活动前，所有参加女子太阳山祭祀的女人都需要净身沐浴，以表达对祖先的尊重。祭祀当天，要在村前大榕树（太阳神树）上挂一个用篾制簸箕作底、圆形铁皮上绘制了黄底红色十二芒纹的太阳图案；树下立放一块中间有圆洞的石头代表太阳神，前方横摆一个绘有“双鸟朝阳”图案的石制长方形香炉、一块用以摆放祭祀物品的长方形石头，上面放着一对红蜡烛、三个杯子、三双筷子。中午12点太阳当顶时举行祭祀。祭祀人员到达太阳山的山顶后，会在山路口横放一截树枝警示闲杂人不得入内。即将到达山顶的道路右侧放置了一口盛满清泉的石制水缸，每个参祭的女人都要喝一口缸中的水，代表神话乜星与女儿的重逢相遇。这些程序完成后，女子太阳山祭祀的重头戏即完成，女人们来到河边休息玩耍，等待男人们为自己呈上丰盛的晚餐。晚餐后开展传统歌舞活动。祭祀日，村里的男人们专为女人服务。①

① 曾燕，《女子太阳山祭祀：壮族文化历史的活档案》，载《云南档案》，2017年第11期，第29-33页。

Item 18: the Folk-belief Custom (Women's Offering Sacrifices to the Sun Mountain)

Item Serial Number: 992	Item ID Number: X-85	Released Date: 2014 (Batch 4)	Category: Folk Custom
Affiliated Province: Yunnan Province	Type: Extended Item	Application Province or Unit: Xichou County, Yunnan Province	

Women's Offering Sacrifices to the Sun Mountain is circulated in Shangguo Village, Xichou County, Wenshan Zhuang and Miao Autonomous Prefecture, Yunnan Province. Shangguo Village is known as "the Village of the Sun", which has retained the only living inheritance of the habit of offering sacrifices to the sun performed by the primitive tribes of the matriarchal society in the world — "the Sun Festival of Women", also known as "the Festival of Women". It originated from the worship of the sun by the ancestors of the matriarchal society. On the first day of the second lunar month every year, all women of the Zhuang nationality who have reached the age of 16 will have a bath and offer sacrifices to the sun.

The sacrificial procedure and ritual of **Women's Offering Sacrifices to the Sun Mountain** mainly include making yellow rice, having a bath and changing clothes, welcoming the sun and seeing the sun off. On the day before the sacrifice, yellow rice needs to be made, representing the golden rays of the sun. Before the sacrificial activity, all women participating in **Women's Offering Sacrifices to the Sun Mountain** need take a bath to show respect for their ancestors. On the day of the sacrifice, a sun pattern with yellow bottom and twelve pieces of red awn painted on a circular iron sheet and with a dustpan made of bamboo strips as the base is hung on a big banyan tree (the Divine Tree of the Sun) in front of the village. A stone with a round hole in the middle is placed under the tree, representing the god of the sun. In front of the stone, a stone-made rectangular incense burner painted with the pattern of "Two Golden Crows Facing the Sun" as well as a rectangular stone for holding sacrifices are placed. A pair of red candles, three cups and three pairs of chopsticks are placed on it. The sacrificial ceremony is held at 12:00 noon when the sun is at its peak. When the sacrificial personnel arrive at the top of the Sun Mountain, they will place a branch at the crossing of the mountain road to warn the unauthorized people not to enter. On the right side of the road that is about to reach the mountaintop, a stone-made vat full of clear spring water is placed. Every woman participating in the sacrifice must take a sip of the water from the vat, representing the reunion of the mythical star and her daughter. After these procedures are completed, the major activities of **Women's Offering Sacrifices to the Sun Mountain** will come to an end. Women arrive at the river side to have a rest and play, waiting for men to present them with a sumptuous dinner. After dinner, traditional singing and dancing activities are carried out. On the sacrificial day, men in the village serve women exclusively.

第19项：茶俗（白族三道茶）

白族三道茶展示

the Display of the Three-course Tea of the Bai Nationality

项目序号：1014	项目编号：X-107	公布时间：2014（第四批）	类别：民俗
所属地区：云南省	类型：扩展项目	申报地区或单位：云南省大理市	

白族三道茶是云南白族招待贵宾时的一种饮茶方式，常出现在大理白族的贵客临门、迎娶新人等重要时刻。白族三道茶以其独特的“头苦、二甜、三回味”的茶道早在明代时已成了白家待客交友的一种礼仪，寓意人生“一苦，二甜，三回味”的哲理，现已成为白族民间婚庆、节日和待客的茶礼。

白族三道茶制作要求严格，有“三道”“六则”“十八序”之说。其中，最核心的是“一苦、二甜、三回味”的“三道”。第一道，“苦茶”，又名“雷响茶”，是白族人最爱喝的白抖烤茶，茶叶被烘烤得微黄时注入沸水，茶罐里隆隆作响，犹如响雷。这一道茶其味香苦，茶味浓酽，寓意做人的哲理“要立业，先要吃苦”。第二道，“甜茶”，以核桃片、乳扇丝和红糖末为佐料，冲入清淡的感通茶水制成，甜而不腻。寓意苦去甜来，代表人生的甘境。第三道，“回味茶”，用蜂蜜加上花椒、姜片和桂皮末，冲苍山雪绿茶煎制而成，其味甜、麻、香、辣，喝后回味无穷。白语中“辣”与“亲”，“麻”和“富”同音，故第三道茶有祝福亲亲热热，大富大贵之意。白族三道茶有提神醒脑、利尿强心、清热降火、预防动脉硬化和降低血压的效果。①

Item 19: the Tea Custom (the Three-course Tea of the Bai Nationality)

Item Serial Number: 1014	Item ID Number: X-107	Released Date: 2014 (Batch 4)	Category: Folk Custom

① 王晓云，《三道茶：大理白族独有的茶道》，载《大理日报》，2016年8月3日第A3版。

Affiliated Province: Yunnan Province	Type: Extended Item	Application Province or Unit: Dali City, Yunnan Province

The Three-course Tea of the Bai Nationality is a way of drinking tea when the Bai people in Yunnan Province entertain distinguished guests, often appearing at important moments of the Bai nationality in Dali City, such as the visiting of distinguished guests and wedding ceremony. With its unique tea ceremony of "bitterness of the first course, sweetness of the second course and aftertaste of the third course", **the Three-course Tea of the Bai Nationality** has become a kind of etiquette for the Bai family to entertain guests and make friends since the Ming Dynasty. It implies the philosophy of life, "first being bitter, second sweet and third memorable", and has become an etiquette of drinking tea at weddings and festivals, and when entertaining guests for the Bai people up to now.

The requirements for making **the Three-course Tea of the Bai Nationality** are strict, and there are "three courses", "six norms" and "eighteen procedures". Among them, the core is the "three courses" of "bitterness of the first course, sweetness of the second course and aftertaste of the third course". The first course, "the bitter tea", also known as "Leixiang (thunderclap) Tea", is the Bai people's favorite Baidou Roasted Tea. When tea leaves are roasted to a slightly yellow color, boiling water is poured into them, and then the tea pot rumbles like thunder. The first-course tea is both fragrant and bitter, having a strong taste, which implies the life philosophy of "enduring hardship before establishing a career". The second course, "the sweet tea", is made with walnut slices, shredded cheese and brown sugar powder as seasonings, light Gantong Tea poured into them, which has agreeable sweetness. The second-course tea implies that bitterness goes and sweetness comes, representing the sweet state of life. The third course, "the tea with aftertaste", is made with honey, prickly ash seeds, ginger slices and cinnamon powder, decocted with Cangshanxue Green Tea. This tea is sweet, numbing, fragrant and spicy, giving people an endless aftertaste after drinking. In the Bai language, "spicy" is homonymous with "close", and "numbing" with "rich", so the third-course tea has the meanings of close relations, great wealth and nobleness. **The Three-course Tea** has the effects of refreshing the mind, promoting diuresis and strengthening the heart, clearing away heat and reducing fire, preventing arteriosclerosis and lowering blood pressure.

一、词汇表 Glossary

第一批：Batch 1
第二批：Batch 2
第三批：Batch 3
第四批：Batch 4
新增项目：New Item
扩展项目：Extended Item
项目序号：Item Serial Number
项目编号：Item ID Number
公布时间：Released Date
类别：Category
所属地区：Affiliated Province
类型：Type
申报地区或单位：Application Province or Unit
民间文学：Folk Literature
传统音乐：Traditional Music
传统舞蹈：Traditional Dance
传统戏剧：Traditional Opera
曲艺：Quyi (a general term for all Chinese talking-and-singing art forms)
传统体育、游艺与杂技：Traditional Sports, Recreations and Acrobatics
传统美术：Traditional Fine Arts
传统技艺：Traditional Craft
传统医药：Traditional Medicine
民俗：Folk Custom

二、云南省国家级（1—4 批）非物质文化遗产项目名称汉英对照
The Chinese-English Versions of the Names of the State-level Intangible Cultural Heritage Items of Yunnan Province (Batches 1-4)

第一章 民间文学 Chapter One Folk Literature

遮帕麻和遮咪麻：*Zhepama and Zhemima Myth*
牡帕密帕：*Mupa Mipa Myth*
四季生产调：The Four-season Production Tune
格萨（斯）尔：*Gesar Epic*
阿诗玛：*Ashima Poem*
梅葛：*Meige Epic*
查姆：*Chamu Epic*
达古达楞格莱标：*Dagu Daleng Gelaibiao Epic*
哈尼哈吧：*Haba (ancient songs) of the Hani Nationality*
召树屯与喃木诺娜：*Zhaoshutun and Nanmu Nuona Poem*
司岗里：*Sigangli (out of the cliff-cave) Epic*
坡芽情歌：*Poya Love Songs*
目瑙斋瓦：*Munao Zhaiwa Epic*
洛奇洛耶与扎斯扎依：*Luoqi Luoye and Zhasi Zhayi Poem*
阿细先基：*Axi Xianji Poem*
黑白战争：*The Battle between the Black and the White*

第二章 传统音乐 Chapter Two Traditional Music

傈僳族民歌：Folk Songs of the Lisu Nationality
哈尼族多声部民歌：Polyphonic Folk Songs of the Hani Nationality
彝族海菜腔：Haicai Tone of the Yi Nationality
姚安坝子腔：Bazi Tone of Yao’an
彝族民歌（彝族酒歌）：Folk Songs of the Yi Nationality (Toasting Songs of the Yi Nationality)
布朗族民歌（布朗族弹唱）：Folk Songs of the Bulang Nationality (Playing and Singing of the Bulang Nationality)
洞经音乐（妙善学女子洞经音乐）：Dongjing Music (Miaoshanxue Maiden Dongjing Music)

弥渡民歌：Midu Folk Songs
纳西族白沙细乐：Baisha Orchestral Music of the Naxi Nationality
剑川白曲：Bai Melody of Jianchuan

第三章　传统舞蹈　Chapter Three　Traditional Dance

锅庄舞（迪庆锅庄舞）：Guozhuang Dance (Diqing Guozhuang Dance)
木鼓舞（沧源佤族木鼓舞）：the Wooden-drum Dance (Cangyuan Wooden-drum Dance of the Wa Nationality)
文山壮族、彝族铜鼓舞：the Bronze-drum Dance of the Zhuang and Yi Nationalities of Wenshan Prefecture
傣族孔雀舞：the Peacock Dance of the Dai Nationality
傈僳族阿尺木刮：Achi Mugua Dance of the Lisu Nationality
彝族葫芦笙舞：Hulusheng Dance of the Yi Nationality
彝族烟盒舞：the Cigarette-box Dance of the Yi Nationality
基诺大鼓舞：the Big Drum Dance of the Jinuo Nationality
傣族象脚鼓舞：the Elephant-foot Drum Dance of the Dai Nationality
彝族打歌：Dage Dance of the Yi Nationality
彝族跳菜：Tiaocai Dance of the Yi Nationality
彝族老虎笙：the Tiger Sheng Dance of the Yi Nationality
彝族左脚舞：the Left Foot Dance of the Yi Nationality
乐作舞：Lezuo Dance
彝族三弦舞（阿细跳月）：Sanxian Dance of the Yi Nationality (Axi Dance in the Moonlight)
彝族三弦舞（撒尼大三弦）：Sanxian Dance of the Yi Nationality (Sani Big Sanxian Dance)
纳西族热美蹉：Remeicuo Dance of the Naxi Nationality
布朗族蜂桶鼓舞：the Bee-barrel Drum Dance of the Bulang Nationality
普米族搓蹉：Cuocuo Dance of the Pumi Nationality
拉祜族芦笙舞：Lusheng Dance of the Lahu Nationality
棕扇舞：the Palm-leaf Fan Dance
耳子歌：Erzige Dance
铓鼓舞：Manggu Drum Dance
水鼓舞：the Water Drum Dance
怒族达比亚舞：Dabiya Dance of the Nu Nationality

热巴舞：Reba Dance

第四章　传统戏剧　Chapter Four　Traditional Opera

花灯戏（玉溪花灯戏）：the Lantern Opera (Yuxi Lantern Opera)
花灯戏：the Lantern Opera
傣剧：Dai Opera
滇剧：Yunnan Opera
佤族清戏：Qing Opera of the Wa Nationality
彝剧：Yi Opera
白剧：Bai Opera
壮剧：Zhuang Opera
关索戏：Guansuo Opera
皮影戏（腾冲皮影戏）：the Shadow Play (Tengchong Shadow Play)

第五章　曲艺　Chapter Five　Quyi (a general term for all Chinese talking-and-singing art forms)

傣族章哈：Zhangha of the Dai Nationality

第六章　传统体育、游艺与杂技　Chapter Six　Traditional Sports, Recreations and Acrobatics

摔跤（彝族摔跤）：Wrestling (Wrestling of the Yi Nationality)

第七章　传统美术　Chapter Seven　Traditional Fine Arts

纳西族东巴画：Dongba Paintings of the Naxi Nationality
傣族剪纸：Paper Cutting of the Dai Nationality
彝族（撒尼）刺绣：(Sani) Embroidery of the Yi Nationality
建筑彩绘（白族民居彩绘）：Architectural Colored Paintings (Colored Paintings on the Residential Houses of the Bai Nationality)
木雕（剑川木雕）：Wood Carving (Jianchuan Wood Carving)

第八章　传统技艺　Chapter Eight　Traditional Craft

傣族慢轮制陶技艺：the Craft of Making Pottery via Slow Wheels of the Dai Nationality

白族扎染技艺：the Craft of Tie Dyeing of the Bai Nationality
苗族芦笙制作技艺：the Craft of Making Lusheng Musical Instruments of the Miao Nationality
阿昌族户撒刀锻制技艺：the Craft of Forging Husa Knives of the Achang Nationality
傣族、纳西族手工造纸技艺：the Craft of Making Paper by Hand of the Dai and Naxi Nationalities
陶器烧制技艺（藏族黑陶烧制技艺）：the Craft of Firing Pottery (the Craft of Firing the Black Pottery of the Zang Nationality)
陶器烧制技艺（建水紫陶烧制技艺）：the Craft of Firing Pottery (the Craft of Firing Jianshui Purple Pottery)
傣族织锦技艺：the Craft of Making Brocade of the Dai Nationality
斑铜制作技艺：the Craft of Making Variegated Copperware
贝叶经制作技艺：the Craft of Making Pattra-leaf Scriptures
普洱茶制作技艺（贡茶制作技艺）：the Craft of Making Pu'er Tea (the Craft of Making Tribute Tea)
普洱茶制作技艺（大益茶制作技艺）：the Craft of Making Pu'er Tea (the Craft of Making Dayi Tea)
乌铜走银制作技艺：the Craft of Making Silver-plated Black Copperware
民族乐器制作技艺（傣族象脚鼓制作技艺）：the Craft of Making National Musical Instruments (the Craft of Making the Elephant-foot Drum of the Dai Nationality)
下关沱茶制作技艺：the Craft of Making Xiaguan Bowl-shaped Compressed Tea
宣威火腿制作技艺：the Craft of Making Xuanwei Ham
蒙自过桥米线制作技艺：the Craft of Making Mengzi Guoqiao Rice Noodles
银饰锻制技艺（鹤庆银器锻制技艺）：the Craft of Making Silver Ornaments (the Craft of Making Heqing Silverware)
红茶制作技艺（滇红茶制作技艺）：the Craft of Making Black Tea (the Craft of Making Yunnan Black Tea)

第九章　传统医药　Chapter Nine　Traditional Medicine

彝医药（彝医水膏药疗法）：the Medicine of the Yi Nationality (the Therapy of Ointments Mixed with Water of the Yi Nationality)

彝医药（拨云锭制作技艺）：the Medicine of the Yi Nationality (the Craft of Making Boyun Pastille)

傣医药（睡药疗法）：the Medicine of the Dai Nationality (the Therapy of Sleeping in Herbs)

藏医药（藏医骨伤疗法）：the Zang Medicine (the Therapies for Bone Injuries of the Zang Medicine)

中医传统制剂方法（昆中药传统中药制剂）：the Preparation Methods of Traditional Chinese Medicine (the Preparations of Kun Traditional Chinese Medicine)

第十章　民俗　Chapter Ten　Folk Custom

傣族泼水节：the Water-splashing Festival of the Dai Nationality

火把节（彝族火把节）：the Torch Festival (the Torch Festival of the Yi Nationality)

景颇族目瑙纵歌：the Munao Zongge Festival of the Jingpo Nationality

独龙族卡雀哇节：the Kaquewa Festival of the Dulong Nationality

怒族仙女节：the Fairy Maiden Festival of the Nu Nationality

傈僳族刀杆节：the Daogan (knife ladder) Festival of the Lisu Nationality

白族绕三灵：Raosanling (worshipping three gods in parades) of the Bai Nationality

苗族服饰（昌宁苗族服饰）：the Costumes of the Miao Nationality (the Costumes of the Miao Nationality in Changning County)

德昂族浇花节：the Flower-watering Festival of the De'ang Nationality

石宝山歌会：the Singing Festival of the Shibao Mountain

大理三月街：Dali March Street

祭寨神林：Offering Sacrifices to Gods of Stockaded Villages

抬阁（通海高台）：Pavilion Lifting (Tonghai High Stage)

苗族花山节：the Flower Hill Festival of the Miao Nationality

彝族服饰：the Costumes of the Yi Nationality

民间信俗（梅里神山祭祀）：the Folk-belief Custom (Offering Sacrifices to the Meili Sacred Mountain)

民间信俗（女子太阳山祭祀）：the Folk-belief Custom (Women's Offering Sacrifices to the Sun Mountain)

茶俗（白族三道茶）：the Tea Custom (the Three-course Tea of the Bai Nationality)

三、一至十章中的文化负载词汉英对照
The Chinese-English Versions of the Culture-loaded Words in Chapters 1-10

第一章 民间文学 Chapter One Folk Literature

天公遮帕麻：the Heaven Father Zhepama
地母遮咪麻：the Earth Mother Zhemima
魔王腊訇：Demon Lahong
厄萨：God Esa
调式：musical mode
十二头魔王：the Twelve-head Demon
锡来河三汗：Three Khans of the Xilai River
蟒古斯喇嘛：Manggusi Lama
昂都拉玛魔汗：the Demon Khan of Angdu Lama
二十一颗头颅魔王：the 21-head Demon King
固么布魔汗：the Demon Khan of Gumobu
那钦汗：Naqin Khan
独唱：solo singing
对唱：antiphonal singing
一人领唱众人合唱：one person leading the singing with others singing in chorus
根谱：the root genealogy
葫芦笙：Hulusheng (a gourd-made musical instrument)
口弦：Kouxian (a kind of buccal reed)
月琴：Yueqin (a four-stringed plucked musical instrument with a full-moon-shaped sound box)
查：*cha* (one "*cha*" refers to one origin of a creature)
阿噻调：the mode of Asai
大四弦：Big Sixian (a four-stringed plucked musical instrument)
茶神：the God of Tea
古老茶农：the ancient tea farmer
红河：the Honghe River
澜沧江：the Lancang River
《窝果策尼果》：*Woguo Ceniguo* (*Twelve Tunes of Ancient Songs*)

《哈尼阿培聪坡坡》：*Hani Apei Congpopo* (*The Epic of the Migration of the Hani Nationality*)
《十二奴局》：*Shi'er Nuju* (*Twelve Chapters*)
《木地米地》：*Mudi Midi* (*The Creation of the Heaven and the Earth*)
佛寺壁画：Buddhist temple murals
经画：scripture paintings
孔雀国：the Peacock Kingdom
金湖：the Golden Lake
神龙：the magic dragon
万能的神灵：the almighty god
小米雀：Xiaomique Bird
坡芽歌书：A Book of Poya Songs
文字之芽：the buds of characters
曲调：musical modes
小调：minor modes
首尾韵：head-and-end rhymes
腰尾韵：middle-and-end rhymes
尾韵：end rhymes
山官制度：Shanguan system ("Shanguan" means the hereditary headman and the presider of sacrificial activities in the villages of the Jingpo nationality)
天神：the god of the heaven
太阳神：the god of the sun
"目瑙纵歌"舞：Munao Zongge Dance
西山地区：Xishan region
东巴经卷：Dongba Scripture
东巴祭司：Dongba, the priest of the Naxi nationality

第二章　传统音乐　Chapter Two　Traditional Music

火塘：the Fire Pit
三弦：Sanxian (a three-stringed plucked musical instrument)
小二胡：Small Erhu (a two-stringed bowed instrument)
正词：main lyrics
衬词：foil lyrics
七绝诗：Seven-character Quatrain

二胡：Erhu (a two-stringed bowed instrument)
嫁调：Jiadiao Tune
宫调式：the mode of Gong (one of the five ancient Chinese musical notes equal to "Do" in western musical scale)
商调式：the mode of Shang (one of the five ancient Chinese musical notes equal to "Re" in western musical scale)
羊皮鼓：the Sheepskin Drum
法铃：Faling Bell (a kind of shaking and percussion instrument)
大三弦：Big Sanxian (a three-stringed plucked musical instrument)
地筒：Ditong (a single-reed blowing musical instrument)
四弦琴：Sixianqin (a four-stringed lute)
妙善学女子洞经（古乐）班：Miaoshanxue Maiden Dongjing (Ancient Music) Troupe
工尺谱：Gongchi musical notation
简谱：numbered musical notation
曲牌：Qupai (the tune name of a melody)
三元宫：the Three Yuan Palace
女子洞经会：the Maiden Dongjing Society
丝竹音乐：Sizhu music (the one performed by using traditional stringed and woodwind instruments)
妙善学女子洞经会：Miaoshanxue Maiden Dongjing Society
赤足舞"跺蹉"：the Barefoot Dance of "Duocuo"
云雀舞"劳马蹉"：the Skylark Dance of "Laomacuo"
弓矢舞"抗蹉"：the Bow and Arrow Dance of "Kangcuo"
白鹤舞"夸蹉"：the White Crane Dance of "Kuacuo"
芦管：Luguan (a traditional Chinese oboe instrument)
苏古笃：Sugudu (a stringed instrument of the Naxi nationality)
小曲项琵琶：Small Quxiang Pipa (a plucked string instrument with a fretted fingerboard)
古筝：Guzheng (a Chinese zither)
二簧：Erhuang (a bow-drawn stringed musical instrument of the Naxi nationality)
胡琴：Huqin Musical Instrument
宴乐之器：the Banquet Musical Instruments
龙头三弦：Dragon-head Sanxian (a three-stringed plucked musical instrument)
山花体：Shanhua Style

第三章　传统舞蹈　Chapter Three　Traditional Dance

木鼓房：the Wooden Drum House
铜鼓：the Bronze Drum
彝族白倮支系：the Bailuo Branch of the Yi nationality
十二调：the Twelve Tunes
“摆”（节日）：“Bai activity” (festival)
关门节：the Door-closing Festival
开门节：the Door-opening Festival
赶摆：Ganbai (going to a fair)
架子孔雀舞：Jiazi Peacock Dance (a dance performed with the racks of peacock wings)
开化古铜鼓：the ancient Kaihua Bronze Drum
四弦：Sixian (a four-stringed plucked musical instrument)
立春：the Beginning of Spring
寨老：Zhailao (a head of a stockaded village)
卓巴（寨老）：Zhuoba or Zhailao (a head of a stockaded village)
小年：the Minor New Year
芦笙：Lusheng Musical Instruments
左脚调：the Left Foot Tune
龙头四弦：Dragon-head Sixian (a four-stringed plucked musical instrument)
红河：the Red River
巴乌：Bawu (a reed-pipe musical instrument)
小三弦：Small Sanxian (a three-stringed plucked musical instrument)
三胡：Sanhu (a three-stringed bowed instrument)
唢呐：Suona Horn (a woodwind instrument)
快三步：the Fast Three-step Dance
青年舞：the Youth’s Dance
玉龙雪山：the Yulong Snow Mountain
金沙江：the Jinsha River
蜂桶鼓：the Bee-barrel Drum
象脚鼓：the Elephant-foot Drum
金芒：Golden Mang Musical Instrument
跳蜂桶鼓：performing the Bee-barrel Drum Dance
跳象脚鼓：performing the Elephant-foot Drum Dance

跳甩手巾：performing the Towel-shaking Dance
尝新节：the New Rice-tasting Festival
春节：the Spring Festival
正步：parade steps
蹉步：Cuobu steps (dance steps where two feet alternately wipe the ground and move forward)
绕步：coiling steps
跳四方：perform Sifang Dance
铓：Mang (a folk copper percussion instrument)
大铓：Big Mang (a folk copper percussion instrument)
单双蹉步：single and double Cuobu steps (dance steps where two feet alternately wipe the ground and move forward)
琵琶：Pipa (a plucked string instrument with a fretted fingerboard)
达比亚：Dabiya (a traditional plucked instrument of the Nu nationality)
铃鼓舞：the Bell Drum Dance
杂剧：Zaju Opera
哑剧：dumb shows
弦子舞：the String Dance
藏传佛教噶举派：the Kagyu School of Tibetan Buddhism

第四章　传统戏剧　Chapter Four　Traditional Opera

土主神：the god of the land owner
土地神：the god of land
崴：Wai (twisted dance steps)
手中花：the Hand Flower
扇花：the Fan Flower
簸箕灯：the Dustpan Lantern
小生：Xiaosheng (the young man's role)
葫芦丝：Hulusi (a wind instrument made of the gourd)
丝弦腔：Sixian tone
胡琴腔：Huqin tone
襄阳腔：Xiangyang tone
秦腔：Qinqiang tone

徽调：Huidiao

汉调：Handiao

湖北高腔：Hubei High Tone

青阳腔：Qingyang Tone

打跳：Datiao Dance

山歌体：the mountain-song style

板腔：Banqiang Tone

联曲体：the joint-tune style

吹吹腔：Chuichui Tone

大本曲：Daben Tune

唢呐曲牌：Suona Qupai (the tune name of a melody)

三弦曲牌：Sanxian Qupai (the tune name of a melody)

道白：Daobai (the spoken part in an opera)

生：Sheng Character (a male role in Chinese opera, usually referring to the role with a beard or a young man)

旦：Dan Character (a female role)

净：Jing Character (a male role in Chinese opera, usually with rough and bold personalities)

丑：Chou Character (a clown)

袍带戏：Paodai operas (the operas in which performers wear the Python Robe and the Jade Belt)

板凳戏：the Bench Opera

灵峰寺：the Lingfeng Temple

药王：the God of Medicine

蜀汉：the Kingdom of Shu Han

江南：regions south of the Yangtze River

湖广：Hubei and Hunan provinces

灯影子：the Lamp Shadow

皮人戏：the Leather-figure Opera

土电影：the Indigenous Movie

东腔：the East Tone

西腔：the West Tone

第五章　曲艺　Chapter Five　Quyi (a general term for all Chinese talking-and-singing art forms)

祭寨神：offering sacrifices to gods of stockaded villages
赕佛：offering sacrifices to the Buddha
孩子满月：a baby's completion of its first month of life

第六章　传统体育、游艺与杂技　Chapter Six　Traditional Sports, Recreations and Acrobatics

丈：*zhang* (a Chinese unit of length, with one *zhang* roughly equal to 131 inches)
火把节：the Torch Festival

第七章　传统美术　Chapter Seven　Traditional Fine Arts

纸幡：the Paper-made Soul-summoning Banners
中原：the Central Plains
扎：Zha (small triangle-shaped colorful paper flags used to worship Buddha)
董：Dong (colorful paper cuttings)
佛幡：banners used in Buddhist temples
吊幢：Diaochuang (hanging streamers)
佛殿：the Buddhist Palace
泼水龙亭：the Water-splashing Dragon Pavilion
上座部佛教：Theravada Buddhism
八舞花：Eight-dance Flowers
羊角花：Sheep-horn Flowers
平绣：Flat Embroidery
镂空贴花：Hollowing and Decaling
抠花：Hollowing Flowers
照壁：the Screen Wall
龙马角：the Dragon-horse Horn
回纹：Huiwen patterns
五华楼：Wuhua Building
人民大会堂：the Great Hall of the People
民族文化宫：the Cultural Palace of Nationalities
座屏：Zuoping (a screen with a base, which cannot be folded)

第八章　传统技艺　Chapter Eight　Traditional Craft

土锅：the Earth Pot
洱海：the Erhai Lake
笙斗：Shengdou (a container in Lusheng Musical Instruments where the air is retained and the reed is caused to vibrate)
石墩：Shidun (a block of stone)
瑞香科丽江荛花：*Wikstroemia lichiangensis* in Latin
泥条盘筑法：the method of coiling clay bars
磬：the Chime Stone
综：Zeng (a device on a loom that separates the warp threads so that the shuttle can pass through)
幅撑：Fucheng (a bamboo stick used to support the woven cloth so that it can maintain a relatively uniform width)
"纹板"（花本）："the Pattern Board" (Huaben)
鼎：Ding (an ancient cooking vessel with two loop handles and three or four legs)
千灯节：the Thousand-lantern Festival
立幡杆节：the Flagpole-erecting Festival
法号：Fahao (a kind of bass wind instruments)

第九章　传统医药　Chapter Nine　Traditional Medicine

气：Qi (vital energy)
青叶胆：Qingyedan Herb (*Swertia mileensis* in Latin)
地胆：Didan Herb (*Elephantopus scaber* in Latin)
茶马古道：the Tea-horse Ancient Road
四塔：the Four Pagodas
五蕴：the Five Aggregates
伤科一号：Trauma No. 1
铁箍散：*Schisandra propinqua*
雪山一枝蒿：*Aconitum racemulosum* Franch.
桑琼丸：Sangqiong Pills
十味乳香丸：Ten-flavor Ruxiang Pills
十八味杜鹃花丸：Eighteen-flavor Azalea Pills
伤科二号：Trauma No. 2

骨碎补：the rhizome of *davallia*
当归：Chinese Angelica
秦皮：ash bark
接骨消炎丸：Pills for Bonesetting and Diminishing Inflammation
八味秦皮丸：Eight-flavor Ash Bark Pills
达尔强散：Da'er Strengthening Powder
五味甘露：Five-flavor Ganlu Medicine
石榴日轮丸：Pomegranate Rilun Pills
巴桑母酥油丸：Basangmu Butter Pills
清肺化痰丸：Pills for Clearing Away the Lung-heat and Eliminating Phlegm
小儿化风丹：Pills for Dispelling Infants' Wind
郑氏女金丹：the Zheng Family's Nüjin Pellets
小儿救急丹：Infant Emergency Pellets
阮氏上清丸：the Ruan Family's Shangqing Pills
保产达生丸：Childbirth-ensuring Pills
姚济资生丸：Yaoji Life-activating Pills
再造丸：Revival Pills
感冒疏风丸：Pills for Curing Influenza and Dispelling Wind
止咳丸：Cough-relieving Pills
桑菊银翘散：Powder of Mulberry Leaf, Daisy, Lonicera and Forsythia
疥疮药膏：Scabies Ointment
生三七丸：Raw Pseudo-ginseng Pills
熟三七丸：Cooked Pseudo-ginseng Pills

第十章 民俗 Chapter Ten Folk Custom

浴佛节：the Festival of Bathing the Buddha
龙舟：the Dragon Boat
孔雀舞：the Peacock Dance
白象舞：the White Elephant Dance
清明节：the Tomb Sweeping Festival
黄道十二宫：the Twelve Signs of the Ecliptic
龙亭：the Dragon Pavilion
丢包（抛绣球）：Diubao (throwing the Embroidered Ball)
孔明灯：the Kongming Lantern

水灯：the Water Lamp

放高升：setting off firecrackers made of explosive, bamboo tubes and bamboo poles by the Dai people

磨担秋：Modanqiu Sport

十二兽舞：the Twelve-beast Dance

“老虎笙”舞：the Tiger Sheng Dance

舞场：the Dance Square

目瑙舞：Munao Dance

喜马拉雅山：the Himalayas

锅庄：Guozhuang Dance

木罗酒：Muluo Liquor

铓锣：Mangluo (a copper percussion instrument used by the ethnic minorities in Yunnan Province)

翻手舞：the Flip-hand Dance

仙女洞：the Fairy Maiden Cave

普化寺：Puhua Temple

点花：Dianhua (offering sacrifices to colored paper flowers by using blood from a cockscomb)

点刀：Diandao (offering sacrifices to knives by using blood from a cockscomb)

刀杆：Daogan (knife ladder)

尺：*chi* (a Chinese unit of length, with one *chi* roughly equal to 13 inches)

天门：the Heavenly Gate

跳嘎：Tiaoga Dance

花柳树老人：the Flower and Willow Tree Elderly

霸王鞭：Bawang Whip

金钱鼓：Jinqian Drum

大理古城：the Ancient City of Dali

城隍庙：Chenghuang Temple

点苍山：the Diancang Mountain (also called the Cangshan Mountain)

崇圣寺：Chongsheng Temple

苍山：the Cangshan Mountain

五台峰：the Wutai Peak

朝阳村：Chaoyang Village

抚民皇帝：Fumin Emperor

南朝（拜）：the Southern Worship

庆洞村：Qingdong Village
神都：Shendu Temple
北朝（拜）：the Northern Worship
扇子舞：the Fan Dance
洱海之神：the god of the Erhai Lake
马久邑村：Majiuyi Village
保安景帝：Bao’anjing Emperor
大襟长衫：long gowns with big Jin (two fronts of an upper garment)
堆沙舞：Duisha Dance
水龙槽：the Water Dragon Trough
浇花舞：the Flower-watering Dance
“阿吒力”佛教音乐：“Azhali” Buddhist music
三弦曲：Sanxian Tunes
霸王鞭舞：Bawang Whip Dance
大白曲（本子曲）：Dabai Tune (Benzi Tune)
白族调：the tunes of the Bai nationality
一字歌：Yizi songs (with one character repeated in each line of lyrics)
石龙霸王鞭舞：Bawang Whip Dance of Shilong Village
“阿吒力”佛教法事活动：“Azhali” Buddhist ritual activities
中央本主：the highest local god
“阿央白”（石刻女阴）：“Ayangbai” (the carved stone pudendum)
庙会：the Temple Fair
三月街：March Street
洋人街：Foreigner Street
辰龙日：the Dragon Day
午马日：the Horse Day
长街宴：Long Street Banquet
文王访贤：King Wen of Zhou Visits the Virtuous
孙渊哭洞：Sun Yuan Cries over the Cave
孟母教子：Mencius’s Mother Teaches Her Son
岳飞出世：The Birth of Yue Fei
三打白骨精：Beating the White Bone Demon Three Times
花果山：The Huaguo Mountain
三借芭蕉扇：Borrowing the Palm-leaf Fan Three Times
许仙借伞：Xu Xian Borrows an Umbrella

水漫金山：The Flooding of Jinshan Temple
鹊桥会：Meeting on the Magpie Bridge
木兰从军：Mulan Joins the Army
毛驴灯：the Donkey Lantern
龙灯：the Dragon Lantern
踩花山：Stepping on the Flower Hill
踩山：Stepping on the Hill
花山：the Flower Hill
蹬脚架：Dengjiaojia (kicking competition)
芦笙舞：Lusheng Dance
右衽大襟短上衣：Youren big-Jin short tops with the left fronts of the tops covering the right ones
马樱花：Maying Flowers (*Rhododendron delavayi Franch* in Latin)
天菩萨：Tianpusa (a strand of hair on top of the head of a Yi man)
英雄髻：Hero's Coiled Hair
对襟窄袖上衣：narrow-sleeved Duijin tops with two fronts of the tops opposite each other
梅里雪山：the Meili Snow Mountain
康巴地区：Kham area
煨桑：Weisang (burning pine and cypress branches)
经幡：Jingfan (prayer flags)
风马旗：Fengma Flags
刀赞：Daozan (a Zang sacrificial talking-and-singing ceremony)
喀夏（说笑话）：Kaxia (telling jokes)
太阳村：the Village of the Sun
女子太阳节：the Sun Festival of Women
女人节：the Festival of Women
太阳神树：the Divine Tree of the Sun
双乌朝阳：Two Golden Crows Facing the Sun
雷响茶：Leixiang (thunderclap) Tea
白抖烤茶：Baidou Roasted Tea
感通茶：Gantong Tea
苍山雪绿茶：Cangshanxue Green Tea

后记 Postscript

本系列文献资料汇编的中文文本主要参考了中国非物质文化遗产保护中心的官网，即中国非物质文化遗产网，相关省、市、自治州、县非物质文化遗产保护中心的官网，相关政府机构的官网，所涉非遗产品生产厂商的官网，权威新闻网站和报纸，以及与所涉非遗项目相关的高质量学术期刊论文和著作等。在此谨向相关版权所有单位和个人表示最真诚的感谢！

具体而言，《四川省国家级非物质文化遗产文献资料汇编（汉英对照）》［The Documentary Compilation of the State-level Intangible Cultural Heritage of Sichuan Province (Chinese-English Versions)］的中文文本主要参考了以下来源的资料：中国非物质文化遗产网、四川省非物质文化遗产保护中心官网、凉山彝族自治州非物质文化遗产保护中心官网、泸州市非物质文化遗产普及基地网、楚雄州图书馆彝族文献数据库系统、西昌市文化馆官网、夹江县文化馆官网、中国人民政治协商会议阿坝州黑水县委员会官网、中国旅游新闻网、腾讯网、中国新闻网、华夏经纬网、成都水井坊股份有限公司官网、普洱茶网、搜狐网、四川新闻网、人民网四川频道、《阿坝日报》、《成都日报》、《宜宾日报》、《四川日报》、《民族论坛》、《现代艺术》、《四川戏剧》、《民族艺术研究》、《四川党的建设》、《四川民族学院学报》、《本草纲目》、《情歌的故乡——康定》等。《云南省国家级非物质文化遗产文献资料汇编（汉英对照）》［The Documentary Compilation of the State-level Intangible Cultural Heritage of Yunnan Province (Chinese-English Versions)］的中文文本主要参考了以下来源的资料：中国非物质文化遗产网、云南非物质文化遗产保护网、迪庆非物质文化遗产保护网、瑞丽市门户网、中国民族建筑研究会中国民族建筑网、楚雄州非遗网、中国·云龙网、蒙自市特产网、昆中药网、保山日报网、中国网、《中国青年报》、《大理日报》、《民族文学研究》、《民族艺术研究》、《民族艺术》、《民族音乐》、《玉溪师范学院学报》、《今日民族》、《建水县非物质文化遗产保护名录》（建水县文化和旅游局编）、《云南省志·医药志》、《云南档案》等。《贵州省国家级非物质文化遗产文献资料汇编（汉英对照）》［The Documentary Compilation of the State-level Intangible Cultural Heritage of Guizhou Province (Chinese-English Versions)］的中文文本主要参考了以下来源的资料：中国非物质文化遗产网、贵州省非物质文化遗产保护中心官网、黔西南州人民政府网、中国铜仁门户网、凯里市人民政府网、安龙县人民政府网、中华人民共和国国家民族事务委员会官网、贵州文明网、贵州百科信息网、多彩贵州网、中国布依网、黔东南新闻网、中华网、人民网、东方资讯网、同济堂官网、国医小镇网、《贵州民族报》、《黔西南日报》、《贵州社会科学》、《贵州民族研究》、《民族文学研究》、《贵州师范大学学报·社会科学版》、《武术研究》、《中华艺术论丛》、《贵州民族学院学报（哲社版）》、《民族学刊》、《安顺学院学报》、《中国山地民族研究集刊》、《中国民族医药杂志》、《当代贵州》、《雷山苗族医药》、《黎平县志》等。[①]

本课题 2019 年 3 月 15 日立项后，年底暴发了新冠疫情，造成课题组成员前往非遗所属地现场搜集文献资料的行程受阻。故在整个课题进行期间，课题组成员仅利用 2019 年暑假（7—8 月）和寒假（2020 年 1 月初）前往四个非遗项目所属地，即贵阳市多彩贵州城、梭戛苗族生态博物馆、中国·贵州花溪镇山布依族生态博物馆和建水县非物质文化遗产保护中心进行文献资料的搜集。在这几次行程中，相关负责人给予课题组成员热情的接待和大力的支持。可以说，这三部文献资料汇编（汉英对照）的顺利完稿离不开以下单位、个人的大力支持，在此课题组谨逐一表示最诚挚的谢意：首先，要特别感谢贵旅艺术团团长、侗族大歌国家级传承人张明超先生为课题组提供了有关侗族大歌和其他贵州省国家级非物质文化遗产的文字和图片资料，并赠与了《指掌间的舞蹈——贵州民族工艺名匠荟萃》（贵州人民出版社出版）这一本非遗著作。这些宝贵的资料为课题组完善贵州省的相关国家级非遗项目的文献资料汇编起到

① 由于行政调整，有些省、市、县的非物质文化遗产保护中心被调整至其他相关部门，其官网地址发生改变，导致编者原来查阅、参考、引用的文章在原网址无法查到，如四川省非物质文化遗产保护中心、凉山彝族自治州非物质文化遗产保护中心、泸州市非物质文化遗产普及基地等；有的企业官网更新，原有文章已不再展示，如成都水井坊股份有限公司官网；由于编者搜集汇编文献时间较早，有些新闻网站或其他网站进行了更新，本书中引用的某些文章在脚注标明网址已无法访问，如腾讯网、四川新闻网、华夏经纬网、人民网四川频道、保山日报网、多彩贵州网、凯里市人民政府网、贵州文明网、安龙县人民政府网、黔西南州人民政府网、中国铜仁门户网、人民网、中华人民共和国国家民族事务委员会官网、贵州百科信息网、中国民族建筑研究会中国民族建筑网、楚雄州非遗网、中国网等。另外，目前在本书编辑出版过程中还能在脚注网址查阅到的文章未来也可能会由于某种原因无法查阅，因此带来的不便敬请谅解！特此说明。

了关键作用。其次，还要特别感谢梭戛苗族老艺人为课题负责人提供了详细了解并亲身体验梭戛苗族服饰的机会。再次，十分感谢建水县文化和旅游局及前建水县非物质文化遗产保护中心对本课题的大力支持。2020 年 1 月初，课题负责人和成员向晓红教授前往前建水县非物质文化遗产保护中心搜集有关建水县的国家级非物质文化遗产铓鼓舞和建水紫陶烧制技艺的文献资料，受到中心唐主任的热情接待，唐主任还赠与课题组《建水县非物质文化遗产保护名录》，为课题组完善这两个非遗项目的文献资料起到了重要作用。最后，还要感谢美国教师 Ann Fouts 女士对本系列文献资料汇编英文文本的润色及提出的修改意见。在后期的审校过程中，课题负责人多次就英译文是否表达地道、用词是否精准等问题向 Ann Fouts 女士请教，Fouts 女士对这些英译文提出了很多宝贵的修改意见，在此谨向 Ann Fouts 女士表达课题组最真诚的感谢！

李新新
2024 年 6 月 30 日于西华大学